Understanding Criminal
Investigation

Wiley Series in

The Psychology of Crime, Policing and Law

Series Editors

Graham Davies and Ray Bull

University of Leicester, UK

The Wiley Series in the Psychology of Crime, Policing and Law publishes concise and integrative reviews on important emerging areas of contemporary research. The purpose of the series is not merely to present research findings in a clear and readable form but also to bring out their implications for both practice and policy. In this way, it is hoped the series will not only be useful to psychologists but also to all those concerned with crime detection and prevention, policing, and the judicial process.

For other titles in this series please see www.wiley.com/go/pcpl

Understanding Criminal Investigation

Stephen Tong

Robin P. Bryant

Miranda A. H. Horvath

A John Wiley & Sons, Ltd, Publication

This edition first published 2009
© 2009 John Wiley & Sons Ltd

Wiley-Blackwell is an imprint of John Wiley & Sons, formed by the merger of Wiley's global Scientific, Technical, and Medical business with Blackwell Publishing.

Registered Office
John Wiley & Sons Ltd, The Atrium, Southern Gate, Chichester, West Sussex, PO19 8SQ, UK

Editorial Offices
The Atrium, Southern Gate, Chichester, West Sussex, PO19 8SQ, UK
9600 Garsington Road, Oxford, OX4 2DQ, UK
350 Main Street, Malden, MA 02148-5020, USA

For details of our global editorial offices, for customer services, and for information about how to apply for permission to reuse the copyright material in this book please see our website at www.wiley.com/wiley-blackwell.

Library of Congress Cataloging-in-Publication Data

Tong, Stephen, 1972–
    Understanding criminal investigation / Stephen Tong, Robin Bryant, Miranda Horvath.
        p. cm.
    Includes bibliographical references and index.
    ISBN 978-0-470-72725-6 (cloth) – ISBN 978-0-470-72726-3 (pbk.)
1. Criminal investigation.   I. Bryant, Robin, Dr.   II. Horvath, Miranda.   III. Title.
    HV8073.T66 2009
    363.25–dc22

                                                                    2009021000

A catalogue record for this book is available from the British Library.

Typeset in 10/12pt Century Schoolbook by Aptara Inc., New Delhi, India

1   2009

Contents

Figures and Tables

Abbreviations

ACCESS	Assess, Collect, Collate, Evaluate, Scrutinise & Summarise
ACPO	Association of Chief Police Officers
APCS	Assessments of Policing and Community Safety
BCS	British Crime Survey
BCU	Basic Command Unit
BIA	behavioural investigative advisers
BSIR	Behavioural Science Instruction and Research Unit
BSIS	Behavioural Science Investigative Support Unit
BSU	Behavioural Science Unit
BTP	British Transport Police
BVPI	Best Value Performance Indicators
CGT	criminal geographic targeting
CI	cognitive interview
CID	Criminal Investigation Department
CJS	criminal justice system
CM	conversation management
CPIA	Criminal Procedure and Investigations Act 1996
CPS	Crown Prosecution Service
CSA	crime scene analysis
CTN	Coals to Newcastle project
DE	diagnostic evaluation
FBI	Federal Bureau of Investigation
FSS	Forensic Science Service
FTO	field training officer
GP	geographical profiling
HMIC	Her Majesty's Inspectorate of Constabulary
ICIDP	Initial Crime Investigators' Development Programme
IMSC	Initial Management of Serious Crime
IO	investigating officer

IP	investigative psychology
IPCC	Independent Police Complaints Commission
IPLDP	Initial Police Learning and Development Programme
MDP	Ministry of Defence Police
MIM	*Murder Investigation Manual*
MO	modus operandi
MPS	Metropolitan Police Service
NCAVC	National Centre for the Analysis of Violent Crime
NCIS	National Criminal Intelligence Service
NCPE	National Centre for Policing Excellence
NCRS	National Crime Recording Standard
NCS	National Crime Squad
NDM	naturalistic decision-making
NIE	National Investigators Examination
NIM	National Intelligence Model
NOS	National Occupational Standards
NPIA	National Police Improvement Agency
NPM	new public management
PACE	Police and Criminal Evidence 1984
PDP	professional development portfolio
PEACE	**P**lanning and preparation, **E**ngage and explain, **A**ccount, **C**losure, **E**valuation
PIP	Professionalising Investigation Programme
POP	problem-oriented policing
PPAF	Police Performance Assessment Framework
RCCP	Royal Commission on Criminal Procedure
SARA	Scanning, Analysis, Response and Assessment
SARC	sexual assault referral centre
SfJ	Skills for Justice
SIO	senior investigating officer
SIODP	Senior Investigating Officer Development Programme
SOCA	Serious Organised Crime Agency
SOP	standard operating procedure
SOS	Specialist Operational Support
STO	specially trained officer
TDC	trainee detective constable
VCIM	ACPO *Investigation of Volume Crime Manual*

About the Authors

Stephen Tong is principal lecturer in policing at Canterbury Christ Church University and director of the BSc (Hons) police studies programme. The police studies degree was created in 2002 and is now a thriving programme with over 100 students. Dr Tong completed his PhD at the Institute of Criminology, University of Cambridge. During his doctoral studies (funded by the National Crime Faculty and the Economic and Social Research Council), on "Training the Effective Detective", he examined detective training and its impact on practice. The research culminated in a report of recommendations delivered to the National Crime Faculty, with further publications in progress.

Robin P. Bryant is Director of Criminal Justice Practice at Canterbury Christ Church University. He has published widely, including a highly successful textbook for trainee police officers, now in its fourth edition. His research interests centre on the application of scientific principles to the investigation of crime and the relationship between new technology and crime.

Miranda A. H. Horvath is a lecturer in forensic psychology at the University of Surrey, where she is also an assistant director of the Crime & Justice @ Surrey research initiative. Dr Horvath's PhD (funded by the Economic and Social Research Council) investigated the role of alcohol and drugs in rape, using information from police case files. The majority of her work is focused on sexual violence and all forms of violence against women, working from an applied social psychological perspective. She has worked on a variety of projects, including assessing the outcomes and impacts of a project which is providing training on domestic violence for criminal justice professionals in Russia; evaluation of the operation and effectiveness of a sexual assault roforral contre in Scotland, and research on men who pay for sex. Dr Horvath has conducted research with a number of police forces and sat on a number of advisory groups. Her work has been both published and presented in a range of arenas, including international peer-reviewed journals and national and international conferences.

Lynsey Gozna is a lecturer in forensic psychology and has practice and research experience in a range of forensic settings, including probation and bail hostels, secure psychiatric units and prisons, in addition to working with numerous police forces in the UK and abroad. She is currently conducting research with the police observing suspect interviews and developing advice on suspect interview strategies and police credibility assessment. She provides training for advanced suspect interview courses specifically on major crime, personality disorder and psychopathy for police and related organisations in the UK. Most recently, she has developed and validated (along with Julian Boon) a holistic and bespoke approach to interactions with clients in forensic settings, entitled the "Chameleon Interview". In addition, she is collaborating on research involving offence-focused post-conviction interviews with personality-disordered sexual offenders, firearm offenders and prolific young offenders.

Series Preface

The Wiley Series in the Psychology of Crime, Policing and Law publishes both single and multi-authored monographs and edited reviews of emerging areas of contemporary research. The purpose of this series is not merely to present research findings in a clear and readable form, but also to bring out their implications for both practice and policy. Books in this series are useful both to psychologists, and to all those involved in crime detection and prevention, child protection, policing and judicial processes.

A little over a century ago, Caroline Luard, the 57-year-old wife of retired Major-General Charles Luard, was murdered. Both the Luards were pillars of Kent society and the circumstances of Mrs Luard's murder achieved national notoriety. On 27 August 1908 she had accompanied her husband on an afternoon walk, but had returned early in order to entertain a visitor. Her route home took her past "La Casa", an isolated summerhouse, and it was on its veranda that her distraught husband came across her body, shot twice through the head. The police arrived within hours of the crime, but already the crime scene had been contaminated by anxious well-wishers and servants, and Mrs Luard's body had been moved. The officer noted that the victim's rings had been wrenched from her hand and her purse had been cut from the pocket of her dress. He gave permission for the body to be taken to lie at her home and left a solitary constable to guard the site from the press and the curious. Signs of a trail leading away from the scene were swiftly obliterated by the stampede of gawpers, handicapping the bloodhounds which were eventually brought in to follow any scent. The chief constable had a force of just four detectives to cover the whole of the county, and these untrained officers showed little initiative or systematic planning in their pursuit of the murderer. Even the arrival of two officers from Scotland Yard, drafted in to aid the investigation, failed to crack the case, and the murderer of Caroline Luard remained undetected (Janes, 2007).

The Luard case displays just how primitive police training and technology were a hundred years ago. The chief constable of the time, another retired military man, appeared to owe his position more to social connections than to any practical experience of policing. He was, however, responsible for the first training courses for police recruits – admittedly voluntary – and instituted an annual athletics cup to encourage physical fitness among his men. As for technology, the police travelled to the scene of the crime by pony and trap; it was only through the enterprise of a local garage that the police were loaned a motor car for the duration of their enquiries (Janes, 2007).

Understanding Criminal Investigation shows how far we have come since the pony-and-trap era. The authors survey a range of areas of modern investigative practice. They highlight the emerging role of science – both physical and psychological – in investigating and solving crime, and the important thinking skills – beyond the sleuth's legendary intuition – which are necessary for effective detection. Eyewitness testimony was central to the Luard case, and this book illustrates both the strengths and vulnerabilities of this form of evidence, as well as the progress that has been made in developing interviewing techniques for eliciting full and accurate accounts from witnesses. Contemporary controversies, such as the effectiveness of offender profiling, the interpretation of crime statistics and performance indicators, and the treatment of rape victims by the police, are all fully described and dispassionately discussed. These themes serve to demonstrate how the police agenda has moved on from what the authors term the "suspect-centred" approach, with its emphasis upon the eliciting of confessions, to an "evidence-centred" approach, which emphasises systematic analysis and an awareness of the benefits which science and technology, properly applied, can bring to the business of crime detection.

The authors, Stephen Tong, Robin P. Bryant, Miranda A. H. Horvath and Lynsey Gozna, are all experienced academics and teachers on the staff of Canterbury Christ Church University and the University of Surrey. Their expertise embraces psychology, law and criminology, central themes of modern police education, and they lecture regularly on police studies programmes as well as more specialised detective-training courses. Their knowledge is grounded not just in academic study, but in first-hand experience of the police station and the holding cell. *Understanding Criminal Investigation* provides an accessible and well-informed text for all those involved in the practical applications of modern investigative procedures, as well as an insight for those not in the front line who wish to understand better the challenges and methods of contemporary policing.

GRAHAM DAVIES
University of Leicester

Preface

Detective work has traditionally been the subject of excitement and intrigue. Literature and entertainment have produced fictional detectives ranging from the intelligent, perceptive investigator through to the slow, uninterested and plodding detective who needs the assistance of an eager private eye. Characters such as Sherlock Holmes, Cracker, Lieutenant Columbo, Charlie Chan, Dr Quincy and Miss Marple present the investigator in a variety of different ways (Clarke, 2001; Reiner, 2000). Their backgrounds and personalities are considerably different, but their interest and determination in finding out "whodunnit" remain consistent. Detective work in fiction regularly appears to be as glamorous, dangerous and interesting, with the detective portrayed as intelligent, skilful and almost always successful in catching and convicting the offender (Reiner, 2000). These detectives sometimes rely on hunches, on scientific fact and evidence, whilst being allowed the luxury of concentrating on only one case rather than a full caseload (Bayley, 2002). However, these imaginary portrayals of detective work find little support in the more prosaic world of academic research.

Although there are a variety of books aimed at assisting detectives in the task of criminal investigation, many focus on legal issues or relevant points of law within the investigative process. Detective training itself has been criticised in the past as being too law-focused without sufficient recognition of the skills or knowledge required beyond the legalistic view of investigation. This book chooses not to focus on legislation or "points to prove", though it could be read alongside legal text; rather, the aim of this text is to bring together some of the literature that provides theoretical explanations of detective practice and a review of policies that impact on criminal investigation, for investigators and those interested in detective work. The broad range of knowledge a detective could draw upon, the variety of agencies, victims, witnesses and offenders involved in the criminal investigation process, and the manner in which investigations are evaluated often reflect the complex and challenging role of the detective.

An ancillary intention of the authors of this book is to enhance the learning experience of the reader, and for this reason there are both review questions and sources for further reading at the end of each chapter.

Acknowledgements

Robin P. Bryant
I would like to thank Roy Murphy, Dr Bryn Caless and Sir David Phillips for their observations on earlier versions of my chapters, and Josephine Bryant, who assisted me in seeking out sources of interest.

Miranda A. H. Horvath
I would like to thank Katarina Fritzon for her observations and advice on an earlier version of one of my chapters. I would also like to thank Lynsey Gozna for co-writing the investigative interviewing chapter. Most importantly I'd like to thank my friends, family (Mark, Helen, Hugo and Milo) and Jo Lewis for their unconditional love and support.

Stephen Tong
I would to thank my family for their support, understanding and patience during the writing up and compilation of this book. The basis of my contribution originated from my PhD; I have been particularly fortunate to have excellent supervisors who have encouraged me throughout the research and provided inspiration, insight and advice. I would like to thank my supervisors Dr Loraine Gelsthorpe, Professor Ben Bowling and Dr Janet Foster for their support and guidance throughout the PhD process. The PhD was based on observing detectives during the training process and their operational duties, and this experience has informed my understanding of criminal investigation. This insight is only possible because of the detectives who allowed me to follow them during their training and day-to-day work. I owe a debt of gratitude to these officers. The ESRC (Economic Social Research Council) and the NCF (National Crime Faculty) funded the PhD research, and without this contribution the research would not have been possible. I am also grateful to Roy Murphy, who offered

valuable advice on previous drafts of my chapters. Finally, I would like to thank Canterbury Christ Church University for granting study leave and providing the time for me to develop this book.

Permissions

The authors would like to sincerely thank the Home Office, Oxford University Press, Pearson Education, Ralph R Frerichs of UCLA and Sally Grover from the Actuarial Profession for permission to use original sources replicated and adapted within this book.

CHAPTER 1

Introduction: A Brief History of Crime Investigation

STEPHEN TONG

Traditionally crime investigation training has focused more heavily on legislation than theoretical contributions (Morgan, 1990; Tong, 2005). This text aims to fill this void by using some of the theoretical contributions from the academic sources and providing an insight into key debates and contemporary issues in crime investigation. An understanding of the investigative process is linked to an appreciation of empirical analysis of investigative decision-making and a critical examination of investigative practice. With this in mind, this text will examine empirical research into police investigative issues and illustrate the practical relevance of theoretical contributions to crime investigation while providing an accessible text intended for a broad audience, including professionals and undergraduate and postgraduate students.

THE DETECTIVE STORY

The origins of the modern detective can be found in the thief-takers of the 18th and 19th centuries. Thief-takers were individuals prepared to recover stolen property for a reward, announced by the town crier (Rawlings, 2002). The thief-taker has been described thus:

The rank and file of these recruits constituted a distinct brood, but two clear-cut differences in motivation set some apart from others. One kind were hirelings; with mercenary motives, they would play both sides of the street. The other kind were social climbers who, in order to move into respectable society, would incriminate their confederates.

(Osterburg & Ward, 2000, p. 15)

That the detection of the offence and the recovery of property were the central functions of the thief-taker (Gilbert, 1993) makes them similar to the modern-day detective (Eck, 1999). A crucial difference, however, was that payment was forthcoming either through agreement with the owner of stolen property or through a financial "parliamentary reward" (Emsley, 2002; Goddard, 1956). In this sense the thief-taker was a private investigator working directly for clients to recover specific property, or working for rewards offered by the courts. However, it seems clear that the entrepreneurial craft of investigation was found among contemporary detectives in Hobbs's (1988) ethnography of East End detectives. Hobbs's research shows that negotiation, exchanging favours, deception and deals are done as part of the process of convicting felons and the recovering of stolen property. There are therefore similarities between the methods used by thief-takers and those used by contemporary detectives.

No doubt some commentators would frown upon some of the practices employed by thief-takers, but given the circumstances of the time and the conditions in which they worked, one should not be surprised at their methods (Wright, 2002). The public dissatisfaction with the practice of the thief-takers' "craft", and the novelist and author Henry Fielding's determination to improve the policing provision in London, instigated a movement away from the monopoly of the entrepreneurial thief-taker. The creation of the Bow Street Runners in 1744 by Fielding offered a more co-ordinated and structured approach to policing (Osterburg & Ward, 2000). However, despite training, the methods of investigation and detection remained similar to those of the craft practised by the thief-taker.

The methods of the Runners went beyond the practices of watchmen or constables who were representative of the police at the time; the Runners attempted to solve the criminal cases to which they were assigned:

[The Runners'] method of detection was essentially the rapid pursuit and arrest of suspects indicated by the earliest information of any crime, and the use of information from petty criminals. To this day the use of informants remains central to detective work.

(Fido & Skinner, 1999, p. 42)

The "suspect-centred" approach is more likely to be successful if a witness or informant names a suspect (Bayley, 1998; Greenwood *et al.*, 1977; Reppetto, 1978). Bayley (2002) suggests that a traditional suspect-orientated approach has only recently been challenged by more scientific approaches to investigation. However, in 1786 this organised approach to suspect-centred response to crime was a significant diversion from the approach previously adopted by entrepreneurial thief-takers. With a "suspect-centred" approach to establish their reputation, the Bow Street Runners were set to expand.

The Runners were considered one of the first organised attempts at policing and provided a basis on which to create the Detective Branch of the Metropolitan Police. Henry Fielding took his obligations seriously, and introduced new approaches to investigation. He ordered proactive[1] raids by his men, and advertised in local newspapers to encourage victims of robbery to come forward and identify the suspects in custody (Rawlings, 2002). When he died in 1754 his brother, Sir John Fielding, succeeded him and continued to develop the Runners (Goddard, 1956). On his appointment, John Fielding established a criminal records office and a gazette that contained details of the activities of the Runners, with pictures of wanted suspects (Goddard, 1956). These initiatives – managing information relating to the investigative process, the use of proactive strategies, compiling and storing intelligence – reflected scientific approaches to investigation. The Runners were disbanded in 1839. Ten years after the creation of Peel's "New Police", they had finally relinquished their investigative role (Fido & Skinner, 1999). They were succeeded by the Metropolitan Detective Branch a few years later.

Although the Home Secretary Robert Peel eventually introduced his reforms for the New Police, this was on the basis of a preventive role rather than a plainclothes investigative function. This served to extend the existence of the Bow Street Runners. There was considerable suspicion over the role of a public police service and its relationship with the state. These concerns were fuelled by practices in France perceived as "political policing", leading to accusations of corruption, conspiracy, and spying on behalf of the state (Brown, 2006; Emsley, 1996). It was not until 1829 that Robert Peel finally passed a Police Bill introducing legislation for the New Police, against the recommendations of the parliamentary committee of 1822 (Edwards, 1999). The Commissioners of the Metropolitan Police, Charles Rowan (1829–55) and Richard Mayne

(1829–60), were in agreement with Peel that the main task of the New Police would be the prevention of crime (Fido & Skinner, 1999).

Lieutenant-Colonel Edmund Henderson (1869–86) succeeded Richard Mayne as Commissioner. He increased the detective force dramatically, to 216 officers, and introduced divisional detectives (Begg & Skinner, 1992; Rawlings, 2002). In 1878 Charles Edward Howard Vincent, a barrister,[2] was appointed Director of Criminal Investigation. This position was previously held by police officers in the rank of Assistant Commissioner (Begg & Skinner, 1992). Vincent was critical of Commissioner Henderson's detectives on the grounds that they were ill-suited and ill-equipped to perform well. As he described it:

> The divisional detectives consisted for the most part of illiterate men, many of whom had been put into plain clothes to screen personal defects which marred their smart appearance in uniform. They were but nominally controlled by a sergeant, little superior to themselves. Every Inspector gave them orders, and in reality they were employed as much as messengers, as in detectives duties, which they discharged pretty much as they liked. They never were withdrawn from duty so long as they committed no flagrant breach of discipline and with some exceptions lived a life unprofitable to themselves, discreditable to the service, useless to the public.
>
> (Charles Vincent, cited in Begg & Skinner, 1992, pp. 66–67)

This period was thus not only marked by the substantial increase in public service detectives, but also by continued suspicion and concerns over their competence (Morris, 2006, 2007). Worse was to come as corruption scandals made the headlines and the integrity of the police was questioned more generally (Morris, 2006).

The history of detective work has received less attention than social anthropological accounts of other groups, and as a result there are periods where an array of credible sources of research does not exist. This is the case particularly from the 1880s through to the mid 20th century (Wright, 2002). However, Morris (2007) describes the history of the detective in distinct periods of development. These include the "Heroic" (1829–78) and "Organisational Specialisation" (1878–1932) periods, characterised by the early development of the organisational and institutional creation of the detective within the public police. Morris (2007, p. 17) describes the "bureaucratisation" and "professionalisation" of the "investigation function" of the police, referring to the establishment of the Criminal Investigation Department (CID), the introduction of detectives into the Metropolitan Police and other forces in the UK, the emergence of the Special Branch and the use of science to assist with investigation. Despite these developments, the use of science was still at a relatively early stage, and scandals, including the "Turf Fraud" (1877) and the failure to catch the Ripper (1888), brought into question the integrity and competence of detectives. Furthermore, to add to Charles Vincent's views on the ability of his detectives in 1878, some time later the Desborough Committee (1919) reported that detective training was not required, as any learning requirement would be acquired through "experience and practical work", a recommendation that Morris (2007, p. 24) argues amounted to "investigation remaining as an artisan craft devoid of any higher intellectual content". In short, this period of development of the detective's role was considered not sufficient to merit higher status, and the competence of detectives was still in question.

Morris's third and fourth periods – "Central Leadership" (1933–80) and "Central Initiative and Control" (1981–present) – reflected a change in the organisation of the investigative function within the UK. Morris (2007, p. 28) argues that during the third period there was a recognition that the "fragmented" organisation of investigation was not meeting public demands and that change was required. This in part was the battleground for attempting to address the need for consistency between police services. An eight-week regional detective training period was recommended (1938) by a Home Office committee, and more consistent approaches to crime investigation were attempted (Morris, 2007). The Metropolitan Police introduced a laboratory for forensic exhibits in 1935, but this was met with initial resistance from detectives (Morris, 2007). However, despite the changes, from the 1960s to the 1980s the "old regime"[3] of seasoned detectives still characterised the notion of detective work as a "craft". It was during this period that Sir Robert Mark (Metropolitan Commissioner 1972–77) attempted to curb corruption. Sir Robert believed that the CID was "a firm within a firm",[4] and that malpractice had become commonplace. As a result he threatened to return all detectives back to uniform (Fido & Skinner, 1999; Mark, 1978). During Sir Robert's period as Commissioner, 470 officers left the Metropolitan Police, one in six of all Metropolitan Police detectives (Fido & Skinner, 1999). Mark is remembered for his stand against corruption in the CID, his most significant contribution during his tenure as Commissioner. The challenge for the police has consistently been the difficulty of controlling corruption and the reluctance to value education and training within the organisation's ranks.

The "Central Initiative and Control" period has seen significant change, Royal Commissions, and attempts at substantial reorganisation of the policing services. The introduction of the Serious Organised Crime Agency (SOCA) in 2004 brought together the intelligence

capacity of the National Criminal Intelligence Service (NCIS) and
the National Crime Squad (NCS) under one roof. In many ways the
introduction of SOCA was representative of the increasing centralisa-
tion of police services joining other national organisations such as the
National Police Improvement Agency (NPIA), Her Majesty's Inspectorate of Constabulary (HMIC), the Forensic Science Service (FSS),
and Skills for Justice (SfJ). Further to this there were failed attempts
to merge the 43 police services of England and Wales into 12 larger
regional forces. Attempts to merge forces have been justified by the
contention that police services in their current format are not "fit for
purpose" (HMIC, 2005). The argument presented for change focuses on
the belief that change is required to respond to terrorism and organised crime. The crime-fighting argument is continually put forward,
whether as the justification of regionalisation or of the enlargement
of the UK DNA database as means for the police to become more
effective (McCartney, 2006). Despite government aspirations for larger
police services and the increasing use of surveillance technologies,
there has been resistance to these ideas (Chakrabarti, 2007). Sir
Ian Blair has argued for a public debate on policing, presenting the
question "What police service do you want?" (Blair, 2005). Yet despite
the acknowledgement that policing is changing at a rapid pace, with
increasing demands symbolic of late modern society, there has been
resistance to a Royal Commission on policing (Blair, 2005).

Police reform at different points of the 20th century allows us in
part to see how policing has changed, but the available evidence also
reveals the criticisms that have been repeatedly aimed at detectives.
Events and cases that have coloured perceptions of detectives include
those of the "Birmingham Six" (1975), the "Guildford Four" (1975),
the "Yorkshire Ripper" (1981), and the cases of Stephen Lawrence
(1993), Michael Menson (1997), Victoria Climbié (2000), Damilola
Taylor (2000), Harold Shipman (2000) and Ian Huntley (2003), to name
a few. These have revealed failures in investigative decision-making,
lack of transparency, and poor supervision, use of intelligence and
information management, in addition to discrimination, corruption and
incompetence. These failures are perhaps related to concerns over the
lack of skills and abilities brought on by the failure to develop detective practices and reliance on dated methods (Morris, 2007; Stelfox,
2007). This is perhaps inevitable with the detective training of the past
focusing on the practice of the law rather than on subjects that encourage an understanding of the social and operational context in which
detectives work (Bowling, 2007; Morgan, 1990; Tong, 2005). Furthermore, the consistent theme that has perhaps dogged the development of
investigation, from thief-takers to modern detectives, is the emphasis

on learning how to undertake investigative work primarily in the work-place. As Stelfox and Pease argue,

> The choice of heuristic must be made explicit and its drawbacks fully understood. Heuristics enable officers to make sense of crime scenes and the accounts of victims and witnesses to take action. In this they are no different to other occupational groups which have been found to develop experiential working rules for the processing of information. However, there are a number of dangers for the police in using this type of reasoning. The most obvious is that decisions are influenced by factors which are not relevant to the situation but which leak from officers' experience or from the wider police culture into the decision making process.
>
> (2005, p. 192)

Bowling (2007) argues a similar point: that in order to attempt to achieve "fair and effective" policing, an understanding of social inequality and the context of the operational environment in which officers work must be achieved. These concerns have been heavily influenced by the working culture, lack of supervision, limited education and training, and a belief that traditional approaches of learning on the job are valued over book learning (Chan, 2003; HMIC, 2002; Hobbs, 1988; Tong, 2005). The terms "art", "craft" and "science" all help to characterise criminal investigation and articulate a practice that is sometimes portrayed as "instinctive" or "mysterious" (Reppetto, 1978; Tong & Bowling, 2006). An examination of the history of crime investigators illustrates the development of practice, and describes typologies of investigation associated with detectives. It is the typologies of the art, craft and science of investigation that provide the basis for understanding detective practice.

DETECTIVE WORK: ART, CRAFT, OR SCIENCE?

There are competing perspectives regarding the nature of detective work. Indeed, the terms "art", "craft" and "science" all help to characterise criminal investigation (Reppetto, 1978; Tong & Bowling, 2006). Debate has suggested that investigative work ranges from any one of these approaches to a combination of all three (Reppetto, 1978). The "old regime" perspective of the seasoned detective highlights the notion of detective work as a "craft". The "craft" is seen as emerging from experience on the job, an understanding of the suspects, victims and police involved in the process of crime investigation and an ability to craft or organise the case in a manner considered suitable by the detective (Hobbs, 1988). Hobbs also illustrates the craft in the context of interpreting the reality of detective work in a way that fits with the requirements of the court. The "craft" here is to ensure the transfer of the reality of police work into the courtroom context in a manner that meets the crime-control objectives of the police. Manipulation of and negotiation with victims, suspects, police managers and supervisors to achieve either organisational ends or a form of justice considered appropriate by the detective may all be seen as relevant characteristics of the craft of detective work (Chatterton, 1995; Corsianos, 2001; Ericson, 1993; Rose, 1996).

The "art" of detective work concerns intuition, and instinctive feelings and hunches regarding problem-solving in an investigative capacity. Ericson (1993) and Sanders (1977) argue that the "art" lies in the ability to separate the false from the genuine, but also in identifying effective and creative lines of enquiry. These lines of enquiry are not only posted by leads from forensic information but also developed from the "reading" of criminal behaviour and those who commit or witness crime. An officer who can practise the "art" of detective work not only reads the behaviour of those surrounding the crime but also considers motivation and strategies to avoid detection. Although this perspective on detective work has been shrouded in mystery, the RAND study[5] criticised detectives for their inability to solve crime unless the public provided information of a suspect or lead (Greenwood *et al.*, 1977). Bayley (1998) reaffirmed this view by arguing that the detective approach to investigation is routinely "suspect-centred". This is to say that when the public provide detectives with a name, the case is built around the suspect rather than other evidence that may be available. This critique of detective work disputes the notion of "art". The RAND study clearly identifies detective work as a process that relies upon the public identification of offenders rather than the intuitive insight of detectives.

The failure of the police service to clearly articulate and develop the detective "art" of investigative decision-making has led to the belief that only some detectives can be recognised for their brilliance within the detective hierarchy. Simon (1991) identifies and contrasts the different elements required of the good detective:

> the homicide unit of any urban police force has for generations been the natural habitat for that rarefied species, the thinking cop.
>
> It goes beyond academic degrees, specialized training or book learning, because all the theory in the world means nothing if you can't read the street. But it goes beyond that, too... Inside every good

detective are hidden mechanisms – compasses that bring him from a dead body to a living suspect in the shortest span of time, gyroscopes that guarantee balance in the worst storms.

(Simon, 1991, p. 18)

Simon identifies the "art" of detective work as the "internalised and instinctive" mechanisms that guide detectives. There is a clear distinction in Simon's interpretation between routine police work, specialised knowledge and "something more". This "art" of detective work appears from Simon's perspective to be a quality that only experience can provide, as theory in classrooms and books does not help the detective "read" the streets. Not only are few detectives perceived as being able to practise the "art", but the manner in which they achieve this is shrouded in mystery. In short, this view sees the detective as an "artist" who can demonstrate brilliant insight and intuition which ultimately results in the crime being solved (Reppetto, 1978). However, there is no script or method available to trainee detectives on how they may reach this elevated cultural status. Rather, the "art" of detective work is acknowledged through colleagues' perceptions on the basis of results, and a reputation as a good thief-taker (Hobbs, 1988). Therefore, recognition of quality in terms of practising the "art" of detective work is not open to external scrutiny, but is rather internalised and admired by detectives themselves.

A perspective in direct opposition to the concept of the detective as artist is one of the investigator as scientist. In this conception of detective work, detectives are skilled in scientific approaches, crime scene management, social sciences, the use of physical evidence, investigative interviewing, informant handling, offender profiling and managing the investigative process (Osterburg & Ward, 2000; Rachlin, 1996). The detective here is one who requires an advanced level of knowledge and instruction in interview technique. The scientific detective is not confined to forensic science but also has an appreciation of the psychology of interview technique, and of the social sciences of crime analysis and policing. Bayley (2002) argues that the use of science in the context of DNA evidence has initiated a shift away from a "suspected-centred" towards an "evidence-centred" approach. The scientific approach to detective work points to a potentially evolving "professional" detective significantly different from the detectives of the past. Both the "old"-style detective (as "artist" or "craftsman") and the professional detective (as "scientist") are "ideal types". In the cultural perspective of the detective as an "artist", of course, it is implicit that only a few officers will attain the status of detective. In the perspective of detective as "scientist", there is an inherent expectation that many will be able to attain the status of detective, as science can be taught to exact principles in the classroom and the workplace. Essentially, detective work as a science arguably removes some of the mythical and cultural barriers to learning and practising detective work.

The art, craft and science debate is reflected in the changing nature of detective work and the variety of methods available to the police. Although rapid development in science has provided an argument that the modern detective will have the attributes aligned with the "scientific detective", these claims are not new. Arthur Conan Doyle, the author of the Sherlock Holmes mysteries, argued: "Detection is, or ought to be, an exact science, and should be treated in the same cold and unemotional manner" (cited in Wright, 2002, p. 75).

The increasing prominence of scientific methods (Morgan, 1990; Tilley & Ford, 1996) and the changing police environment challenge traditional approaches to policing (Morgan, 1990; Southgate, 1988). The analytical distinction between an art, a craft and/or a science is particularly useful in highlighting the different processes involved in detective work (Guyot, 1991). The distinction leads to a number of questions: Can the art of detective work be introduced to trainee detectives through education and training, or are detectives born rather than made? Is detective work just a matter of matching DNA profiles with little requirement for investigative work? Or do the notions of the art and craft of detective work still have currency in the work of the modern detective? Is there a risk of detectives being "deskilled" (Maguire *et al.*, 1992) with a move towards the scientific approach at the expense of the traditional skills of the artist or craftsman typologies? Although there are no direct answers in the literature, these types of questions are of particular importance to the issue of the effectiveness of detective work. It is apparent that art, craft and science skills all play an important part in detective practice (Ericson, 1993; Reppetto, 1978; Sanders, 1977; Simon, 1991) and this leads us to consider the appropriate skills, abilities, competence and training required for future detectives.

OVERVIEW OF THE BOOK

This book will attempt to articulate detective practice and investigative processes using empirical research and theory. Chapter 2 outlines a brief historical overview of the various attempts to "model" criminal investigation (ACCESS and SARA models); the chapter also examines the current thinking in the professional sphere. Chapter 3, "Forms of Reasoning and the Analysis of Intelligence in Criminal Investigation", will provide an overview of knowledge generation, decision-making and the drawing of inferences and reasoning. The use of the hypothetico-deductive approach and inductive reasoning is examined, both within the original scientific context and in its application to criminal investigation. "Geographical and Offender Profiling" is the subject of Chapter 4, outlining the range of psychological models of profiling and providing a critical commentary on the value or otherwise of each approach. The chapter concludes by focusing on the role of offender and geographical profiling as an investigative tool. Chapter 5 examines eyewitness testimony, providing an overview of the empirical research on the subject and outlining the emerging areas of research and development in its use. Chapter 6 provides a brief history of interview techniques in the UK, including the introduction of audio and video taping. The use of the PEACE technique is outlined, using illustrations from a Thames Valley interview of a rape victim. Chapter 7 examines the issues around performance measurement, considering the viability of outcome-based measures. This chapter examines the evidence from empirical research together with British Crime Survey (BCS) statistics and police-recorded crime. Chapter 8 identifies key challenges to modern-day detectives, particularly weaknesses and shortcomings in contemporary investigations. The limitations of adversarial criminal justice, challenges to police investigation into sexual offences, evolving technologies and the implementation of scientific methods are evaluated against the "search for the truth" debate in the context of crime investigations. Chapter 9 begins with a brief history of police training before describing the some of the challenges facing the police in their attempts to achieve professionalisation. Finally, Chapter 10 draws together the key issues raised throughout the book.

NOTES

1. Crime investigation can be labelled as proactive or reactive. Proactive investigation is used when the police predict a crime is going to take place and seek to arrest suspects as they commit the crime. This type of operation is usually informed by intelligence, for example the use of informants. Reactive investigation is when the crime has occurred and the police respond by seeking out evidence after the offence has been committed.
2. The significance of the appointment of a barrister reflects the perceived importance of law to the role of criminal investigation and the detective.
3. A term used by Rose (1996) in describing detective culture, supported by the work of Young (1991).

4. "Firm within a firm" was a phrase coined by *The Times* newspaper. It referred to the relationship between organised crime and detectives from the Metropolitan Police in the 1960s. Essentially detectives were taking bribes from organised criminals and facilitating the pornography business in Soho, London (Mark, 1978).

5. The RAND study was an extensive two-year study conducted in the early 1970s in America and focused upon the effectiveness, organisation and contribution of police investigation (Greenwood *et al.*, 1977).

CHAPTER 2

Theories of Criminal Investigation

ROBIN P. BRYANT

INTRODUCTION

Although the "Detective Branch" was formalised into the New Police in 1842, it was not until the 1870s that criminal investigation took a firmer foothold with the introduction of the Criminal Investigation Department (CID) (Fido & Skinner, 1999; Newburn *et al.*, 2007a, p. 3). From that time on, and until relatively recently, criminal investigation was dominated by a reactive model of investigation, which emphasised "thief-taking", "points to prove" case construction (that is, at a relatively early stage of an enquiry, directing all efforts towards establishing a persuasive case against a suspect) and, most controversially of all (in retrospect at least), the widespread reliance on confession as means to secure a conviction. However, by 1982 the Byford Report[1] into the investigation of the crimes of Peter Sutcliffe, the so-called "Yorkshire Ripper", highlighted a number of significant shortcomings in investigative approaches. During the late 1980s and the early 1990s the traditional approach to criminal investigation came under increasing scrutiny and criticism (although not always, it must be acknowledged, by the wider public itself). This increasing concern stemmed, at least in part, from a series of miscarriages of justice, some notorious cases of police corruption (often involving plainclothes CID officers), the "backwash" emanating from the uncovering of abuses during interrogation of prisoners in Northern Ireland and, latterly, the flawed investigation into the death of Stephen Lawrence. Wright (2002, p. 96) argues that the miscarriage of justice cases in particular offered important insights into the "mindset" of the police at the time and (citing McConville *et al.*, 1991) clearly demonstrated the unfortunate consequences of an overwhelming emphasis on case construction. Likewise, in the 1980s, a number of other dubious practices became evident, including the inappropriate use of the "sus" laws (s. 4 of the Vagrancy Act, 1824) to arrest a person "suspected of being loitering with intent to steal" (in many forces the number of arrests attributed to a police officer was a criterion for appointment as a detective). Other practices at the time included falsely attributing an adverse comment to a suspect on arrest or during interview (known colloquially as a "verbal"), systematically but discreetly "hiving off" undetected crime reports to maintain extraordinarily high rates of detection (known as "cuffing") and claiming false clear-up rates by undertaking prison visits to serving prisoners to encourage them to admit to crimes[2] ("cleaning the slate").

Hence, by the mid to late 1990s, the emphasis within criminal investigation, particularly in the training of new detectives, had begun to move away from the "points to prove" philosophy to one that stressed instead "seeking after the truth". This is a more subtle distinction than may first appear. For example, whereas "points to prove" presupposes a crime or crimes, an offender or offenders and a prosecution case (that is, crime-solving), "seeking after the truth" tacitly acknowledges other possibilities such as "no crime" or the possibility of restorative justice outcomes for the victim. However, as Brandl notes, "not surprisingly, most studies which have examined the effectiveness of the criminal-investigation process have used 'crime-solving' as the criterion on which to make performance judgments" (cited in Bailey, 1995, p. 163). It follows that there is little available, as yet, to help the researcher evaluate the utility and effectiveness of these more recent "truth-seeking" models of criminal investigation, and this chapter should be read in that light.

"Seeking after the truth" requires the investigator to explore those lines of enquiry that point towards the innocence of a suspect with as much vigour as they are inclined to use to explore those that suggest guilt. Indeed, by 1996 the Criminal Procedure and Investigations Act s. 23(1)(a) required that all "reasonable lines of enquiry" be pursued, and reflected in statute at least some aspects of this "new wave" in criminal investigation. Likewise, if there was a move away from reliance on confession, at the same time advances in forensic investigation (notably the use of DNA) meant that the defence in a criminal case would focus as often on the process of the police investigation as it would on evidence exonerating the accused. Put simply, from a prosecution perspective a culture of suspect-centred investigation invariably leaves other explanations for events (in particular, those that potentially point away from guilt) untested and hence open to exploitation by the defence. These tactics of "active defence" (Ede & Shepherd, 2000) were more effectively countered within a context of truth-seeking than one of case-building. This is discussed further in Chapter 8.

Hence by the turn of the last century there appeared to be a genuine desire to recast criminal investigation into a new shape that would be more in keeping with the complexities and expectations of modern life, and more likely to lead to the guilty being punished and the innocent exonerated. But, given an impetus for such reform, just what shape should this new approach to "seeking after the truth" take? Perhaps inevitably, analogies were made with other professions (notably the medical profession) that draw upon, sometimes with dramatically successful outcomes, a "corpus of knowledge" that guides and informs the work of its members. However, as Adrian West and others noted at the time, the problem such a project has is that, "in contrast to many other investigative fields of enquiry, a corpus of knowledge of the history and methods of the art and science of investigation within [the UK] does not exist" (West, 2001, p. 15). The reform of criminal investigation thus became one of the development of investigative theory, which would embrace a corpus of knowledge unique to the profession itself. This theory would, it was argued at the time, lead naturally to the creation of a "model" of criminal investigation that the new wave of professional investigators would utilise to both fulfil their professional role and develop their profession still further.

THE DEVELOPMENT OF THEORY

One of the problems in the context of discussing criminal investigation is that the term "modelling" itself may assume a variety of distinct meanings. Of all of these perhaps the least common is "model" used in its scientific sense when applied to an attempt to emulate, using underlying scientific principles, an observable phenomenon. This is most familiar to us in a forensic context – for example, the modelling of vehicle collisions using equations of motion and Newton's laws.[3] In this case the model is tested by comparing its predictions with what actually happens. The model may then be accepted as a sufficiently accurate representation of reality, or modified to improve its representation, or even abandoned altogether. However, in another (more frequently occurring) sense, "model" refers to an idealised "template" for best action, as in the "model answer" to an examination question, of which a good illustration is the *Murder Investigation Manual* (MIM, see the section on the manual below). This "idealised model" approach to investigative theory can often lead to the use of routines and checklists, common features of many models such as the MIM. For example, Cook and Tattersall (2008, p. 457) claim that "investigative theory always requires a standard structure for assessment, prioritisation, and review to ensure that essential work is completed and unnecessary work is discarded".

Despite Burrows *et al.*'s observation that "it is clear that there is no single, universally applied model of investigation" (2005, p. 24), we may nonetheless infer that the development of investigative theory has been influenced by two distinctive but interrelated approaches. One approach is, in effect, to research the work of successful detectives and discover those skills, that knowledge, which have led to their success; a second discernible theme is the "cultural borrowing" from other disciplines and professions. Investigative theory usually emanates from a synthesis of these two approaches combined with an evaluation of lessons learned from the past, much as the armed forces might do after a war or military engagement.

Studying What Works

A beguilingly attractive approach to establishing investigative theory is to "study what works". Inevitably there are differences between investigators in how well they do their jobs; so what is it that makes the "effective detective" (Smith & Flanagan, 2000)? Leaving aside how we measure "effectiveness", what do successful detectives have in common and how do they differ from less successful ones? There is no shortage of advice in this respect, with *Blackstone's Senior Investigating Officers' Handbook* offering the suggestion that "successful SIOs must be able to reason logically, think clearly, analyse material, and extract significant information from minute detail" (Cook & Tattersall, 2008, p. 2). Much of the research conducted into the skills and knowledge of investigators has identified the existence of both general skills (e.g. communication and "people skills") and specific skills (e.g. the ability to formulate lines of enquiry). Barrett, for example, notes that "if, for example, expert investigators use particular strategies or focus on particular issues which help them solve crimes more quickly than less competent detectives, this may enable us to begin to specify means of accelerating the development of investigative decision-making expertise" (2005, p. 50).

Indeed, effective decision-making is often seen as a key quality for the investigator to possess (e.g. Wright's "sequence of decisions from action

at the initial scene of a crime through to case disposal": 2002, p. 85).
An example of the "studying what works" approach is the use of
naturalistic decision-making (NDM)[4] techniques for understanding
investigative practice and "capturing the experiences" of those
involved, particularly in the management of critical incidents (see
Alison & Crego, 2008, particularly ch. 7).

This kind of approach to discovering knowledge has a long history,
and can be traced at least to the 17th century and Francis Bacon's
Novum Organum (later developed in the 19th century by John Stuart
Mill in his *System of Logic*). Bacon attempted to understand the nature
of heat by listing all occurrences of the phenomenon, for example from
a candle's flame, from the rays of the sun and so on. Using a scheme
of classification and analysis, he hoped to discover what made "heat"
heat and what made "not heat" not heat. There are, however, obvious
limitations to such an approach, notably the circularity involved in
attempting to define a phenomenon ("effectiveness" in criminal investigation) by using occurrences of the phenomenon itself. Nonetheless, this
"distillation" of good investigative practice has been influential in the
development many of the models of investigation, such as the MIM
and ACPO Core Investigative Doctrine[5]; see the section on this below.

Cultural Borrowing

A parallel tradition within the establishment of investigative theory
has been the "borrowing" of ideas and approaches from other professions, most notably those professions with a theoretical basis in the
physical and biological sciences. An obvious parallel is with medicine.
After all, the challenges of clinical diagnosis, prognosis and treatment
are mirrored in those challenges that confront the investigator: what
crime, what suspect, what evidence? The task of criminal investigation is at least as complex: it too involves the uncertainties of human
beings, the subtleties of decision-making, the testing of evidence, the
skills of communication. The medical profession has a corpus of knowledge (literally), it has its scientific methods, its registers and all the
other hallmarks of a profession. Fundamentally a clinician seeks
the truth and learns to be wary of the "hunch". Medicine has also
been, in many key respects, a resounding modern-day success story.
Could this success not be replicated, through the replication of similar
theory and methodology, within criminal investigation? Such questions
are not new, for by the mid 1970s Greenwood *et al.* (1977) were already
questioning O'Hara's influential *Fundamentals of Criminal Investigation* (O'Hara & O'Hara, 1973) and its couching of investigation as an
"art form". In the preface Greenwood states: "The detection of crime is,

after all, not a science but an art, whose secrets are not likely to be captured in any great part between the covers of a book" (Greenwood *et al.*, 1977, p. 37). His adherence to the belief that routine investigations are more art than science encourages the idea that criminal investigation should be guided by individual intuition rather than by a rational and systematic method of enquiry.

But by 2000, in an equally influential book, Osterburg and Ward felt confident enough to assert that

> Most working detectives hold that their work is unique, that few tasks even come close. The authors of this text, on the other hand, maintain that the criminal investigators' job is simply another kind of inquiry – a reconstruction of the past. Because others with a similar concern for the past (ranging from historians to geologists) employ the scientific method in their endeavours, so too must the detective.
>
> (Osterburg & Ward, 2000, p. 347)

However, it becomes apparent when reading these various accounts and calls for change that the concept of the "scientific method", so often invoked, is rarely defined. In some cases (e.g. the ACPO Core Investigative Doctrine – see the section on this below) it will mean the adoption of the hypothetico-deductive method in order to take an investigation forward. In others, it would be more accurate to say that specific "methods of research" are required, rather than the more general "scientific method" (in the sense used by Karl Popper[6] and others). The main stages in the research process typically consist of stating the problem, forming the hypothesis, research design, measurement, data collection and analysis and hypothesis decision-making. Hypothesis formation and testing (features of most theories of investigation) are thus stages of a research paradigm rather than the "scientific method" per se. This is discussed in more detail in Chapter 3. Perhaps what "scientific method" really means in the context of investigative theory is the maintenance of an objective and open mindset, the unremitting pursuance of all "lines of enquiry" no matter whether they lead to innocence or guilt, the application of reason, the mistrust of intuition and the seeking after truth.

Synthesised Models of Investigation

Models of investigation frequently synthesise the approaches of studying best practice and cultural borrowing (particularly of the scientific method) together with the outcomes of evaluating past investigative failures, and, to a much lesser extent, past successes. The ACPO Core Investigative Doctrine is a clear example of such a model (see the section on the Doctrine below). The "lessons learned" are drawn in part from the now familiar inquiries into the deaths of Stephen Lawrence and Victoria Climbié;[7] and, from an earlier era, the Byford Report. Understandably, the media interest at the time of the publication of the Macpherson Report into the death of Stephen Lawrence concerned itself with the claims of "institutional racism", but the conclusion of the Stephen Lawrence inquiry clearly points to investigative incompetence as well as institutional racism and poor leadership (Macpherson, 1999, ch. 46).

These synthesised models often invoke what Burrows et al. (2005, pp. 23–24, and discussing volume crime investigation) refer to as the "procedural" and "discretionary" forms of investigation. Procedural approaches utilise pre-defined sets of prescriptions of actions to be taken and emphasise adherence to standardised approaches as the case is passed from one specialist to the next.[8] On the other hand, discretionary forms of investigation involve individuals taking responsibility for investigating the "whole case" and require generalist all-round investigative skills. Ironically, given its origins in a more general desire to "professionalise" the police service, the focus on synthesised models may have inadvertently undermined these more clinician-orientated discretionary approaches.

INVESTIGATIVE MODELS IN PRACTICE

Aide-mémoires, mnemonics, unpublished handbooks, standard operating procedures (SOPs) and less formal means have often been used by investigators to help guide an investigation. We begin this section with an appreciation of some of these methods. We move from this to examine in detail some of the more recent and developed investigative theory that has emerged in the last two decades.

ACCESS and SARA

There have been a number of what might be termed "acronym-based" approaches to assist in structuring the whole investigation, or critical parts of it. ACCESS (Assess, Collect, Collate, Evaluate, Scrutinise and Summarise) was a system usually attributed to Eric Shepherd (Ede & Shepherd, 2000, pp. 256–268) and taught to trainee police investigators from a number of police forces from the mid 1990s, including Kent Police. (Shepherd however initially devised the model as a means of testing the police case – see Ede & Shepherd, 2000, pp. 255–268). At the outset of an investigation is the assessment stage, in effect a needs analysis linked to the aims and objectives of the investigation. This is followed by collection (of data) and collation (the ordering of the data), evaluation (both in terms of reliability and validity) and scrutiny. Interestingly, Shepherd recommends employing a hypothesis-testing approach at the "scrutiny" phase. The first round of the cycle is concluded with summarising, although this in turn might well lead back to the assess phase, and so on.

SARA (Scanning, Analysis, Response and Assessment) was a problem-solving model used by some police forces to train police recruits (student police officers undertaking training towards qualification) in the fundamentals of investigation, adapted from a methodology within community policing and problem-oriented policing (POP). SARA as a model for investigation has now been replaced by the IPLDP (Initial Police Learning and Development Programme) crime investigation model, which consists of seven stages: instigation, initial response, investigative assessment, suspect management, evidence assessment, charge and post-charge activity and, finally, court (Bryant, 2008a, p. 567).

The ACPO Murder Investigation Manual

First published in 1998, the ACPO *Murder Investigation Manual* (the MIM, or sometimes simply the ACPO "murder manual") was one of the first major attempts in the UK to produce a comprehensive theory of investigation.[9] At over 300 pages it was certainly more detailed, comprehensive and longer than any previous "official" attempt to delineate investigative practice. Another departure from the past was that the MIM was not as dominated by a description of law and procedure as many previous manuals had been. Despite its title, the manual was soon adopted as a guide to the investigation of most forms of serious crime, not only murder. It was produced under the guidance of the ACPO Homicide Working Group and a third revised edition was produced in 2006. NPIA confirms that the MIM is "now seen, by practitioners and policy makers alike, as the definitive guide on homicide investigation" (NPIA, 2008b). Throughout this section we refer to the 2000 (second) edition of the MIM, which was distributed to interested parties on CD ROM in Adobe format.

The MIM presents itself as based on "scientific model" of investigation (ACPO, 2000, p. 15), and it is clear from the body of the manual that this actually refers to phases within the process of investigation (the use of hypothesis testing) rather than scientific testing of the model itself.

The MIM posits five stages of an investigation:

1. fast-track actions/initial stages;
2. theoretical process or investigative theory;
3. planned method of investigation;
4. suspect enquiries;
5. the disposal, of which there are two phases: post-charge and investigative maintenance (ACPO, 2000, pp. 17–18).

It is obvious from the introduction (ACPO, 2006, p. 15) that the manual was intended for practising, or even experienced, investigators, rather than trainees. However, much of the content of stages 1, 4 and 5 of the MIM is likely to have been familiar to experienced SIOs, although the authors of the manual clearly believed that a reiteration and explanation of good investigative practice was still necessary (such as awareness of the "golden hours" immediately after a crime which yield the best harvest of forensic materials). Stage 3 outlines forensic, search, arrest, interview, identification and communication strategies, and although much of this material could have been sourced by investigators in other ways, its gathering together in a single manual was of obvious value and utility, particularly as a means to train SIOs. However, the inclusion of stage 2, describing the theoretical processes used during a murder investigation, marked a significant development on previous manuals. The investigative theory outlined in the MIM is described under seven main headings:

- introduction (problem-solving approach, evidence and facts, and statistical information);
- crime scene assessment/process (location, victim, offender, scene forensics and post-mortem);
- offender profiling;
- behaviour patterns;
- geographical profiling (criminal geographical targeting, applicability of geographical profiling and requirements to produce a geographical profile);
- synthesis/analysis (mental reconstruction, the logical approach/ critical approach, hypothesis/theoretical process);
- lines of enquiry.

The synthesis/analysis phase of stage 3 sets out, in effect, the reasoning and analytical processes available to the SIO. This was a new departure an apparent attempt to overtly explain processes of decision-making to the SIO.[10] In that respect, the MIM does represent a move

from "artisan to professional" as the manual's introduction claims
(ACPO, 2006, p. 15). However, there is a tendency towards uncritical
presentations of the theory. For example, it is clear that the "Crime
Scene Assessment/Process" (ACPO, 2000, p. 22) is based on Routine
Activity Theory, but this is not made clear to the reader. In other professional contexts, the theoretical basis of an assertion (or practice advice)
is made clear to the user, and they are able to draw their own informed
conclusions. It is also unclear why certain techniques feature within
stage 3 while others are omitted. For example, almost four pages of the
MIM (ACPO, 2000, pp. 30–33) are devoted to "geographical profiling"
and this is a largely uncritical résumé of one particular type of software,
the "Rigel" system, of the four that are commonly available (Bryant,
2008b). On the other hand, the use of inferential databases in homicide
investigation (e.g. CATCHEM) is "relegated" to barely one page under
"Other Investigation Considerations", and presented in a manner that
means the inexperienced SIO is unlikely to appreciate its importance.

The ACPO *Investigation of Volume Crime Manual*

Published in 2001, the ACPO *Investigation of Volume Crime Manual*
(the VCIM) was produced for "front line staff including those working in
communications, crime desks, uniform, CID and scenes of crime work
to ensure that each fully play their part in the investigation" (ACPO,
2001, Foreword). "Volume crime" is defined as crimes such as street
robbery, burglary, theft (including shoplifting), vehicle crime, criminal
damage and "drugs" (ACPO, 2001, p. 9). The VCIM proposes five areas
involved in the investigation of volume crime:

1. call handling and initial response;
2. scene assessment;
3. evidence gathering;
4. witness management;
5. suspect handling.

It contains little in the way of new "theory" (this was presumably
not its intention) and is in effect an extended checklist of actions and
good practice advice, together with guidance on the law and procedure.
There is only limited content on how to conduct a volume crime investigation, the processes and forms of analysis and reasoning that could
be used, or the model to be employed (scientific or otherwise); it instead
emphasises meeting professional standards.[11]

The ACPO Core Investigative Doctrine

The ACPO Core Investigative Doctrine[12] (the "Doctrine") was developed under the direction of Sir David Phillips (2003) and under the auspices of the National Centre for Policing Excellence (the NCPE, now subsumed within the National Police Improvement Agency, the NPIA). The Doctrine "forms the basis of SIO training in the UK" (Roycroft, 2007, p. 94) and has informed the development subsequent "good practice" advice from ACPO (e.g. the *Road Death Investigation Manual* in 2007).

The authors describe the Doctrine as a "strategic overview of the investigative process, providing a framework for investigative good practice. Its purpose is to provide investigators with the skills and knowledge they require to conduct investigations in a competent manner, inspiring confidence in the investigator and the wider criminal justice system" (ACPO Centrex, 2005, p. 7). The Doctrine constitutes practice advice, and hence is not "mandated", which means that its adoption is at the discretion of chief police officers in a force. However, there is some evidence in recent HMIC inspections of monitoring of the implementation of the Doctrine by forces, as with HMIC's observation on Derbyshire Constabulary in July 2008 that their "staff and first responders are aware of the 'golden hour' principles contained within the 2005 practice advice on core investigative doctrine" (HMIC, 2008, p. 30). In its Professionalising Investigation Programme (PIP) Investigation Guidance to forces, NPIA makes it clear that a force's "Policy should reinforce that the investigation model detailed within Core Investigative Doctrine will be utilised for all investigations within the force" (NPIA, 2008a). However, it is also clear that the authors of the Doctrine do not intend it be "doctrinaire" in the sense of being overly prescriptive.[13]

The Doctrine (ACPO Centrex, 2005) covers six main areas, within two broad themes:

Part I. *Underlying Principles and Knowledge*
- Investigative knowledge
- Legal framework
- Criminal investigation process

Part II. *Process of Investigation*
- Investigative decision-making
- Investigation strategies
- Management

Further, the doctrine proposes conceptualising investigation in terms of:

- Activities
- Decisions
- Outcomes

Part I sets out the roles of key players within criminal investigation (e.g. the forensic investigator), but is largely devoted to the legal background (e.g. the Criminal Procedure and Investigations Act 1996, CPIA). However, Part I also discusses the relationship between "taught knowledge and experience" (ACPO Centrex, 2005, p. 23), employing a model attributed to Stewart (1998). This describes a number of routes to professional investigative competence, consisting of different combinations of learning through experience and learning through formal tuition. This suggests to the authors of the Doctrine that investigators "must have the desire and skills to learn" (ACPO Centrex, 2005, p. 24), a theme later developed in the Flanagan Report, which desires a police service "which emphasises individual professionalism" and recognises "the need to move away from training towards education" (Flanagan, 2008, p. 53). The content of Part I is also linked to the underlying knowledge and understanding required for the National Occupational Standards (NOS) that underpin initial investigation (see 2 4 below), although these links are not made explicit.

Part II was of particular interest to the academic community, as it provided, *inter alia*, a model of the investigative process, explanations of how investigators make decisions, the investigative "mindset", investigative and evidential evaluation, and developing and testing hypotheses (ACPO Centrex, 2005, pp. 41–73). In this sense the Doctrine was a development of the MIM (see the section on the *Investigation of Volume Crime Manual* above) with a more detailed theoretical basis. In particular, there is much more in the Doctrine on the decision-making process but also on the issue of identifying and avoiding bias (e.g. the "verification bias" and the "availability error").

However, it would appear that some of the more theoretical aspects of the Doctrine could be further developed, particularly in terms of depth and detail. Of particular note is the need for a more developed doctrine of reasoning, heuristics and hypothesis setting and testing. For example, although decision-making is examined in some detail it is not linked to more theoretical understandings of argumentation and "classical" (as distinct from naturalistic) decision-making.

TRAINING AND EDUCATION

Establishing models for investigation and the desire for increased "professionalisation" of criminal investigation inevitably leads to a consideration of the place of training and education in the development of investigators.[14] Until relatively recently, detective training was the remit of the local police force, although by the 1980s it was increasingly based on national (ACPO) guidelines (e.g. Brownie, 1982). In the 1980s and 1990s the core syllabus for detective training was dominated by law (e.g. the law surrounding theft, burglary) and evidence and procedure (e.g. investigative interviewing), and it remains so today. Currently, investigator training is officially delivered to every new recruit to the police service ("every police officer is an investigator") through the IPLDP. More advanced investigator training, largely for trainee detective constables (TDCs), is undertaken through the Initial Crime Investigators' Development Programme (ICIDP).

The IPLDP

The NPIA Initial Police Learning and Development Programme is undertaken by all new police officer recruits to the police service as part of their two-year progression to attested police constable status. The IPLDP is linked with the 22 National Occupational Standards for initial policing as described by the Sector Skills Council, Skills for Justice. A subset of the 22 NOS is associated with the PIP Level 1, namely the three NOS units: CI101, to "Conduct priority and volume investigations"; CJ101, to "Interview victims and witnesses in relation to priority and volume investigations"; and CJ201, to "Interview suspects in relation to priority and volume investigations". Each unit is then subdivided into a number of elements. As with all occupational standards, the PIP Level units are competence-based and emphasise the achievement of measurable behavioural outcomes. Table 2.1 shows how the investigative content of IPLDP is linked with the Core Investigative Doctrine.

IPLDP does not have a "syllabus" of content in the conventional sense, but instead a series of learning outcomes clustered together as either "core" or "optional". Police forces have significant responsibility in how they choose to deliver these learning outcomes. In terms of investigation, the relevant core learning outcomes are concerned with "problem-solving", the "initial investigation of crime" and "investigative decision-making". As these learning outcomes suggest, IPLDP essentially aims to ensure that police constables are able to investigate

Table 2.1 Occupational standards

Core investigative doctrine activity	Example of activity	Linked NOS units
Initial report	Control room instruction, incident log, etc.	1B9
Police response	Risk assessment, recording the incident, etc.	1B9, 2H1, 2I1, 2I2, 2C1
Scene attendance	Provide immediate support to victims etc.	4G2, 4G4
Crime scene assessment	CPIA 1996, protecting the scene, minimising contamination, etc.	2C1
Witnesses	Identify and question witnesses, CCTV, etc.	2G2
Information/intelligence	Force intelligence reports, CHIS, etc.	2G2
Suspect?	Initial lines of enquiry, description, names, etc.	2G2
Enquiries to trace offender	PNC, NDNAD	2G2
Arrest	Arrest strategy, PACE/SOCPA 2005 powers of arrest, etc.	2C3
Searches	Legal authority, seizure of items, proportionality, etc.	2J1, 2J2
Custody procedures	Escort to custody, give grounds for detention, etc.	2K1, 2K2
Interview(s)	PEACE, interview strategy, etc.	2H1, 2H2
Charge, caution, bail, NFA (no further action), etc.	CPS charging standards, prepare case files, evaluate investigation, etc.	2J1, 2G4, 2J2

Source: Bryant, 2008a, pp. 567–568.

reports of crime and in some cases carry out the investigation into a number of categories of volume and signal crimes. In more complex or serious cases they are expected to complete a "handover package" (essentially a collection of materials, such as records of interviews) to be passed to PIP Level 2 investigators.[15]

The ICIDP

The NPIA ICIDP (sometimes referred to as the National ICIDP, the NICIDP) is a programme designed for trainee detective constables and provides the basis for the investigation of more serious and complex cases. ICIDP is linked with PIP Level 2. As with PIP Level 1, Level 2 is linked with the Skills for Justice NOS for investigation (namely CI102, to "Conduct serious and complex investigations"; CJ102, to "Interview victims and witnesses in relation to serious and complex investigations"; and CJ202, to "Interview suspects in relation to serious and complex investigations").

ICIDP consists of three phases. Phase 1 is a period of self-study by the trainee investigator, using printed materials, and taking a minimum of 14 weeks (NPIA, 2008c, p. 1). The recommended textbook is *Blackstone's Police Investigators' Manual* together with its associated workbook. Content is law-based and covers: property offences; assaults, drugs and firearms; sexual offences and offences against children and other vulnerable persons; and evidence (Sampson *et al.*, 2008). This is followed by candidates for Phase 2 of ICIDP sitting the National Investigators Examination (NIE), which tests knowledge of the four sub-areas of property offences; assaults, drugs, firearms and defences; sexual offences; and evidence (NPIA, 2008c, p. 3). The NIE is a multiple-choice examination: each question has four possible answers, of which only one is correct; and in order to pass candidates must achieve 48.5% or more (NPIA, 2008c, p. 14). Random guessing will gain a candidate on average 25% of the marks and thus 48.5% represents a relatively low pass mark. Compensation between the four sub-areas tested also appears to be condoned and hence it would appear possible for a candidate to score above average on one sub-area in order to compensate for a very low mark in another. Questions are also marked using a simple rubric of 1 (correct) and 0 (incorrect). This in contrast with some other forms of professional training, such as medicine, which have utilised negative marking schemes to discourage guesswork, for obvious clinical reasons. (However, practice does vary amongst medical schools.) Finally, the policy on cheating in examinations explains that "A candidate found to be copying responses from another candidate, or otherwise obtaining assistance from another candidate, will be warned of their behaviour that it is inappropriate and may be subsequently disqualified from the examination" (NPIA, 2008c, p. 11), but there would appear to be no restriction on retaking the examination at a later stage and continuing with the ICIDP. In contrast, students applying to train as solicitors, after completing a qualifying law degree, must inform the Solicitors' Regulation Authority of any instances of cheating in examinations; which, in the absence of mitigating factors, would normally mean a bar to admission (SRA, 2008, p. 5). These are all important issues, for the NIE is the only guaranteed formal and centrally determined check on investigators' knowledge during training towards qualification.

Phase 2 of the ICIDP is typically a six-week taught course. In many forces there is also a requirement to complete a "tier 2" (post-initial training) investigating interview course before commencing Phase 2. There is some flexibility in how forces structure the six-week course (some, for example, base the course on a case study and might also incorporate a Hydra simulation), although all are likely to be linked to the NOS units and elements, subscribe to the NPIA specified aims and objectives, and will at least cross-reference the ACPO Core Investigative Doctrine (see the section on this above). Typical content in the Phase 2 taught element will include aspects of law and procedure (human rights, disclosure, Regulation of Investigatory Powers Act 2000, Serious Organised Crime and Police Act 2005), evidence (burden of proof, similar fact, bad character, hearsay, presentation at court), handling victims and witnesses (including vulnerable witnesses), interviewing suspects, victims and witnesses, crime scene management and forensic investigation and the ACPO Core Investigative Doctrine.

Practice varies between forces in terms of a formal assessment of the knowledge and understanding gained on the course (e.g. whether a formal written examination is set or not). However, in all cases Phase 3 of ICIDP will involve demonstration and assessment of competence in the workplace against the three NOS units. This involves supervision by a tutor (normally an accredited detective constable (Level 2) or an investigative adviser[16]) and collecting evidence in a professional development portfolio (PDP). Experienced investigators (those in position before the advent of the ICIDP) are able to access Phase 3 through APL procedures. On successful completion of Phase 3, investigators are "registered" at the BCU (Basic Command Unit) level as qualified at PIP Level 2.[17]

However, there is some concern that the process of supervision and assessment of trainees undertaking the ICIDP is falling short of initial expectations. As Chatterton observes:

> despite their trainee status, TDCs are not treated as such. Despite their lack of experience they carry a full crime workload. It is not uncommon for TDCs to provide night cover on their BCUs and on these occasions they are not always accompanied by an experienced detective. If they are fortunate enough to have a mentor the amount of support they receive is still limited because of the size of the mentor's own crime load.
>
> (2008, p. vii)

If this is indeed the case, then it is doubtful whether such a lack of proper support and supervision would encourage investigators to develop the commitment to learning that the ACPO Doctrine presupposes.

IMSC and SIODP

The Initial Management of Serious Crime (IMSC) course is designed primarily for detective sergeants and is, in effect, a bridging course between the ICIDP and the more advanced programmes for SIOs. The course is currently under review by the NPIA.

The Senior Investigating Officer Development Programme (SIODP) is designed for investigators already qualified to at least PIP Level 2 (e.g. through the ICIDP, see the section on this above) or its equivalent, who will be responsible for investigating serious crime (such as homicide and rape by a stranger). Students of the SIODP are typically of detective inspector rank or above. As with IPLDP and ICIDP (see the sections above for these) the SIODP is linked with the NOS units of competence, in this case the single unit CI103, to "Manage major investigations", although this unit has a total of five elements. Typically 15 days in duration (although a one-week "Hydra" simulation course – based on the investigation of a serious crime – is also often recommended as a follow-up, and in some cases is a compulsory element), the SIODP is usually delivered on a regional rather than local force basis for the sake of economy of scale (the numbers involved are significantly lower than for the ICIDP) and access to specialist inputs. Typically, the course includes the ACPO Core Investigative Doctrine (particularly in terms of initial response, gathering information, use of forensic investigation), inter-agency working, family liaison, resource management, the use of intelligence, record-keeping (particularly in policy logging and disclosure), self-evaluation and the evaluation of others, and handling the media.

The course is followed by the gathering of evidence in a PDP to claim competence against the NOS unit, leading to the achievement of PIP Level 3. NPIA is currently consulting on a professional register for SIOs (NPIA, 2008d) which, it is envisaged, will contain the details of all those accredited through the SIODP or through other means of demonstrating competence at PIP Level 3. In order to remain "live" on the register, an SIO will be required to provide details of the CPD activity they have undertaken in order to maintain their expertise. This is similar to the new requirements on medical practitioners (see the section on "cultural borrowing" above) who, to retain their places on a professional register, will be required after 2009 to show evidence that they have kept up to date and are fit to practise (GMC, 2008).

SUMMARY

The past decade has seen increasing emphasis on the development of investigative theory to inform the process and conduct of criminal investigation. This has arisen partly through a stated need to "profes-sionalise" criminal investigation, but also as a response to the perceived inadequacies of the past and as a response to a changing legal landscape (see Chapter 9). Theories of investigation have emanated from studying both what works and what doesn't, but also from borrowing approaches from other professions which share similar demands and constraints, and in many cases attempting to synthesise these two philosophies into a single model. A major contribution to investigative theory has been the ACPO Core Investigative Doctrine, whose influence has been felt in a number of revised training programmes for investigators. These programmes represent a further stage in the attempt to professionalise investigation. However, concerns remain over the depth of the profes-sionalisation process and in particular the commitment to supporting trainees, their opportunity to develop, and establishing rigorous forms of assessment.

NOTES

1. In December 1981 Sir Lawrence Byford of HMIC produced a confidential report on the investigation into the series of attacks and murders by Peter Sutcliffe, the "Yorkshire Ripper". An excised version of the report was released by the Home Office in 2006 under a Freedom of Information request.
2. In 1986 Constable Ron Walker of Kent Constabulary (now Kent Police) made a detailed complaint to the Metropolitan Police that over 60 fellow police officers were engaged in soliciting bogus confessions from convicted prisoners in order to improve clear-up rates. Walker alleged that in one case a serving prisoner admitted committing 87 offences, despite the fact that 34 of these occurred while he was in prison or under other forms of close supervision. When Scotland Yard finally raided a number of police stations in Kent in August 1986 (McCarthy, 1986), they found that, "with the exception of one single document, every item of paperwork it needed had been destroyed" (Davies, 2003). Subsequently one detective was dismissed and 34 police officers disciplined (Horsnell, 1989).
3. Sir Isaac Newton's laws of motion, first described in the 17th century, are concerned with the relationship between force, momentum, velocity and acceleration. They are still widely used today when attempting to analyse events in the physical world.
4. NDM is often contrasted with "Classical Decision Making (or Theory)", the latter being based upon a normative and ostensibly rational system involving the estimation of likelihood and

outcomes. NDM, however, recognises that decisions in the "real world" are often made by people with only incomplete information and under pressure of time and resources, and derive from more informal "naturalistic" methods.

5. There has also been a plethora of "good practice" guidelines from the NPIA in other aspects of policing, such as search, domestic abuse and criminal assets recovery.

6. Popper's major contribution to the philosophy of science was an elucidation of the scientific method, marking a break from the classical inductivism of the past. One important criterion for a hypothesis to be scientific is that it should be capable of being falsified through the use of experimentation or observation. So, for example, the basic tenets of astrology would fail to meet this requirement; whereas hypotheses in astronomy are usually such that they would pass the falsifiability "test".

7. Victoria Climbié was 8 years old when she was murdered by her guardians. The Victoria Climbié inquiry found shortcomings in the investigation of her murder and, in the words of one witness to the inquiry, the MPS Deputy Assistant Commissioner William Griffiths, "In the A to Z of an investigation, that investigation did not get to B" (Laming, 2003, para. 1.19).

8. There has been a noticeable growth in the number of "specialist units" within police BCUs and a rise in the attendant problems with "demarcation" and assuming responsibility.

9. The National Crime Faculty's "aide-mémoire for senior investigating officers" was produced in 1996 and contained some of the subject matter later to be found in the MIM.

10. Earlier descriptions of investigative theory were strong on detail (typically different crimes, law, procedure, interview techniques, forensic science and courtroom skills) but offered little in the way of explanation of the process of investigation itself. It was as if a recipe for baking a cake listed the ingredients and proportions but failed to explain to the reader just how they should go about the process of baking.

11. This emphasis is possibly at the expense of a more detailed analysis of the variability of volume crime in terms of its "solvability".

12. The use of the term "doctrine" is an oblique reference to both the military and religious meanings of the word, and this ambiguity was probably intended. Organised religions often have doctrine as a collection of beliefs and systems that in turn underpin religious instruction and teaching. When used in its military sense, "doctrine" refers to detailed strategies and tactics to be employed

during conflict and reflects how the enemy is likely to conduct its offensive or its defence.

13. This is not to say that the results of following the Doctrine should be unrecorded. The military will often undertake an evaluation of a campaign conducted according to doctrine, which requires a detailed recording of courses of actions taken (or left untaken), together with a justification from those issuing orders.

14. For a more general discussion of police training see Chapter 9 below. The remainder of this chapter is largely devoted to the training and education of trainee investigators. From the 1980s onwards there was an increasing decentralisation of "specialist" training to BCU level. In some forces this had the effect of reducing the (typically five-yearly) routine updating of the knowledge and skills of investigators, and it is now possible for an officer to serve up to 15 years of continuous service without further training.

15. However, the quality of "handover packages" frequently raises concern during internal police reviews (see, for example, Northamptonshire Police, 2007).

16. The tutors are normally expected to have completed a three- to five-day training course on coaching and assessment skills.

17. However, it is relatively common practice for the investigator, once qualified, to move to one of the many "specialist roles" such as public protection, "hate crime" or Tactical CID. This means that the more "public facing" investigatory work is often conducted by inexperienced and unqualified trainee investigators.

REVIEW QUESTIONS

1. What has influenced the development of investigative theory in the UK?
2. How are investigators trained in England and Wales and how does investigative theory feature in their training?
3. What are the issues that might be inhibiting a deeper professionalisation of criminal investigation?

QUESTIONS FOR FURTHER RESEARCH AND ANALYSIS

1. What other examples of "borrowing" from other professions can you identify within criminal investigation practice?
2. How do other countries train their detectives?

3. What evidence is there for a decline in the attractiveness of detective work?

RECOMMENDED READING

ACPO Centrex (2005) Practice advice on core investigative doctrine. Camborne: NCPE.

WEBSITE

National Policing Improvement Agency: http://www.npia.police.uk/

CHAPTER 3

Forms of Reasoning and the Analysis of Intelligence in Criminal Investigation

ROBIN P. BRYANT

INTRODUCTION

When undertaking the analysis of intelligence within criminal investigation there is a parallel version of the "Johari Window", the famous psychological model of self-awareness: there are forms of intelligence that we both know about and know that we know; and there is intelligence that we do not know but we know that we do not know; But there is also intelligence that we do not know exists but others do (our blind spots), and, perhaps most potentially damaging of all, intelligence that we think we know is true, but which is actually not the case at all.[1] It is perhaps for this reason that, as Heuer argues:

> Intelligence analysts should be self-conscious about their reasoning processes. They should think about how they make judgments and reach conclusions, not just about the judgments and conclusions themselves.
>
> (1999, p. 31)

There is also what we might term the "myth of the *gestalt*": that somehow a jigsaw can be successfully completed by assembling a sufficient number of small pieces of intelligence in the expectation (or even hope) that they will form a coherent whole picture. But there is much evidence from history to demonstrate clearly that intelligence failures usually occur not because of a lack of sufficient information but for the lack of sufficient analysis, and that often there is not a "complete picture" to be had.

A problem with any chapter on intelligence reasoning within criminal investigation is that, as Trent *et al.* (2007, p. 76) note, "the cognitive work of intelligence analysts has not been studied as much as one might suppose", and this absence of published research within intelligence is paralleled within crime investigation as a whole. For example, Stelfox and Pease (2005, p. 191) note that "there has been surprisingly little empirical research into the way in which individual officers approach the task of investigating crime". Although books and articles on intelligence often begin by citing the work of the first-century military strategist Sun Tzu and the often asserted claim that "intelligence is the second oldest profession", in fact intelligence (as opposed to espionage, which is clearly what Sun Tzu meant) is a comparatively recent phenomenon and did not develop as a "profession" until the 1940s and 1950s (Rathmell, 2002, p. 90), this might be one reason, apart from concerns of security, why there is little in the way of a culture of publishing research in this area.

This chapter therefore considers more general forms of reasoning and argumentation, placing these in the more specific context of intelligence analysis and theories surrounding criminal investigation.

It is important to study the reasoning processes used within intelligence analysis for a number of reasons. Firstly, there are only particular ways in which the conclusions of an intelligence argument built upon rational methods are likely to give rise to sound conclusions, and these are discussed below. It is important that these are recognised, discussed and evaluated by the investigator and analyst. By and large (certainly in non-military examples of analysing intelligence), final decisions concerning intelligence "products" are still made by people using cognitive processes, and not by machines using programmed instructions. Secondly, errors of intelligence analysis that arise through fallacious forms of reasoning will always be with us. What is important therefore is to "train people how to look for and recognize these mental obstacles, and how to develop procedures designed to offset them" (MacEachin, 1999, p. ix). It is particularly important that unjustified confidence in intelligence analysis conclusions is minimised. Ironically, copious quantities of information available to the analyst do not of themselves increase the accuracy of such analyses. In this context more is not better. However, more can lead to increased but unreliable confidence in the intelligence "product" (Heuer, 1999, p. 54). Furthermore, having a truly "objective" approach (the "open mind") and a relentlessly rational frame of mind ("Mr Spock") is effectively impossible, hence it is important that preconceptions are identified so that they can be "factored in" and challenged by others. Surprisingly, given the nature of the job itself, this open and challenging approach to intelligence is not always a feature of the modern intelligence-gathering organisation, for as Sandow-Quirk wryly observes:

> In a bureaucratic and authoritarian milieu, any challenges to the received truths of policy which emerge from disinterested analysis are unlikely to be encouraged; challenges to the mental models of the environment held by management will almost certainly engender resistance.
>
> (2002, p. 138)

INVESTIGATIVE THEORY

Operational intelligence, particularly when used as part of a criminal investigation, usually fits within an overarching investigative theory. For example, in the UK, police forces have been expected to have adopted the principles of the National Intelligence Model (NIM) and, more recently, have been advised to employ the ACPO *Practice Advice on Core Investigative Doctrine* (ACPO Centrex, 2005).[2] However, as with intelligence *per se*, it is worth noting at this point that "there is no commonly-accepted corpus of knowledge within the police service which informs officers' actions in the process of detection" (Stelfox & Pease, 2005, p. 192). The past two decades have seen a number of attempts at theorising investigative practice, particularly the use of intelligence; it is what, in Chapter 2 above, we described as "Doctrine".

First, there have been the various attempts to distil the essence of successful investigatory work, including the work of Nicky Smith and Conor Flanagan (amongst others) on the qualities of an "effective detective" (Smith & Flanagan, 2000). Secondly, there is a particularly noticeable tradition, evident within both the NIM and the new investigative doctrine, of the cultural borrowing of ideas and approaches from other disciplines, particularly science and medicine. However, whenever ideas are "transplanted" from one location to another we have to be wary of the differences in context. The context in which criminal investigation must operate is not the same as that of a medical investigation. Thirdly, there is an approach to formulating theory through a synthesis of these two approaches, coupled with the assimilation of lessons learned from errors made in the past – for example, the importance of the "golden hour" and forensic awareness. The new ACPO Core Investigative Doctrine is essentially this kind of synthesis. However, it is debatable whether what we see in the Doctrine is actually what we recognise as theory within the physical, biological or even social sciences. In some senses it is closer to Piaget's delineation of intellectual development than it is to Einstein's Special Theory of Relativity. That is, it describes how a successfully conducted investigation should develop under normal circumstances rather than being a theory which helps us predict how to respond under new and untested circumstances. This doesn't invalidate the Doctrine, just as, despite subsequent developments in theory, Piaget's work still retains its importance in understanding how children develop; it simply makes the Doctrine something other than a theory.

Against the backdrop of the development of the Doctrine, we have also seen a debate concerning what we could perhaps classify as the "art, craft and science" of detective work. "Art" here means instinct, involving "hunches" and the mysterious "detective's nose" – within this paradigm, detectives are born, not made. This is what makes good TV, and in turn links with the idea of investigation as a form of "craft", which emphasises learning on the job, is suspect-centred (for example, "points to prove"), adversarial and based solidly in police "routine and process". This sees detectives as made through experience. The "science" of investigation, by contrast, is posited as inquisitorial in nature, seeking after the truth, emphasising evidence and promoting hypothesis testing. This latter approach is, we would argue, the paradigm of the ACPO Doctrine, where detectives are trained in the scientific method.

In part, the Doctrine's emphasis on scientific and justifiable approaches to investigation (particularly in terms of the law surrounding disclosure) and intelligence-gathering is a reaction to the perceived inadequacies of the past. For example, in the Home Office report *Reviewing Murder Investigations* (Nicol *et al.*, 2004), poor judgement was identified as one of the main sources of investigative weakness leading to failures in an enquiry. The Macpherson Report (1999) into the circumstances surrounding the murder of the black teenager Stephen Lawrence in London, amongst a litany of other police failures, also uncovered major shortcomings in investigatory approaches. A common factor appears to be that the quality of reasoning affected the investigative process, and it is timely to look now at what is involved in reasoning – both in investigation and in intelligence.

FORMS OF REASONING

Reasoning is a feature of most forms of sound argument and the exercise of judgement – it could be argued that reasoning skills are therefore key to good intelligence analysis. Although reasoning, argument and judgement are by no means identical concepts, they all refer to what are primarily cognitive processes to arrive at conclusions and decisions when analysing intelligence. We examine, from this point, a number of notable forms of human reasoning, and those most commonly encountered when utilising intelligence products.[3]

Inductive and "Commonsense" Reasoning

Inductive reasoning involves generalising from a number of previous examples to establish a "rule" or "theory". This form of reasoning is very common in everyday life and was the basis for much scientific discovery in the past. (There are some suggestions that this form of reasoning is "hard-wired" into our brains, since most people appear able to use this form of reasoning without being taught it.) For example, early humans undoubtedly realised that there is a cycle, "day/night–day/night", and generalised from this pattern to conclude that night would always follow day. On a certain intellectual level, most of us are probably content that induction provides sufficient grounds for us to retain our acceptance of the "day/night–day/night" cycle. We do not necessarily require convincing with the use of cosmological arguments concerning the motions of the earth and sun, or the entropy of the solar system. The more this confidence is reinforced by subsequent events, the more we are persuaded by the truth of the generalisation.[4]

However, despite being a widespread technique for reasoning, induction has an inherent weakness. As Bertrand Russell, Karl Popper and others have demonstrated, there is no logical reason why a generalisation should follow from particular observations. A famous example concerns swans. If every example of a swan that we have seen is coloured white then, not unnaturally, we conclude that all swans are white (our "working" hypothesis). This is all very well until we observe our first black swan.[5] Often this is the point at which textbooks and websites stop when discussing the strengths and limitations of induction. However, continuing our example of the colour of swans, in practice we do not abandon altogether our inductive theory concerning their colour. Instead we modify our thinking to suppose that *most* swans encountered *in the UK* are *likely* to be white. In practice therefore, most inductive reasoning is also "probabilistic" reasoning, and what is crucial is to have a reliable understanding, as far as is possible, of the probabilities attached to the conditional nature of a hypothesis. Hence intelligence hypotheses, which lead in turn to more substantial theories, are sometimes built from incremental improvements (elaborations embracing inconsistencies) rather than the paradigm shift which is sometimes required.[6]

Hence it is not the case that inductive reasoning has no value because of its inherent weakness, but rather that we should be cautious in its application. The danger for investigators and intelligence analysts when using inductive methods resides in the problem of generalisation from observation, particularly if these observations are limited in number or unrepresentative. For example, consider the white detective investigating gun crime within inner London. In all likelihood, given the social demography of the area, these crimes are likely to involve members of ethnic minorities, indeed "disproportionate" numbers when compared with the social demography of the whole UK. (Just as the numbers of ethnic minority citizens from such an area making contributions to charities will be "disproportionate".) Areas with a high ethnic minority population also tend to feature amongst some of the poorest in Britain – for example parts of Manchester or Birmingham. A false generalisation here would be for our detective to conclude, using induction, that gun crime is endemically "black" in nature rather than symptomatic of other social phenomena that gun crime and "being black" are independently linked with. In some senses, the incorrect reasoning of the detective is a "natural" response, and this demonstrates the need for an understanding of the nature and limitations of reasoning.

Allied to induction are those heuristics[7] built upon experience, which may be called "commonsense reasoning", and the use of "schemata" of previous examples that we attempt to fit new intelligence discoveries to. Reasoning by analogy looks for previous examples which appear to match (in what we deem to be the "key" characteristics) a current and partially unknown situation. We also tend to simplify explanations for events into a relatively small number of possibilities and assign (usually mentally) "relative likelihoods". This is common to many professional contexts where clinical judgement is required. For example, Falvey et al., referring to mental health diagnoses, note that:

The mind uses a variety of heuristics (i.e., cognitive shortcuts) to handle the information overload that is characteristic of complex judgments. These heuristics tend to reduce the complexity of problems by assessing probabilities based on a limited number of variables across many cases at the expense of considering innumerable variables germane to one individual.

(2005, p. 292)

This can be a powerful and effective approach. There are, however, further dangers that may lurk with commonsense heuristics, even those based upon more sophisticated applications of likelihood. These dangers reside in an individual's inevitably limited experience of low-incidence events, often mediated by media representations of crime. For example, consider the crime of child abduction and murder by a stranger with a sexual motive.[8]

Suppose we were asked to read a number of statements and score them using a scale of 1 to 5. We are told to allocate a score of 1 if we judge that there is no basis to the statement and 5 if we believe that it is almost certainly correct, using the numbers 2, 3 and 4 to estimate the accuracy of the statement if it falls between these two extremes.

The first statement is:

IF the crime is sexually orientated child homicide THEN the offender is most likely to be male.

Our commonsense reasoning here would suggest an answer of 5: almost every case of this kind we have heard or read about has involved a man as an offender.[9]

Now suppose we have some additional information and are asked to assess the following statement:

IF the crime is sexually orientated child homicide AND the victim is female THEN the sex of the offender is equally likely to be male or female.

We are not likely to change our previous conclusion hence are likely to give an answer of 1: that is, we know of no reason why the sex of the victim should have any bearing on the sex of the offender in this case, and in any case would not move our estimate from almost 100% to 50%.

A more complex set of statements to assess would read as follows:

IF the crime is sexually orientated child homicide AND the offender is not within the family THEN the crime is probably part of a series.

IF the method of killing indicates ritualistic killing THEN the crime may be, or become part of, a series.

Perhaps surprisingly, the answer to both statements is "1" (based upon analysis of the 358 cases in the CATCHEM database since 1960). Whereas the first two examples we gave are successfully addressed using experience-based heuristics (largely inductive reasoning), the third and fourth are not. However, in our experience, *trainee detectives are often as confident in their wrong answers as they are in their correct ones.* This is a crucial point. Given the nature of this type of crime and its low incidence, we need the CATCHEM database as a form of reliable inductive reasoning: our own experience or commonsense are simply not reliable enough. (It is unlikely that even the most experienced investigator would encounter more than one or two of these crimes in his or her career.) Furthermore, it is the combination of the variables of the offence and victim that give rise to "predictions" concerning an unknown offender: change just one of the input variables and it may be a markedly different prediction for, say, the likelihood that the offender lives within five miles of the victim. We can easily overestimate our ability to deal with this complexity. For example, most people find it difficult to juggle more than a few variables in their heads when the variables interrelate, but for the five CATCHEM "offender variables" there are a possible 10 combinations, and the number of combinations increases according to $n(n-1)/2$ where n is the number of variables.

Deductive Reasoning and Argumentation

In contrast with inductive reasoning, deductive approaches start with assumptions (or a general rule) and deduce other conclusions from these starting points. For example, we may assume that all human beings have DNA. If we arrest John, a human being, then we can conclude that John has DNA. Deductive reasoning forms part of a wider set of concepts and methods known as "logic". There are two main schools of logic, known as "formal logic" or sometimes "symbolic logic" which is mathematically derived (using, for example, set theory), and "informal logic" which uses everyday language. Deductive reasoning is often associated with the wider field of argumentation. In modern intelligence analysis, the examination and construction of arguments is often part of the field of "intelligence and security informatics" research.

Deductive reasoning also has its drawbacks. In essence, it helps us to extend what we already know by demonstrating the consequences of our assumptions rather than adding directly to the pool of "new" knowledge. Further, although the logic is impeccable, the value of our conclusions ("inferences") is entirely dependent on the truth of our assumptions, or the "premises" as they are often called. For example, consider the two premises and the conclusion below:

Premise: An imam of the local mosque is a Muslim.

Premise: All Muslims are extremists.

Conclusion: The imam is an extremist.

Here the argument is deductively valid (correct) but not necessarily true, as the second premise is certainly *invalid* (false) and hence the conclusion can either be valid or invalid: we cannot say, based on these premises. Now consider the argument:

Premise: The suspect, Dave Jones, was seen outside Tesco supermarket talking to Abu Hamza al-Masri.

Premise: Abu Hamza al-Masri is a well-known extremist.

Conclusion: Dave Jones is an extremist.

Both premises could well be valid, but the argument used to establish the conclusion is not (it does not follow) and hence, as before, the validity of the conclusion is unknown. The validity of arguments using deductive logic is summarised in Table 3.1. A more prosaic way of expressing this is GIGO (Garbage In – Garbage Out) (more precisely this should be GINCC – Garbage In – No Clear Conclusion).

Table 3.1 Validity of arguments

Premises	Argument	Conclusion
Valid	*Valid*	*Valid*
Invalid	*Valid*	*Valid or invalid (don't know)*
Valid	*Invalid*	*Valid or invalid (don't know)*
Invalid	*Invalid*	*Valid or invalid (don't know)*

The validity of one's premises is a major concern in all intelligence analysis, as the information that forms the basis of an inference is rarely completely reliable. Police forces in the UK have a system (derived from the national agencies) to reflect these uncertainties, referred to as *"5x5x5"*, where intelligence on one of the three axes ranges from "known to be true without reservation" to "suspected to be false or malicious".

In practice, intelligence arguments (which may be called hypotheses in some literature) are probably made up of complex sets of inferences leading to a conclusion. That is, they are often extended arguments rather than the simple three-part arguments discussed above.[10]

An example of an extended argument is given in Figure 3.1, where P1, P2, P3 and P4 are premises, C1 an inference and C2 a conclusion.

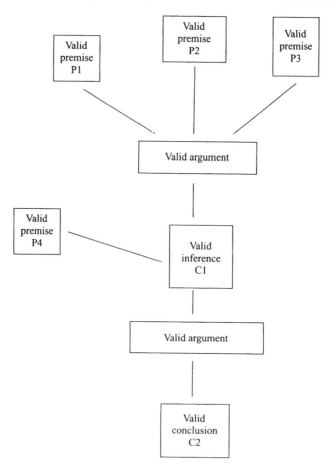

Figure 3.1   Logical propositions

Within logic, arguments are usually distinguished from a beguiling, similar-looking statement called a *conditional proposition*. These take the form of IF, THEN statements (see the CATCHEM examples above) and allow for degrees of certainty to be introduced rather than the categorical true/false dichotomies discussed in the examples above.

INDUCTIVE VERSUS DEDUCTIVE REASONING

Inductive and deductive forms of reasoning are often described, at least tacitly, as being in some form of conflict. Inductive reasoning is commonly viewed as being useful in uncovering new insights within an investigation, but inherently untrustworthy. Deductive reasoning, by contrast, is seen as inherently reliable but somewhat restricted in application, and by some authorities (Canter, 2000, p. 24) as exhibiting "fundamental weaknesses". Popular writers (such as Turvey, 1998) can often seem to imply that the investigator should be wary of inductive methods. There are a number of problems with this "inductive versus deductive" debate. Firstly, it ignores the empirical observation that most practising investigators employ a variety of inductive and deductive forms of reasoning, and not just the classical syllogisms reproduced in the literature ("All men are mortal. Socrates is a man. Socrates is mortal"). For example, investigators are likely to employ the two main forms of deduction often termed *modus ponens* and *modus tollens*.[11]

In *modus ponens* the argument takes the following form:

IF P, THEN Q (premise)
P (premise)
THEREFORE Q (conclusion)

Modus tollens deductions have the structure:

IF P, THEN Q (premise)
NOT Q (premise)
THEREFORE NOT P (conclusion)

A practical example of the application of *modus tollens* would be:

If the suspect's alibi is true (P), then he must have been observed by the CCTV camera (Q).

The suspect cannot be seen on the film taken from the camera (not Q).

The suspect's alibi is probably not true (therefore not P).

Or, more prosaically, here is Sherlock Holmes's famous application of *modus tollens* from the short story 'The Adventure of Silver Blaze' by Arthur Conan Doyle:

The Simpson incident had shown me that a dog was kept in the stables, and yet, though someone had been in and had fetched out a horse, he had not barked enough to arouse the two lads in the loft. Obviously the midnight visitor was someone whom the dog knew well.[12]

In practice most people have an understanding of *modus ponens* but may lack the mental rule for *modus tollens* (e.g. Braine & O'Brien, 1991). This was earlier confirmed in research by Rips and Marcus (1971, cited in Rips, 1994, p. 42).

Secondly, the "mistrust" logicians express for inductive reasoning ignores the likelihood that in many intelligence applications it provides a perfectly good basis for initial conjecture. The danger here is not inductive reasoning of itself, but rather its application without recognition of its limitations. For example, an experienced intelligence analyst supporting an investigation into a series of linked burglaries in the centre of Anytown would start with two initial hypotheses based on inductive reasoning (which the analyst may term "commonsense" or as being "down to experience" or even "intuition"):

1. That in all likelihood the perpetrator is currently resident, or was recently resident at the time of the crimes, somewhere close to the centre of Anytown.
2. That the perpetrator probably has previous convictions.

The combination of these hypotheses leads the investigator to focus the investigation on those known criminals living close to the location of the offences.[13] In fact both 1 and 2 find support in the research literature. A number of research studies have noted the domocentric nature of much crime, and the phenomenon of high-volume recidivist offenders is widely acknowledged. Application of inductive reasoning to high-incidence crimes will often lead to the same conclusions as the experientially derived approaches favoured by the "apprenticeship" model of investigation. As we illustrated earlier, the danger arises if this largely successful inductive reasoning is applied to circumstances rarely encountered by investigators, such as low-incidence crimes or burglary by artifice.

Abductive Reasoning and Hypothesis-Testing

Abductive reasoning,[14] when used as part of criminal investigation, is essentially an examination of "competing" hypotheses and deciding between a "null" and any alternative hypothesis. It involves testing according to likelihood and looking for evidence which either confirms or refutes an alternative when compared with the null hypothesis.

Perhaps surprisingly, the ACPO Core Investigative Doctrine recommends that "hypotheses should only be used when absolutely necessary" (ACPO Centrex, 2005, p. 72), implying perhaps that hypothesising somehow represents a less valid form of reasoning. That suggests the authors of the Doctrine are taking "hypothesis" as meaning some form of guesswork whereas, in its true scientific sense, it is nothing of the kind.[15] The "hypothetico-deductive" scientific model is characterised by a number of stages. Although we will now describe these stages in a sequential order, in practice the process may be somewhat more fluid. First, *data* (information) are collected and collated – often in the form of communications information, reports from informants, open sources of intelligence and so on. *Conjectures* are made – perhaps in the mind of the investigator, for example: "What role does this person play in the criminal organisation?" A *pair of competing hypotheses*, normally at a more detailed level than a conjecture, is established – these are opposite to one another but also exhaustively comprehensive. For example a pair of hypotheses may be concerned with whether or not the person concerned "launders" the proceeds of crime for the organisation.

First, hypotheses are tested. There are a number of ways that tests may be carried out. Interestingly, with hypotheses used within the physical sciences, the onus is on *seeking evidence which might refute the hypothesis* rather than focusing on evidence that may support it.[16] Within investigation in general, and intelligence analysis in particular, there are number of ways in which this testing might progress, often used in conjunction with each other, including:

- What are the consequences that would logically follow from the null hypothesis?
- What would follow from the alternative?
- What antecedents would we expect to find if the null hypothesis was correct?

According to the results of the testing, hypotheses are supported or refuted – does the evidence support the null hypothesis? Do the logical consequences of a hypothesis give rise to a contradiction of known fact (*reductio ad absurdum*)? Are the expected antecedents to be found? "Successful" hypotheses then form the building blocks of a more comprehensive and embracing *theory*.

Less experienced investigators may instead start with a theory and attempt to derive hypotheses. For example, consider:

H_0: John Smith is the source of the fake passports (the null hypothesis)

H_1: Somebody else is the source (the alternative)

Although technically correct, H_0 and H_1 are a particularly unhelpful initial pair of hypotheses, as hidden within them (particularly within

the alternative hypothesis) are too many complex and potentially
ambiguous possibilities. Instead, if we are to draw the analogy with
science and medicine more accurately, then H_0 and H_1 should start
at a deeper level of detail and precision and build instead towards
theories. The decision between these lower-level hypotheses is based
upon a weighted average of the results of testing each null hypothesis
against its alternative.

As an example, consider the investigation into the rape of a woman
by an unknown male. A consideration here might be the age of the
offender (A). The information available to the enquiry would probably
include attributes of the offence (location, time, events), the offender
(build, personal hygiene, method of hiding identity) and the victim (age,
ethnicity). The age of the unknown offender could be estimated through
hypothesis testing. Here a simple starting point could be a null hypothesis that the offender is under 21 ("young") against the alternative that
he is 21 or over ("not young").[17] In mathematical notation we have:

$$H_0: A < 21$$
$$H_1: A \geq 21$$

There are likely to be a number of ways of testing this pair of hypotheses. For example, a single eyewitness description of a man seen
driving a way from the location of the rape indicates an offender in his
early to mid thirties, provisionally supporting H_1, but with no great
reliability. Driving *per se* is more likely to be found as evidence arising
as an abductive consequence of H_1 (about one-third of drivers pass the
practical driving test under the age of 21).[18]

The victim reports that the offender smelled of rolling tobacco, which
lends some support to H_1 but has a low discriminatory value as a
test. (Although smoking self-made cigarettes from rolling tobacco and
papers was often associated with older smokers, this would appear now
to be less the case.)[19]

Psychological theory, on the other hand, suggests that the form of
approach used by the offender is more closely associated with younger
offenders, lending support to H_0. A database of previous cases of rape
by a stranger indicates that, for rapes that occur outside, before sunset
and where the victim is aged under 17, there is a probability of 70%
that the offender is under 21 (not actual data), again lending support
to H_0.

There are likely to be a number of other tests that an experienced
investigator (and intelligence analysts) would employ to test the same

pair of hypotheses, most based upon abductive reasoning. These are illustrated in Figure 3.2.

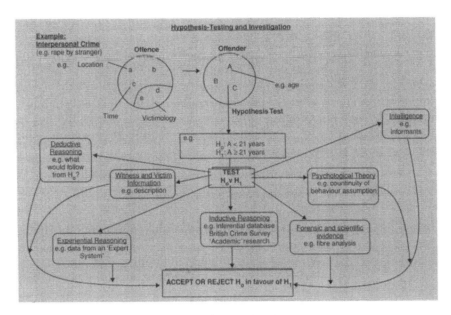

Figure 3.2   Hypothesis-testing and investigation

The results of some tests are likely to be more compelling than others as they will carry a larger weight in the decision between the null and alternative hypotheses. Examples of such tests include clear, reliable and intra- and inter-consistent eyewitness testimony. Note that although decisions are made (need to be made) concerning null and alternative hypotheses, these decisions are likely to be subjected to periodic review in the light of new intelligence that may be derived at a later stage of the investigation.

There are additional problems that may arise when attempting to both formulate and test intelligence hypotheses. Firstly, effective hypothesis-testing requires the use of tests with a high discriminatory or "diagnostic" value to differentiate between pairs of hypotheses (see the example above). Errors occur when tests of a low (or even zero) discriminatory power are used. A recent example occurred, albeit in a different context, during the shooting by Metropolitan Police Service (MPS) officers of the innocent Brazilian Jean Charles de Menezes at Stockwell underground station on 22 July 2005. Although "looking over his shoulder and acting in a wary manner" (IPCC, 2007, p. 55) may be characteristic actions of a would-be suicide bomber, they are also characteristic of many more forms of behaviour, none of which is related to suicide bombing. That is, the hypothesis has a low discriminatory power as a test for a suicide bomber.[20]

It may even be that no test is used at all, but decisions between hypotheses are still made. This is related to the concept of *satisficing*,[21] that is, decision-making by choosing the first hypothesis that fits the facts, often in combination with a form of Occam's razor,[22] the first and simplest possible explanation consistent with intelligence. It is just as important to check whether the same evidence would actually support another hypothesis altogether. Finally, the problem essentially lies in whether the analyst or investigator is able or willing to consider a fuller range of possible null and alternative hypotheses.

THE NATURE OF CHANCE

Investigators are often confronted with questions concerning the likelihood of certain events occurring by "chance" or whether they should be invested with more significant intelligence meanings. This is a particularly pertinent consideration in an area of work known for its deception and duplicity. For example, we may be interested in the likelihood of two people being in one-off phone contact purely "by chance" (for example, through error) rather than as an indication of a meaningful connection between them. The science of chance and likelihood is known as "probability".

Our everyday lives are pervaded by considerations of "chance" – what is the likelihood of a certain event occurring? Sometimes this manifests itself as an assessment of the likelihood of some apparently rare event occurring, such as a "coincidence". The problem is that we have few "natural" (untaught) means of assessing the scientific importance of an example of chance in terms of so-called "risk". We are broadly aware that, for example, we are far more likely to be involved in a road traffic collision than in an accident involving aircraft. But more people, it would appear, fear flying than travelling in a car. It is just that the outcomes of these two events – car or plane crash – are dramatically different in terms of our likelihood of survival and the numbers involved within the confines of a particular incident. We believe, rightly or wrongly, that although road traffic collisions are far more common than mid-air collisions, our chances of survival are much higher in the former. Outcomes often "cloud" our judgement of chance. Another example might be found in playing five-card poker. Imagine being dealt the 10, jack, queen, king and ace of clubs in one poker hand. We are likely to consider it a very rare event, which indeed it is. However, it has exactly the same chance of occurring as any other specified hand of cards (such as the 3 of clubs, 5 of diamonds, queen of hearts, 2 of hearts and 5 of spades), including your previous hand in the game. (Note that this is not the same as saying it has the same *aggregate chance* as all the other possible hands.) We obviously attach greater meaning to this hand of cards than to most others because of its importance to the game. Furthermore, although we have an appreciation of the relative amount of risk involved in taking certain actions, we do not, as a matter of course, know by just how much one chance relates to another.

Finally, we are sometimes just plain wrong about certain chances. For example, we may argue that it will either rain on 29 August 2010 in Oxford or that it will not, and therefore the chances of it doing so are 50:50. However, this is not actually the case. Just because there are two possible outcomes to an event does not mean that they have equal (50:50) chances of occurring. For example, if we enter the UK's national lottery, we either win or do not win the jackpot. However, we would not argue that our chances of winning the jackpot are 0.5, otherwise we would each be expecting to win roughly once every two weeks, which obviously is not likely!

There are two distinct approaches to formalising an understanding of chance and calculating probabilities: *a priori* ("before the event") and *a posterori* ("after the event") approaches. This distinction is an important one for investigation. The *a priori* approach is a more "abstract" method, where we attempt to account for all possible outcomes of an event, ensuring that they have equal probabilities and then selecting out the outcomes that interest us. In this sense the probability is calculated "in a vacuum" using a number of assumptions. For example, take the apparently simple case of throwing a six-sided die and recording the topmost number. If the die is a "fair" one, by which we mean that each of the numbers 1 to 6 is as likely to occur as any other, then we can say, for example, that **Pr** (a number 2) = **1/6**. We can also say that **Pr** (an even number) = **0.5** (as there are three outcomes from six, all equally likely). Note that we have calculated these probabilities without the need to actually undertake any form of empirical research and by using some (quite key) assumptions.

This type of probability is quite rare in intelligence analysis. More common are *a posterori* calculations. For example, suppose we wished to know the probability of a blue cotton fibre being present on car seats in Australia purely "by chance" (this is a real example, see e.g. Kingsley, 2002). It is difficult to envisage an *a priori* approach to this problem. Instead, we would need to conduct some form of practical sampling of cars and their seats and, using evidence-gathering techniques recover, all the blue cotton fibres. The probability would then be estimated using the calculation, and is an example of the "frequentist" approach to estimating probabilities. So, for example, our previous question concerning the likelihood of rain on 29 August 2010 in Oxford is likely to be estimated by looking at past events and to draw upon records of past weather patterns and occurrences, allowing perhaps for the effects of global warming.

However, in intelligence analysis there is more often a third notion of chance, to some extent straddling *a priori* and *a posterori* approaches, which Bowell and Kemp (2005, p. 83) refer to as *rational expectation*. Intelligence analysis, particularly when applied to terrorism, often considers low-probability events with few past examples to generalise from. An analogy would be estimating the likelihood of a major earthquake in south-east England in the next 10 years. Such an estimate would not only be based on the frequency of past earthquakes in the area (the average "return period") but also on what we know of the science of tectonic plate movements in the English Channel. However, the potential problems with "rational expectation" as an approach to intelligence might simply be that an intelligence model based upon reasoning is, from one cause or another, particularly sensitive to the initial "boundary conditions". For example, a slight change in the underlying assumptions may give rise to a dramatically different predicted outcome. The change to one or more assumptions (premises) may be needed as a result of further information becoming available.

The examples considered so far are such that one event is not dependent upon other events. For example, consider the scenario of choosing unseen two balls in succession, not returning the first ball, from a bag containing three red balls and five yellow balls. The probability of choosing a red ball in the first choice is 3/8, a yellow ball, 5/8. This is the simple *probability* of each event. However, the probability of choosing a certain colour at a subsequent selection is "affected" by the outcome of the first choice (as we have not returned the first ball). This is known as *conditional probability*.

In our example the probabilities are fourfold:

Probability (red ball given that first ball was red):	2/7
Probability (yellow ball given that first ball was red):	5/7
Probability (red ball given that first ball was yellow):	3/7
Probability (yellow ball given that first ball was yellow):	4/7

The phrase "given that" is often used in probability to mean "under the assumption that", and is usually abbreviated with the symbol |. In general terms we consider the probability of event A occurring given that event B has already occurred, written as **Pr(A|B)**. Conditional probability occurs frequently in forensic investigation.[23]

However, as a further illustrative example, consider the two events:

A: The person has a police warrant card.

B: The person is a Kent police officer.

Now **Pr(A|B) = 1** (all Kent police officers have warrant cards) but **Pr(B|A) = 0.02** (approximately), as having a warrant card applies to all members of the UK police forces.

Or, using an example where it is difficult to evaluate the probabilities but the argument still holds, consider the two events:

A: A search of the home of an arrested person uncovers a copy of *The Anarchist Cookbook*.

B: The person is involved in terrorism.

Here **Pr(A|B)** and **Pr(B|A)** are not equal, although the values of each would be difficult to determine. When they are erroneously held to be equal in the courts, it is known as the "Prosecutor's Fallacy".

COINCIDENCE AND THE NATURE OF RANDOMNESS

Coincidence is both a blessing and a curse for the investigator. It can be a compelling indicator of meaning, or simply a chance event. As we noted with the above example of two hands of poker, the low probability of an event occurring is not sufficient for us to be impressed and to invest it with added meaning. That said, we assign meaning to some low-probability events but not others. As Griffiths and Tenenbaum (2007) argue, coincidence is attached to events which have both a low probability of occurring *and* which are assigned meaning (of a causal nature). The first quality is mathematical, the second within the psychology of the investigator. Griffiths and Tenenbaum go on to argue a distinction between "mere" coincidence (usually dismissed with the phrase "just a coincidence") and "suspicious" coincidence where some as yet undetected causal factor is at work. One type of coincidence may give rise to "false conclusions", the other to "significant discoveries". Further, some forms of coincidence are much more likely than we may intuitively believe. For example, if we gather a group of 30 people together it might appear "obvious" to the casual observer that the likelihood that two of them share the same birthday

(day and month rather than year) is low, given there are 365 or 366 days in a year. Perhaps if we asked over 180 people we might encounter a match. However, rather surprisingly the probability of a match with 30 people is actually just over 70%, so it is more likely than not to occur. "Littlewood's Law of Miracles" explains that in fact most coincidences are a frequently occurring phenomenon (with a "miraculous" coincidence happening to each of us with a frequency of approximately once every 35 days) that require no further causal explanation than chance (Littlewood, 1953).

Hence we may see patterns and meaning where they do not exist, particularly in terms of the unusual and unexpected. Likewise, we may not spot patterns and links where they do exist, particularly if we assimilate knowledge within an existing investigatory paradigm in a gradual manner. On the one hand there is an overall tendency for us to perceive "order" where there is none, particularly in terms of cause and effect; on the other hand we have a limited understanding of what "randomness" actually means. During the autumn and winter of 1944, hundreds of V1 rockets ("flying bombs")[24] were launched from occupied mainland Europe towards London and south-east England, causing damage and injury (one V1 attack alone led to the deaths of over 160 people in south London in October 1944). As Clarke noted later, "During the flying bomb attack on London, frequent assertions were made that the points of impact of the bombs tended to be grouped in clusters. It was accordingly decided to apply a statistical test to discover whether any support could be found for this allegation" (1946, p. 481). Londoners' impression that the attacks were not spatially random in nature was supported by the fact that in some areas of less than 1 km^2 there had been over four attacks, whereas in others close by there had been none. Table 3.2 below shows the number of flying bomb attacks per 0.5 km^2 in a 144 km^2 area of south London.

Table 3.2 Flying bomb attacks

No. of flying bombs per square	No. of squares
0	229
1	211
2	93
3	35
4	7
5 and over	1
Total	576

Source: Clarke, 1946, p. 481; reproduced with the permission of the Institute of Actuaries.

The statistical test Clarke applied involved testing the null hypothesis that the attacks followed a particular model of randomness (known as the *Poisson distribution*) against the alternative hypothesis that they were non-random. The results are shown in Table 3.3. As can be seen, there was a very good fit between the predicted and observed values, lending strong support to the null hypothesis that the V1 attacks followed a form of randomness.[25] Indeed, a similar form of spatial randomness occurs when sand is thrown on to a horizontal surface.

Table 3.3   Analysis of flying bomb attacks

No. of flying bombs per square	Expected no. of squares (Poisson)	Actual no. of squares
0	226.74	229
1	211.39	211
2	98.54	93
3	30.62	35
4	7.14	7
5 and over	1.57	1
Total	576.00	576

Source: Clarke, 1946, p. 481; reproduced with the permission of the Institute of Actuaries.

It is a common misconception that "randomness" means an even spread and is some generalised reference to a phenomenon that, by definition, cannot be understood. As Clarke's example illustrates, randomness knows several forms and is susceptible to some level of understanding. Randomness may also give the misleading appearance of order. (The "arrangement" of the stars in the night sky is entirely mathematically random but this does not prevent people seeing "patterns" in terms of the constellations.)

The objective of an intelligence analysis is to separate the important signal from the background of random white noise, a skill that operators developed in the early days of sonar and radar (Laming, 2004). Of course, analysing intelligence information is not the same as modelling V2 attacks or learning to use radar, but there are more relevant examples of the use of "leading indicators" as a way of separating the important and telling information about crime from the background noise and transmuting it into intelligence. For example, those individuals who choose to park in disabled bays but have no right to do so are not representative of road users as a whole, but are much more likely to have a history of wider criminality (an example of the offender "self-selection" phenomenon – see Chenery et al., 1000); and Roach (2007) discusses those individuals who do "big bad things" but are only spotted when doing "small bad things".

MORE GENERAL FORMS OF BIAS AND FALLACY

We have identified a number of potential hazards for the investigator and intelligence analyst lurking within forms of reasoning, argument, hypothesis-testing, chance, coincidence and the supposedly random. There are also other, more general, forms of bias and fallacy lying in wait for the unwary. Indeed, it is perhaps more important that the investigator studies the origins of error than it is that he or she fully comprehends the subtleties of sound reasoning; for, as Shulsky and Schmitt note:

> [while] it may not be possible to lay down rules that will inevitably guide us to analyze intelligence information correctly, it is nevertheless useful to try to identify intellectual errors or deficiencies that may be characteristic of the analytical process.
>
> (2002, p. 72)

Putting aside discussions concerning individual intellectual and cognitive abilities, it would appear that we succumb to fallacious reasoning for a number of reasons, some of which are particularly important for the investigator, including the abstract nature of the premises (Wason & Johnson-Laird, 1968, p. 124, citing Wilkins, 1928) and the emotive quality of the material of the material being assessed (Lefford, 1946). Researchers have identified a number of more general sources of possibly erroneous reasoning and argumentation in intelligence analysis (e.g. Trent et al., 2007, p. 81, and reviewing the literature on problems identified in military intelligence analysis). These include the "mental set" of the investigator, where strategies for the present and future are based upon successful strategies used in the past. Related to this is "fixation", where preconceived notions are adhered to even in the face of contradictory evidence (with various psychological tactics to countering the "cognitive dissonance" that might ensue). However, perhaps the most pervasive and potentially damaging error in reasoning is *verification bias*. Stelfox and Pease (2005, p. 197), citing Tweney and Chitwood (1995), explain that there are number of identifiable components to verification bias. Firstly, there is the failure to seek disconfirmatory evidence. As we explained earlier, the hypothetico-deductive approach to intelligence discovery requires the active seeking of evidence that would contradict the hypothesis;

whereas our "natural" tendency might be to note that information which agrees with our favoured working hypothesis but ignore, or "explain away", that which doesn't. Secondly, there is the reluctance to test the alternative hypothesis, in the ways we described earlier. For example, best practice would be to consider whether evidence supporting a favoured hypothesis supports alternative hypotheses just as well. One subtle aspect of the verification bias, perhaps of particular importance when analysing intelligence, is the difference between *wanting to see* and *expecting to see*, the latter being much more pervasive, the former not as great an issue in practice (Heuer, 1999, p. 9).

Fallacies of argument are myriad (note that they are often referred to in the literature as "informal fallacies"). Some are so common (and infamous) that they have acquired their own name. Indeed, it is a long list: affirmation of the consequent, anecdotal evidence, *argumentum ad antiquitatem, non sequitur, argumentum ad baculum, argumentum ad hominem, argumentum ad ignorantiam, argumentum ad misericordiam, argumentum ad populum, argumentum ad verecundiam,* complex question, converse accident/hasty generalisation, *post hoc ergo propter hoc,* denial of the antecedent, *dicto simpliciter, ignoratio elenchi* (irrelevant conclusion), the Natural Law, *non causa pro causa* and *petitio principii* (begging the question) are just a few.

To take one example: *non causa pro causa* (false cause and effect). This fallacy often occurs when we mistake correlation for causation. Just because two events occur together does not mean that one necessarily caused the other. A close relation of *non causa pro causa* is *post hoc ergo propter hoc*. This is the error of assuming an event to be the cause of another event simply because it happened before that event. *Non causa pro causa* and *post hoc ergo propter hoc* may also occur in the analysis of information and data, and not just as informal fallacies in spoken or written argument. The discipline of aetiology (*etiology* in the American spelling) originated within medicine (for example, to discover the causes of a disease) but is now a more general examination of cause and effect. In the analysis of two or more variables we must be careful to differentiate between a statistical and mathematical correlation and, for this reason alone, inferring a form of cause-and-effect association. A mathematical correlation could be the beginnings of a "suspicion" that there are underlying causal factors at work but is not sufficient by itself to demonstrate the existence of such a link. Put more succinctly, correlation is not the same as causation.

This is not, however, to decry the potential use of correlation as the basis for further investigation. Consider the famous early example of the application of epidemiology by Dr John Snow in 19th-century London. In 1854 London experienced a particularly harmful outbreak of cholera. Although at the time cholera was not unknown, having occurred previously, for example, in 1040–40, the summor had been particularly warm and more Londoners than usual had taken to drinking cold water from the street water pumps rather than boiling it for tea. (There were few houses with running water.) In the 19th century it was erroneously believed that cholera was the result of inhaling "bad air" and so the potential consequences of drinking unboiled water were not understood. However, the anaesthesiologist John Snow suspected that cholera was in some way associated with contaminated water; that it was a waterborne rather than an airborne disease. He tested his hypothesis in the summer of 1854 by collecting information concerning the homes of cholera victims and the locations of street water pumps they had utilised. His research indicated that the outbreak was roughly centred on a water pump on the corner of Cambridge Street and Broad Street in the Soho district of London.

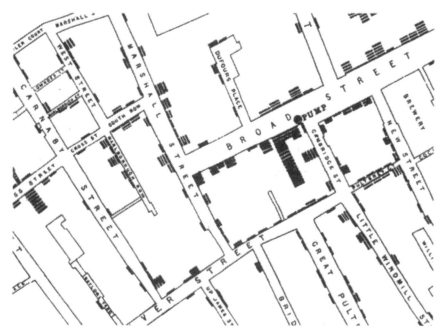

This shows a part of John Snow's map of the cholera outbreak of 1854. The number of deaths in each household is represented by the number of black rectangles. Reproduced with permission from the University of California, Los Angeles website http://www.ph.ucla.edu/epi/snow/snowmap1_highres.pdf from the original by Snow,1855.

Figure 3.3   John Snow's map of the London cholera outbreak, 1854

On Snow's advice the pump handle was removed, which meant that no more water could be drawn from the Broad Street supply, and thereafter the number of cases of cholera went into a steep decline (the numbers were already reducing before the handle was removed). Interestingly, Snow himself was careful not immediately to infer a causal link between the two, noting in 1855 that:

> There is no doubt that the mortality was much diminished, as I said before, by the flight of the population, which commenced soon after the outbreak; but the attacks had so far diminished before the use of the water was stopped, that it is impossible to decide whether the well still contained the cholera poison in an active state, or whether, from some cause, the water had become free from it.
>
> (Snow, 1855, cited in Buck *et al.*, 1988, p. 417)

Although the story of the cholera outbreak of 1854 and the removal of the handle of the water pump in Broad Street is well known (in the UK it often features on the curriculum of secondary school science), Snow went on to conduct further research on both the 1854 and earlier outbreaks of cholera in the capital. As part of his "Grand Experiment" he examined not only the geographical aspects of the epidemiology but also the correlations between the per capita numbers of cholera cases and the companies that supplied the water and the water's source (such as from the Thames).

Table 3.4   Analysis of cholera outbreak

Company	No. of houses	Expected no. of deaths by cholera	Actual no. of deaths by cholera
Southwark and Vauxhall Company	40,046	345.5	1263
Lambeth Company	26,107	225.2	98
Rest of London	256,423	2212.3	1422
Totals	322,576	2783.0	2783

Source: Based on data in Snow, 1855, p. 53, with expected numbers of deaths calculated by the author assuming no association and using Snow's implicit assumption of a constant proportion of deaths per household.

In modern terms this would be described as a hypothesis test with the null hypothesis representing no association between the locations supplied by a company and the number of cases of cholera. The evidence, however, strongly supports the alternative hypothesis of an association.[26] Indeed, the Southwark and Vauxhall Company was known to draw its water supply from the polluted Thames.

As a contrasting example, consider four neighbouring counties in eastern England, comparing the number of violent crimes against the person taking place in them and the number of churches in each county.

Table 3.5 Number of violent crimes against the person and number of churches in four neighbouring counties, 2006/07

County	No. of churches	No. of violent crimes against the person 2006/07
Bedfordshire	140	9,139
Cambridgeshire	190	10,421
Essex	413	22,823
Hertfordshire	263	16,890

Sources: Genuki church database statistics: http://www.genuki.org.uk/org/ ChurchStatistics.shtml (accessed 14 Nov. 2007); Nicholas *et al.*, 2006/07, tables in ch. 6. Available at: http://www.homeoffice.gov.uk/rds/ crimeew0607.html

Plotting a scatter graph of the number of violent crimes against the number of churches results in the pattern shown in Figure 3.4. The graph suggests a strong positive mathematical correlation between the two variables, an impression confirmed by statistical testing.[27] However, we are not likely to conclude, on this evidence alone, that violent crime against the person in these four counties is "caused" by churches. Instead, we are likely to look for and test alternative explanations.[28]

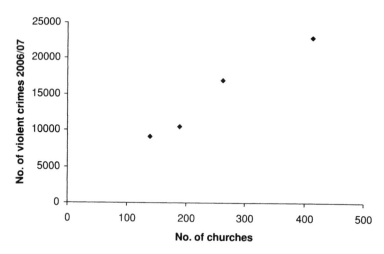

Figure 3.4 Number of violent crimes against the person plotted against number of churches in four neighbouring counties

In this case the "controlling" and so far hidden variable could be population size – that is, both the number of churches and the number of violent crimes relate to the number of people living in these counties. If this were so, then population size would constitute a third "lurking" (or "confounding") variable.

In much intelligence analysis the situation becomes even more complex, as one variable may in fact be controlled by combinations of more than one other variable, rather than the bivariate example we considered above. This applies equally to spatial and temporal network analysis (for example, in the case of linked terrorist cells) as it does to relationships between variables expressed on a linear scale. Statistically, an intelligence analysis may therefore require the elimination of any spuriously correlated variables and the "unveiling" of any lurking variables before multivariate regression analysis is conducted: a major challenge. For example, a 2005 study attempted to measure the latent support for terrorism in a number of countries and found that the level of support (the dependent variable) related to four other factors (the independent variables), namely demography (e.g. gender), views about Islam, opinions about democracy and attitudes towards the US (Wike, 2006).

THE DETECTIVE'S "NOSE": THE PLACE OF INTUITION IN INVESTIGATION

In all this discussion concerning inductive, deductive and abductive forms of reasoning, bias and fallacy, is there no place for an appreciation of the detective's "nose" for a case? That is, intuition, hunches, instinct, gut feelings and other non-cognitive (often emotion-based) means of taking an investigation forward or analysing intelligence? Perhaps the reluctance to include such an appreciation until the end of this chapter stems more from concerns over issues such as legal disclosure, formal accountability and the possibility of prejudice and bias (see Chapter 2) than it does from a perceived lack of value in these "traditional" forms of emotional intelligence (often the subject of fictional and media portrayal of the detective). Certainly, investigators are usually warned about the dangers of using intuition:

> investigators must guard against relying on their intuition, which involves the emergence of views of a case based on the investigator's own personality characteristics, past experiences, and subjective reactions to people and circumstances. Intuition is not based on a

rational analysis of facts and evidence collected through effective investigative techniques.

(Rossmo, 2006, p. 1)

It is true that no serious investigator would rely solely on intuition as the basis for an investigative strategy. However, a general disapproval of the use of intuition (as conveyed, for example, during a training programme) will not guarantee that individuals, in the private recesses of their minds, will not at least consider putting their hunches to the test. What is important, therefore, is that we understand the strengths, weaknesses, advantages and limitations of the gut reaction rather than deny its existence. Part of the problem resides in the ambiguous meanings of "intuition". Standard dictionary definitions often emphasise the bypassing of cognitively based reasoning processes to achieve the direct acquisition of supposed knowledge. However, in practice (and in the past within criminal investigations) we often use the word as a form of shorthand to represent a complex set of interrelated observations and arguments, usually based upon past experience and proven problem-solving heuristics. In this meaning, "intuitive" does not imply "impulsive". Rather, it is simply too difficult, if not impossible, and simply too time-consuming to express rationally the grounds for the hunch, but it may be no less rational for that (Innes, 2003, p. 10). After all, it is effectively mathematically impossible for even an expert chess player to calculate rationally all the possible moves and countermoves available to the player and his or her opponent. And yet in some senses they do so, and highly effectively.

Gut reactions and the hypothetico-deductive scientific methodology are therefore not necessarily incompatible and in some cases may even be complementary. For example, Gigerenzer (2007) has written a number of accounts of how relatively simple and largely informal heuristics have proved successful in decision-making. As an example, suppose you were confronted with the following question (the author's example, adapted from the work of Gigerenzer & Goldstein, 1996):

In terms of population, which is the bigger English city: Canterbury or Portsmouth?

You might know the answer, but if not use Table 3.6 to guess ("intuit") the answer.

You probably came to the conclusion that Portsmouth has the bigger population and this is correct (c.190,000 compared with Canterbury's c.43,000). If required, detailed arguments could be produced to explain

Table 3.6 Comparison of the cities of Canterbury and Portsmouth

	Canterbury	Portsmouth
Has a cathedral	Yes	Yes
Has a university or universities	Yes	Yes
Has a premier league football (soccer) team	No	Yes
Has a ground suitable for first-class cricket	Yes	No
Has a daily local newspaper	No	Yes
Has a high-speed inter-city rail service	No	Yes

why and how we judged Portsmouth to be the larger of the two cities based on the information in the table. Even more formally, we could build a mathematical linear regression model based upon the correlation between each of the binary variables (cathedral or not, university or not and so on) and population size. However, research has shown (Hutchinson & Gigerenzer, 2005, p. 98) that the much quicker informal decision heuristic that you probably used to decide between Canterbury and Portsmouth is at least as good as the complex mathematical linear regression approach. Of course, a simple exercise such as this lacks the complexity of actual criminal investigation, and the decision-making systems employed are more transparent than with most forms of intuition, but it does illustrate that at least some "gut reactions" are worth further thought.

SUMMARY

Criminal investigation invariably involves the use of reasoning and the analysis of intelligence. Indeed, reasoning and analysis feature within a number of models of investigative theory, including the ACPO Practice Advice on Core Investigative Doctrine. There are a number of forms of reasoning available to the investigator and analyst, including inductive and "commonsense" reasoning, deductive reasoning and argumentation, and abductive reasoning. In practice these forms of reasoning are often complementary rather than working in opposition to each other. Reasoning forms part of the process of hypothesis-setting and testing, a key approach to modern investigation. However, investigation can also be hindered by misunderstandings of the nature of chance, coincidence, randomness and more general forms of bias and fallacy.

NOTES

1. This concept of intelligence being concerned with what you don't know was famously expressed by Donald Rumsfeld. The former US Secretary for Defense said this at a news conference on 4 September 2002: "Reports that say that something hasn't happened are always interesting to me, because as we know, there are known knowns; there are things we know we know. We also know there are known unknowns; that is to say we know there are some things we do not know. But there are also unknown unknowns – the ones we don't know we don't know."

2. See Chapter 2 for further discussion of the ACPO Core Investigative Doctrine and of the development of investigative theory.

3. Note that the terms used for some of the concepts examined below may vary: for example, US Homeland Security refer to inductive methods as "data mining" and deductive methods as "data fusion".

4. This is known as "the rule of inductive generalisation".

5. Swans coloured black are common in Australia but not in Europe.

6. It is worth noting at this point, and in what follows later, that we use "theory" in its scientific sense. In everyday language a "theory" is normally a speculative proposition put forward. In science, however, it is an explanation for events which has been repeatedly tested and found to stand up to scrutiny.

7. Heuristics (from the Greek *heuriskein*, to find) is the process of finding out by trial and error or learning through experience.

8. The data that follow are taken from Aitken *et al.*, 1995, and refer to the CATCHEM database; the examples are from Adhami & Browne, 1996.

9. Rosemary West is a very rare exception, though it has been argued that she was much under the influence of her serial killer husband, Frederick. Other females engaged in sexually orientated child homicide may have been complicit rather than active.

10. These logical propositions are called syllogisms, and syllogistic logic is often used in making intelligence cases, where a common or "middle" term is present in the two premises but not in the conclusion. There are dangers in such structures since quite false conclusions can be arrived at; for example we could argue that all humans have legs, birds have legs, therefore all humans are birds (or all birds are humans). It looks stark set out in this way, but such "proofs" are regrettably common.

11. These descriptions of reasoning may be explained (from the Latin) thus: *modus ponens* ("mood that affirms") is "the way of supposing

or making assumptions", whilst *modus tollens* ("mood that denies") is "the way of proving an opposite, absent or contrary state".

12. Holmes is speculating on the identity of the murderer, and in particular whether the murderer is a stranger to the location of the crime. His conclusion, using *modus tollens*, is that the murderer was no stranger.

13. The late Stuart Kind, a forensic scientist who assisted the police investigation during the "Yorkshire Ripper" enquiry, used the terms "frame" and "form" to describe these assumptions (Kind, 1987).

14. "Abductive" from the Latin *abducto*, literally meaning "I lead out" or "I extrapolate from".

15. "Hypothesis" comes from Greek, literally meaning "under" (*hypo*) "proposition" (*thesis*), and strictly is "a proposition made as a basis for reasoning, without the assumption of its truth" (*Oxford English Dictionary*, 1996).

16. It could be argued that the "null" or "invalid" hypothesis (Latin *ne* + *ullus*: not any) should be given more prominence in police investigations: essentially it asks *What evidence must there be to disprove the existing hypothesis?* This will usually be the defence position as far as the evidence is concerned.

17. Of course, the choice of 21 is somewhat arbitrary: essentially the test is concerned with placing the age of the offender in one of several general categories.

18. Authors' calculation based upon Department for Transport data submitted for the Seventh Report of the House of Commons Select Transport Committee (2008).

19. This relates to an interesting set of questions concerning our inductive knowledge of such matters. When teaching trainee detectives the authors have noted that most students believe, for example, that the appearance of the back of the hands gives a clear indication of the age of the person (in the case of a masked offender). However, simple but unscientific testing in the classroom indicates that very few students achieve better results than random guesswork.

20. There is another point in this particular case, as was brought out by the Independent Police Complaints Commission (IPCC) investigation report: the victim (de Menezes) got off a bus at Brixton underground station and immediately got back on the bus. Surveillance proposed that this was suspicious and erratic behaviour. In fact it was entirely logical, since Brixton underground station was shut for maintenance work. The surveillants did not register this fact and so the hypothesis received false "confirmation" (IPCC, 2007).

21. Meaning an explanation is good enough for normal purposes, see for example http://www.utilitarianism.com/satisfice.htm for its every-day use.

22. Named after William of Occam (1288–1349), the English philosopher and Franciscan friar who proposed it; it means not creating more complex explanations than meet the facts or are sufficient to account for something. The razor cuts out superfluous explanation. This was also Henry David Thoreau's test for the persuasiveness of some circumstantial evidence.

23. See Chapter 8 for an example of the misuse of conditional probability in a forensic setting.

24. "V" weapons were missiles used in the latter stages of the Second World War against the British Isles. V stood for *Vergeltungswaffe* (reprisal weapon): V1 was a small flying bomb powered by a simple jet engine (the bomb was colloquially known in the UK as the "doodlebug"), whilst V2 was the first ballistic missile deriving from rocket research by Dr Wernher von Braun, who went on to help the Americans in rocketry and the space race post-war. Several thousands of V1 weapons were launched against London, Antwerp and other cities during the course of 1944–45, and hundreds of V2 rockets were launched, primarily against London, in late 1944 and 1945, the last falling on 1 April 1945. The V2 was most feared because its arrival was silent and largely undetectable (it fell at great velocity), so much so that the British government did not confirm the existence of the rockets for some time, preferring to explain the explosions away as gas leaks or plane crashes. There was apparently a V3, a long-range gun, designed to fire "nuclear shells", but it was never used. See e.g. Jones, 1978 (chs. 44–46 (pp. 413–464)); Howard, 1970 (ch. 9, "Bombing and the Bomb" (pp. 141–153)); and Gardiner, 2004 (ch. 23, "The War Will Not Be Over By Christmas" (pp. 638–658)).

25. We might note, for context, that 6,184 people were killed by V1 bombs and 15,258 people were seriously injured, whilst 2,754 were killed by the V2 and 6,523 were injured. 23,000 houses were totally destroyed by the two weapons and nearly a million homes were damaged. Conventional bombing, in the Blitz and "Baedeker" raids, killed more than 50,000 civilians between 1940 and 1945 (Gardiner, 2004, p. 653).

26. The calculations, conducted by the author to confirm this, are based on the test of a 3 by 2 contingency table using the chi-squared distribution at a 5% level of significance with 2 degrees of freedom.

27. The Pearson product-moment coefficient of correlation between the two variables is 0.984.

28. This doesn't in itself invalidate the potential use of the number of churches as a form of predictive device for estimating the expected number of recorded offences of violence against the person in a fifth county.

REVIEW QUESTIONS

1. Outline the strengths and weaknesses of inductive, deductive and abductive forms of reasoning.
2. What are the null and alternative hypotheses when used as part of an investigation?
3. What are the most common forms of error encountered when using reasoning within a criminal investigation?

QUESTIONS FOR FURTHER RESEARCH AND ANALYSIS

1. Are random events beyond understanding?
2. Is the use of "intuition" ever justifiable in a criminal investigation?
3. Could investigative reasoning be systematised or even mechanised?

RECOMMENDED READING

ACPO Centrex (2005). *Practice advice on core investigative doctrine*. Camborne: NCPE.

Copi, I. & Cohen, C. (2004). *Introduction to logic*. Upper Saddle River, NJ: Prentice Hall.

Heuer, R. (1999). *Psychology of intelligence analysis*. Washington, DC: Center for the Study of Intelligence, Central Intelligence Agency.

Innes, M. (2003). *Investigating murder: Detective work and the police response to criminal homicide*. Oxford: Oxford University Press.

Newburn, T., Williamson, Y. & Wright, A. (2007). *Handbook of criminal investigation* (pt. 4). Cullompton: Willan Publishing.

Stelfox, P. & Pease, K. (2005). Cognition and detection: Reluctant bedfellows? In M. Smith & N. Tilley (eds.), *Crime science: New approaches to preventing and detecting crime* (pp. 191–207). Cullompton: Willan Publishing.

CHAPTER 4

Offender Profiling

MIRANDA A. H. HORVATH

INTRODUCTION

Offender profiling is one of the most written about, discussed and debated applications of psychology to the forensic field. It has been the focus of significant media attention and interest from the general public for many years. This is a consequence of the involvement of profilers in notorious serial murders and rapes and the fictionalisation of the role in films such as *Manhunter* and *The Silence of the Lambs* and television programmes such as *Wire in the Blood, Criminal Minds* and *Cracker*. As a result there can be a great deal of misinformation in circulation. This chapter will provide an introduction to a range of psychological models of profiling, and equip the reader with a basic knowledge of the topic and an understanding of the role of offender profiling as an investigative tool.

Profiling has been described by many authors in a variety of different ways (see e.g. Douglas *et al.*, 1986; Geberth, 1996; Turvey, 1999). Essentially, profiling can be defined as the use of various techniques to provide investigators with information (such as personality and behavioural characteristics) about an individual who is responsible for committing criminal acts based on information from the crimes they have committed. McGrath (2000) argues that profiling can be described as a process designed to assist criminal investigative efforts. However it is defined, and there are many overlaps in the definitions available, it is crucial to understand that profiling should never be used as

the sole investigative tool. Profiling should be used in combination with
and complement other investigative techniques (Holmes, 1989). Most
simplistically, profiling can be defined as the combination of analysis
of available information and the application of relevant psychological
theories to provide investigators with clues about the likely characteristics (such as where they might live or their occupation) and the type
of person who would have committed the offence.

Typically profilers' services are requested in cases where it has not
been possible to identify the offender through traditional investigative techniques (e.g. when there are few clues or leads on potential
suspects) or when the offender has committed serious crimes, such as
murder or rape, particularly if the crimes are a part of series. Profiling
is used in these crimes for a number of reasons, for example they cause
the greatest concern to the public and generate a lot of media attention, so there is maximum pressure on the police to catch the offender
as quickly as possible. Further, in comparison to volume crime (e.g.
burglary), the motivation and underlying personality of the offender
might manifest themselves through the way crimes such as rape and
murder are committed. In the UK the use of profilers is now included in
national guidance manuals such as the *Murder Investigation Manual*
(ACPO, 2006) and promoted in senior detective training programmes
(Rainbow, 2008).

Profiling is not suitable for use in all types of crimes; Wilson *et al.*
(1997) and Pinizzotto (1984) have proposed that it is most suitable
for crimes that involve some form of psychopathology.[1] Geberth (1996)
states that murders, rapes, ritualistic crimes and torture usually
involve high levels of psychopathology. Profiling is most frequently
used for these types of crimes.

Profiling is also often used when a series of crimes has occurred
that the police believe may be linked. Rossmo (2000) identifies three
main methods used by police investigators to link crimes prior to an
offender's apprehension: (1) physical evidence; (2) offender description;
and (3) crime scene behaviour, which also incorporates (a) proximity in
time and place, (b) modus operandi[2] and (c) signature. Each method
has its strengths and weaknesses. It is not uncommon for a series of
crimes to be connected through a combination of these means.

WHAT IS THE PURPOSE OF PROFILING?

It is crucial to stress that the purpose of profiling is not to provide the
specific identity of an offender but to identify their major personality
and behavioural characteristics (Hagan, 1992). Holmes and Holmes

(2002) highlight three ways in which profiling can aid the investigative process:

1. Provide a social and psychological assessment of the offender – including the core components of the offender's personality. It should help to reduce the number of possible perpetrators the police are investigating, in other words to focus their investigation. It could also predict possible future attacks.
2. Provide a psychological evaluation of possessions found with suspected offenders – the profile may suggest items offenders may have in their possession. This is particularly useful if the rest of the available evidence is directing the police to a prime suspect. A profiler can also use analysis of the offender's possessions to advise the police about interview strategies.
3. Provide advice concerning interviewing strategies with suspects – the profiler should be able to provide police with advice about different personality types and possible effective interview strategies depending on the characteristics of the offender. The maximum amount of information may then be elicited.

Another benefit that profiling can offer is to help investigators avoid linkage blindness. Linkage blindness is the inability on the part of investigators to recognise and identify connections between crimes which are part of a series (Rossmo, 1997). Ted Bundy[3] is a good example of an offender who was able to utilise jurisdictional boundaries to impede investigators from linking his crimes and therefore slow down the investigation.

In summary, profiling can help investigators summarise a case, map the case against known "types", enable linkage between offences and target interventions or resources.

PROFILING ASSUMPTIONS

Profiling is based on four main assumptions: consistency within individuals, discrimination between individuals, homogeneity of types, and data reliability. In order for profiling to be effective, the individuals being profiled must be consistent in their behaviour over time. It is also crucial that we can discriminate between individuals. There must also be what is sometimes referred to as the "homology assumption": this refers to the supposition that the more similar offenders in the same category of crime are in their demographic or personality characteristics, the more similar their behaviour during an offence will be

(Molios & Alison, 2002). Finally, and perhaps most importantly, the data that the assumptions are based on must be reliable.

APPROACHES TO OFFENDER PROFILING

Part of the difficulty in providing a comprehensive overview of profiling as a tool for assisting in crime investigation is concisely summarised by Gudjonsson and Copson:

> Profiling is neither a readily identifiable nor a homogeneous entity . . . Little has been published to shed light on what profilers actually do or how they do it.
>
> (1997, p. 76)

In other words, profiling is not one thing; it is a combination of different approaches that do not necessarily link or complement each other. As time passes more material becomes available that provides insight into the different approaches to profiling. Unfortunately the age-old problem remains that the majority of people working as profilers on a day-to-day basis do not choose to, or do not have time to, write about their experiences. Often when they do write about the cases they have worked on, they only discuss the ones in which their profiles were successful. This means it is almost impossible to evaluate how reliable and effective the different approaches are. The four most developed and widely used approaches to profiling will be outlined in this chapter. First, it is worth noting that all approaches can be broadly categorised as using either an inductive or a deductive technique.

Inductive Profiling

Inductive profiling is a process of profiling criminal behaviour, crime scenes and victims from known behaviours and emotions suggested by other criminals, crime scenes and/or victims. Essentially the process is reasoning from initial statistical data from other similar crimes, offenders and/or victims to the specific case being profiled. The reasoning and the justification for the judgement in an inductive profile come from cases outside the one being profiled.

There are elements of inductive profiling in the approaches taken by the Federal Bureau of Investigation (FBI, crime scene analysis) and investigative psychology. For example, the FBI will base (some) of its profile on the "organised/disorganised" typology that in turn is based on research with convicted offenders. In investigative psychology, data from previous crimes are routinely analysed and the results published in peer-reviewed publications; these findings are then used to guide and inform the profiling process.

Deductive Profiling

Deductive profiling is the behavioural evidence analysis of a specific criminal, crime scene(s) and victim(s) exclusively from forensic evidence relating to the crime scene(s) and victim(s) of that offender alone. Therefore the information used to build up the profile focuses on the specific behaviours of the individual rather than considering a wider set of crimes perpetrated by other offenders (as is the case in inductive profiling). The FBI (crime scene analysis) approach is also characterised by some deductive elements, for example the emphasis on the investigator's experience and intuition. However, the deductive approach is best demonstrated in a UK context in the work of Paul Britton (diagnostic evaluation).

The selection of the four approaches to profiling which this chapter will consider is supported by their inclusion in many other texts on profiling (e.g. Ainsworth, 2001; Jackson & Bekerian, 1997). The four approaches are:

1. *Crime scene analysis (CSA)*
   This is when the profiler attempts to find behavioural clues from the crime scene and the victim. This approach is most famously taken by the FBI in America.
2. *Investigative psychology (IP)*
   Associated with David Canter and the University of Liverpool, this approach attempts to take a scientific approach (with an emphasis on statistics) to profiling and focuses on many aspects of the crime (e.g. geographical as well as behavioural clues as to offender characteristics).
3. *Diagnostic evaluation (DE)*
   The profiler attempts to use their clinical experience and judgement to understand the motivation behind an offender's actions. This approach is used in the UK by (amongst others) Paul Britton and by the current behavioural investigative advisers (BIA) working at the National Policing Improvement Agency (NPIA) within the Specialist Operational Support (SOS) team.
4. *Geographical profiling (GP)*
   A group of techniques under the umbrella of geographical profiling which focus on the probable spatial behaviour of the offender within the context of the locations of and the spatial relationships between

the various crime sites. Kim Rossmo, who is based in Canada, is
probably most associated with this approach.

CRIME SCENE ANALYSIS

In 1978 Robert Ressler began a serial murder project that provided the
basis of the FBI method of profiling and led to the establishment of
the Behavioural Science Unit (BSU) (Cook & Hinman, 1999). Initially
the BSU focused on researching the behaviours, crimes and motivations
of serial killers where there were sexual aspects to the crimes they had
committed, although many people have since disputed whether what
the FBI does can be called research because it has published very few
empirical findings (Kocsis, 2003). The main approach used by the BSU
to do this "research" was for agents attached to the unit to interview
convicted serial murderers to help with investigative techniques. In
addition to this research the FBI emphasises the importance of experience and intuition as part of the profiling process. It concentrates on the
most serious, bizarre and extreme crimes. As well as producing profiles,
FBI agents will work closely with the local police investigation team
(e.g. advising on how to respond to communication, interview strategy,
etc.) (Howitt, 2001).

In 1984 it was announced that it had been decided to establish a
National Centre for the Analysis of Violent Crime (NCAVC), whose aim
was to consolidate the available skills and resources to provide support
more effectively to federal, state and local law enforcement agencies.
NCAVC was to be administered by the BSU and physically located at
the FBI Academy. As a result, in 1986 the original BSU was divided
into two units: the Behavioural Science Instruction and Research Unit
(BSIR) and the Behavioural Science Investigative Support Unit (BSIS).
The overall aim of NCAVC was to reduce the amount of violent crime
in the USA. For further details about this see Ressler *et al.* (1988).

The BSU has conducted two major projects. The first collected data
from 36 sexual murderers (who had killed on average five or six victims
each) and the second expanded the work to 41 serial rapists (who had
raped between 10 and 59 victims each). The data from the study of serial
killers were combined with knowledge from "years of experience" to
develop a classification system, which allows offenders to be classified
as either organised or disorganised. The study of the 36 sexual murderers enabled the FBI to identify the personality patterns and examine
some of the factors believed to influence the development of these
patterns. The FBI looked at childhood attributes, social environment
(including family functioning, relationship with parents and siblings),

formative events (e.g. history of parental discipline, history of abuse and neglect, sexual experiences, childhood sexual abuse and family relationships), behavioural indicators and outcome: performance (i.e. academic, employment and military). The focus for the FBI was what these characteristics tell us about the men themselves and how these things may lead the offenders to develop a motivation to murder. It also focused on the role of fantasy for the offenders (distinguishing between fantasies from before the first murder and those that developed afterwards). It looked in detail at three phases: the antecedent behaviours that occur directly before the murder, the actual murder and, finally, what happens after the murder. The FBI also used this information to propose a motivational model for sexual homicide (the details of which can be found in Ressler et al., 1986 and Ressler et al., 1988). A simple summary of the key components of the organised/disorganised classification system is shown in Table 4.1. It should be noted that Douglas et al. (1992) introduced a third classification: "mixed". However, this has received little attention; for a detailed discussion of the problems with it see Canter et al. (2004).

FBI profilers also examine the crime scene for information that reveals the characteristics of the offender. The FBI's approach works from the belief that certain patterns of the offender's personality can be detected through the examination of crime scene evidence. So FBI profilers provide a behaviourally based suspect profile founded on years of experience in the field, the knowledge base that develops with that, and familiarity with a large number of cases. Profiling according to the FBI method has six stages: profiling inputs; decision process models; crime assessment; the criminal profile; the investigation; the apprehension. For a further explanation of these stages see Ressler et al. (1988, ch. 9). Amongst its other achievements the BSU is believed to have coined the term "serial killer" (Howitt, 2001).

Criticisms of Crime Scene Analysis

The sample that was originally used in the FBI "research" was small, consisting of only 36 offenders. Additionally, until 2004 it had not been tested, leading to the conclusion that the reliability and validity of the organised/disorganised typology was unknown. Canter et al. (2004) tested the typology empirically using the third crime in the series for 100 convicted serial killers from the USA. Their hypothesis was that the features proposed to be characteristic of organised crime scenes should be distinctly different to those characteristics of a disorganised crime scene. Canter et al.'s findings do not support the dichotomy:

Table 4.1   FBI organised/disorganised classification scheme

Offender type	Crime scene characteristics	Offender characteristics
Organised non-social	Planning Victim a targeted stranger Personalises the victim Controlled conversation Crime scene reflects overall control Demands submissive victim Restraints used Aggressive acts prior to death Body hidden Weapon/evidence absent Transports victim/body	Sexually competent Lives with partner High intelligence Socially adequate Skilled work preferred High birth order status Father's work stable Inconsistent childhood discipline Controlled mood during crime Use of alcohol with crime Precipitating situational stress Mobility Has car in good condition Follows crime in news media May change job or leave town
Disorganised asocial	Spontaneous offence Victim or location known Depersonalises victim Minimal conversation Crime scene random and sloppy Sudden violence to victim Minimal use of restraints Sexual acts after death Body left in view Evidence/weapon often present Body left at death scene	Sexually incompetent Lives alone Average intelligence Socially immature Poor work history Low birth order status Father's work unstable Harsh discipline in childhood Anxious mood during crime Minimal use of alcohol Minimal situation stress Lives/works near crime scene Minimal interest in news media Minimal change in lifestyle

Source: Information taken from Ressler *et al.*, 1986; Ressler, *et al.*, 1988.

all serial killers are likely to exhibit some aspects that are organized and some that are disorganized, but the differences between them are, more than likely, differences in the particular subset of disorganized variables that they exhibit.

(2004, p. 313)

Caution should of course be exercised, as Canter *et al.*'s study is just one attempt to test the typology and their methodology is not without flaws. However, it nonetheless appears overly simplistic to suggest that all offenders will fall into one of just two categories. Furthermore, the specific methods used by FBI profilers are difficult to validate because typology and techniques are intertwined with other aspects of the investigation.

Kocsis (2003) criticises the FBI approach for the lack of availability of data and accounts of its techniques, saying that the validity is almost impossible to estimate because the information that is available is tightly controlled by the FBI. Further, the work that has been published has appeared in non-peer-reviewed journals or autobiographical memoirs (e.g. Douglas & Burgess, 1986; Douglas & Olshaker, 1996; Ressler & Schachtman, 1992).

FBI profilers have been criticised by the courts and other researchers for many reasons, including failure to base opinions on data that can be tested; treating investigative theories as fact; failure to carefully track profiles they generate; and failure to compare profiles with actual offenders when outcomes are known (Homant & Kennedy, 1998; New Jersey v. Fortin, 2000; Poythress *et al.*, 1993; Turvey, 1999).

INVESTIGATIVE PSYCHOLOGY

Investigative psychology was created by David Canter when working at the University of Surrey and his work on it continued when he moved to the University of Liverpool. Canter started working on crime relatively late in his career, having primarily been an environmental psychologist. He was approached in the mid-1980s by the police for help in solving a series of rapes for which John Duffy was convicted (he later became known as the "Railway Rapist"). The profile Canter produced for that case was devised working from psychological theories (Canter, 1995). He pioneered investigative psychology with consideration of criticisms of the FBI approach to "profiling": IP is based on scientific methods of investigation and rigorous methodological principles. It also purports not to be a new approach to profiling but instead to use psychology for a very practical purpose, and draws on many psychological theories to understand offending. The basis for a lot of Canter's reasoning is that human beings are actually very consistent in their behaviour.

Investigative psychology can be argued to be similar to the FBI approach because they are both largely statistical in nature, but IP claims to exclude the use of the elements of intuition and experience in investigating crime. Furthermore, IP continually updates its database of offender populations and publishes its research and methodologies in peer-reviewed publications so they are open to examination and scrutiny (e.g. Canter *et al.*, 2003, Goodwill & Alison, 2005; Salfati & Taylor, 2006; Snook *et al.*, 2006). Put simply, by analysing offending behaviour IP has identified five factors that it claims are crucial to producing profiles that can aid investigations:

1. residential location;
2. criminal biography;
3. domestic/social characteristics;
4. personality characteristics;
5. occupational/educational history (Ainsworth, 2001).

Investigative psychology has also done considerable work on geographical profiling; this is discussed later. One principle that IP works from is that the way in which crimes are committed displays characteristics that are routine in the behaviour of the offender. The belief is that behaviour is consistent whether an offender is committing criminal activity or non-criminal activity (Ainsworth, 2001). Actions are dictated by an individual's mental maps and internal narratives, which provide boundaries and limits, essentially a "script" to guide behaviour.

Investigative psychology uses a broad range of statistical analysis techniques, including multidimensional scaling[4] (such as Smallest Space Analysis). In combination with these techniques, investigative psychology draws heavily on facet theory.[5] For a comprehensive introduction to these techniques see Howitt (2001).

More recent work has looked at a wider range of offences than just rape and murder and drawn on other frameworks and concepts not previously applied to offending behaviour. For example Fritzon *et al.* (2001) applied an action systems framework to terrorism and arson; while in their offender profiling series of books, Canter and Alison incorporate organised crime, equivocal death and investigative interviews.

Investigative psychology has two main strengths. Firstly, the methods it uses and its findings are made widely available in publications; as a result, they can be replicated, discussed and evaluated by other people. Secondly, the profiles offered by IP are based on probabilities rather than certainties.

Criticisms of Investigative Psychology

The fact that investigative psychology does not claim to be a new approach to profiling can also be used as a basis for the criticism that it is just an adaptation of older theories. IP is further criticised because it relies very heavily on statistical procedures, and it can be argued that its findings might be specific to the statistics they are based on.

Investigative psychology's profiles are potentially limited in their readability and usability. The accounts of the techniques used and of the academic research involved can be quite dense and difficult to understand – particularly for a non-academic audience. This is in part because of their use of statistics, which unless the reader has a basic understanding of data-analysis techniques can be incredibly challenging.

DIAGNOSTIC EVALUATION

As previously mentioned, this approach to profiling is used by the behavioural investigative advisers working at the NPIA. However, it is best exemplified by the work of Paul Britton, who trained and worked as a clinical psychologist, focusing on treating behavioural disorders and mental illness; before became a psychologist, he spent time as a police cadet, although he has admitted that the latter did not give him much relevant insight for his role as a profiler. He has published two well-known books based on his experiences in profiling: *The Jigsaw Man* (1997) and *Picking Up the Pieces* (2000). Like Canter, Britton became involved in profiling by chance, when in 1984 he was asked by Leicester police to advise them on the investigation into the murder of Caroline Osborne[6] (for more detailed insight into this case see *The Jigsaw Man*). His work on this first case was successful, and as a result he was asked to assist on further cases. Britton describes his approach as examining photographs from the crime scene and the post-mortem and any other information that could be provided by the police and then, "Folding a foolscap page, I began writing down a list of psychological features that I could draw from the material" (Britton, 1997, p. 50).

Put simply, using the material he is provided with and his experience working as a clinical psychologist, Britton (1997) endeavours to answer four basic questions:

1. What happened?
2. How was it done?
3. Who was the victim?
4. What motivated the killer/s?

This approach means that he treats each case as "unique" so in theory he has no preconceptions or prior hypotheses that he brings to it. His profile should therefore be based on details from the specific incident rather than statistical inductive techniques, meaning that his approach is primarily deductive. However, as has already been mentioned, because he draws on his clinical experiences (although they do not relate to prior crimes) he is also using one inductive element. Britton provided profiling services to many police forces during the 1980s and 1990s, in very high-profile cases, such as the murder of Jamie Bulger in 1993, as well as many that have not pricked the public conscience. He has not published accounts of the techniques he uses in the academic literature, so they have not been open to scrutiny by his peers. The other result of this is that, although it is possible to give some general indications about the techniques he uses, it is not possible to describe them in such a way that they could be replicated.

Britton's books only give insights into the cases in which his profiles were successful, so it is impossible to work out how effective his approach to profiling is. This criticism has been levelled at many profilers who have produced autobiographies and/or engaged with the media, for example Douglas and Olshaker (1997), by many other people writing about profiling (see Canter & Alison, 1999). Probably the most famous exception to profilers' tendency to publicise only their successes is Britton's work on the murder of Rachel Nickell, a very widely publicised case.

Rachel Nickell was murdered on Wimbledon Common in July 1992. She was sexually assaulted and stabbed 49 times. The police had identified a suspect (Colin Stagg – a jobless loner who walked his dog on the common three times a day and had a previous conviction for a sex offence), but were having difficulties gathering evidence. Britton "advised" the police that an undercover officer should write to and meet Stagg. An officer, "Lizzie James", wrote to and met Stagg over a 28-week period (Turvey, 1999, points out how unethical this use of profiling was as the policewoman involved resigned because she never fully recovered from the trauma). The logic advocated by Britton was that Stagg might confess to the fantasies that might have led him to kill Rachel Nickell. Stagg did write about violent sexual fantasies; however, he did not admit to anything that linked him directly to the murder of Rachel Nickell, and numerous questions were raised about whether Britton had effectively set a "honey trap". Stagg was charged with murder (he consistently denied it), but the case was thrown out of court when the judge ruled that the evidence gained through the covert operation was inadmissible.[7] Forensic psychologist Gisli Gudjonsson appeared in the trial for the defence to disagree with Britton's actions and opinions about Stagg (Gudjonsson & Haward, 1998).

This case is frequently mentioned as an example of bad profiling practice because Britton overstepped the guidelines laid down by the British Psychological Society for good ethical practice as a psychologist.

Britton faced disciplinary charges from the British Psychological Society in 2002 for professional misconduct, but the charges were dropped because it was deemed he could not get a fair hearing (BBC News, 2002). Perhaps he was given too much power by the detectives involved in the case to direct the lines of investigation? A profile, and indeed a profiler, should be used as an investigative tool by the investigatory team; the senior investigating officer should decide which lines of enquiry to pursue. This can be a difficult balance to strike, but personality and ego cannot be allowed to dominate. The Rachel Nickell case is discussed in depth by Ormerod (1999); the main point to draw from his assessment is that the abuse of profiling techniques has only damaged the development of profiling as a credible tool for crime investigation.

Criticisms of Diagnostic Evaluation

Apart from the criticisms levelled at Britton as a result of the Rachel Nickell case, his approach has also been criticised for a number of reasons. In the profiles he produces he does not cite any psychological research that he drew on to create his profile (Ainsworth, 2001), a criticism that can also be levelled at the FBI. Britton's approach is based around treating every case as unique, so in theory he brings no preconceptions to it (whether this possible is debatable), but this means that profiling as a technique does not develop. Furthermore, and again like the FBI, Britton does not publish empirical papers so his theories and techniques have not been validated and tested (Ainsworth, 2001).

GEOGRAPHICAL PROFILING

This chapter has focused on psychological profiles which can provide insights into an offender's likely motivation, behaviour and lifestyle, all of which are directly related to spatial activity and the environment and locations an offender lives in and encounters. There is a group of techniques under the umbrella of geographical profiling which focus on the likely spatial behaviour of the offender within the context of locations and the spatial relationships between the various crime sites. Usually psychological and geographical information work in tandem to provide a picture of the person responsible for the crimes in question. Rossmo defines geographical profiling as "An investigative methodology that uses the locations of a connected series of crimes to determine the most probable area of offender residence" (2000, p. 1).

Typically geographical profiling and its associated software are used to assist in the investigation of distances travelled by offenders committing serial crimes such as murders, rapes, arson, robbery and bombing, analysing crime locations and providing an estimate of the most probable residential location of the offender (Canter *et al.*, 2000; Rossmo, 1993). It has been used with less frequency in single crimes that have multiple sites.

Geographical profiling combines quantitative (objective) and qualitative (subjective) components. Typically the objective component uses scientific geographic techniques and quantitative measures to analyse and interpret the pattern created from the location of the target sites. The subjective element is based primarily on the profiler's reconstruction and interpretation of the offender's mental map (Homant & Kennedy, 1998). In order to understand GP it is necessary to understand its background in research on behavioural geography and the geography of crime: for example environmental criminology, the interaction between people and the environment that surrounds them, routine activity theory, rational choice theory and crime pattern theory (Brantingham & Brantingham, 1998). For a detailed introduction to the theoretical background see Rossmo (2000).

Computerised GP software uses information from the locations of the different sites involved in crime. The amount of information available varies: in some crimes, victim encounter, attack, murder and body dump site may all be in the same location whereas in others they could be in four completely separate locations. Perhaps unsurprisingly, the key location to be identified in most cases where GP is used is the offender home. However, it must be remembered that there is a small minority of offenders who have "no fixed abode" and who, when encountered, will complicate any attempt at geographical profiling. How offenders use locations can also aid in understanding the characteristics of the offender. For example locations can give clues to how they search for a victim and the associated levels of organisation and mobility they display. It is also crucial to consider that different sites can have varying degrees of relevance for the offender and for different types of crime.

Rossmo (2000) describes five basic assumptions that computerised geographical profiles must work from if they are to be accurate:

1. the profile must be based on multiple crime sites;
2. the crimes must be linked to the same offender;
3. the offender committing the crimes cannot be commuting into the area of criminal activity;
4. the distribution of suitable targets (i.e. target backcloth) must be relatively uniform around the offender's home; and
5. the offender cannot move anchor points (or operate from multiple anchor points) during his or her crime series.

If an offender is targeting a specific type of building, for example an arsonist who prefers shopping centres, they will be affected by the laws in the city that determine where such buildings can be located. Further, an offender who targets prostitutes will focus their search on the areas in towns where these women congregate. If, however, the victims whom offenders are targeting are not clustered in a particular area but instead are evenly distributed through a town or region, then the choice of crime location will not be affected by the victim backcloth. Instead offenders will focus on their activity space and the potential target backcloth. There are a small number of offenders, for example contract killers, for whom the offence location is entirely dependent on the victim's characteristics. Generally, though, this is not the case; but it does highlight the importance of victim characteristics in the creation of an accurate geographical profile. All of the considerations outlined so far contribute to one of the key fundamental assumptions of GP, which is that behaviour is not random: there is an underlying spatial structure which determines how and where people commit crime.

In the UK David Canter is widely recognised as being one of the first people to introduce systematic geographical profiling to major police investigations (Canter & Youngs, 2008b). A wide variety of work has emerged from Canter, his colleagues and students, much of which is brought together in two recent books: *Principles of Geographical Offender Profiling* (Canter & Youngs, 2008a) and *Applications of Geographical Offender Profiling* (Canter & Youngs, 2008b).

Canter's approach to geographical profiling draws on the concept that people have mental maps which are internally generated representations of the world, and that these are useful for understanding offending, particularly its geography. The basic argument is that people tend to stay in areas they are comfortable and familiar with. If they move outside these areas it is because they have got a legitimate reason for doing so (e.g. John Duffy, who worked on the railways) (Ainsworth, 2001). Many of the principles Canter has developed over the years began in his work with Adam Gregory (1994), which attempted to differentiate the geographical patterns of offences committed by rapists by exploring travelling costs, resources of time (e.g. offenders travelling at weekends compared to those travelling during the week) and knowledge of an area. Amongst other findings, they discovered that an offender's home or base was more often than not likely to be in the same area in which his crimes are committed. Canter used this finding in the profile he produced for the investigation into the "Railway Rapist"[8] in London (Canter, 2004). Another key finding was the creation of the "circle hypothesis". In order to work out the area in which an offender's home might be, Canter and Gregory drew a line between the two crimes in a series that were furthest apart, creating the diameter of a circle, and predicted that the home would be somewhere in this circle. Those offenders whose homes are in the circle are labelled "marauders"; those whose homes are not are called "commuters". Considerable work has been done to test these findings, with varying degrees of success (see Canter & Larkin, 1993; Koscis & Irwin, 1997; Lundrigan & Canter, 2001).

Much of the research into geographical profiling has been brought together to develop "decision support systems" – the aim is to collate and organise the information police have to help them to understand crime and combine that information with their local knowledge in an investigation. There is much debate about the utility of the different GP software and systems available. For example Canter (2005) is very critical of the approach used by Brent Snook and his colleagues. Amongst other criticisms he suggests that the models of criminals' spatial behaviour being used to develop the software are over-simplified, and that the understanding of the cognitive processes of those who use the systems is limited (for further details see Canter, 2005). Rossmo (2000) advocates the use of criminal geographic targeting (CGT), which "works on the assumption that a relationship, modelled on some form of distance decay function, exists between crime location and offender residence". This approach can be criticised for only being applicable to non-commuting offenders. Geographical profiling has been successfully used in relation to child murder. Since 1 January 1960 the details of all child sexual homicides in the UK have been recorded in the CATCHEM database (Copson, 1995). This database has revealed numerous useful insights into the geography of such offences, for example that crimes are less likely to be solved the more geographically complex they are (i.e. when there are multiple locations involved).

Criticisms of Geographical Profiling

Geographical profiling is limited in its usefulness if used alone because it does not allow consideration of the social factors which may affect offenders' decision-making. However, it could be argued that it is unlikely that it would ever be used in complete isolation. Canter and Youngs criticise GP because of the limited exploration of its theoretical basis, which is substantially lacking in relation to the significant attention that has been given to its practical applications. They argue that this means that many of the assumptions taken for granted by those working in the area are not clearly stated or understood (see Canter & Youngs, 2008a, for a full discussion of this limitation).

THE PROFILING PROCESS

Most often a profile will be used in an investigation after there has been a series of crimes and the employment of traditional investigation techniques has failed to lead to the apprehension of an offender or offenders. At this point the police might request the assistance of a profiler, who would examine case files, including investigative reports, witness statements and autopsy reports. The profiler might also ask to inspect crime scene and area photographs, have discussions with investigators and crime analysts, and if possible undertake visits to the crime sites. A geographical profiler would be likely to also analyse neighbourhood crime statistics and demographic data, and to study street, zoning and rapid transit maps. In the UK the NPIA employs dedicated geographical profilers within the SOS team that works alongside the behavioural investigative advisers to provide operational support to senior investigating officers dealing with serious crimes.

Both psychological and geographical profilers will then spend time analysing the available information and writing a report. Profilers will present the report in writing to the police, and on some occasions may be asked to have face-to-face discussions with senior investigating officers or to present the key findings to the investigation team. Profilers may also help officers develop new investigative strategies, or the officers may do this independently of the profiler. The basic time taken to produce a profile has been estimated to be at least 40 hours (Boon, 1997; Gudjonsson & Copson, 1997).

Typical Components of Profiles

A profile can take many forms. Typically a profiler will provide a written report to the senior investigating officer which lays out the profiler's suggestions about the case and provides justification for each of the conclusions or recommendations they have made. The profile may also provide suggestions about interview strategy once the suspect has been apprehended. However, the specifics will vary based on the personal style of the profiler, the requests the officer has made and the information available about the case. As well as providing a written report, a profiler may have informal discussions with the officers involved before the report is delivered, and present the contents of the report to the investigative team (if appropriate). In the working conditions introduced by the ACPO Sub-Committee for Behaviour Science in 2001 (that all BIAs were invited to sign up to in order to retain ACPO-approved status), the minimum requirements for a report's content were made explicit (see Rainbow, 2008 for details). Perhaps the most important criterion to highlight is that. "Interpretations/investigative suggestions [must be] supported by evidence/rationale" (Rainbow, 2008, p. 91).

While it is not possible to provide an exhaustive list of the components of a profile, some of the things that might be included about the offender are: age, gender, ethnicity, lifestyle; marital status and intelligence; academic achievement and parental environment; social adjustment and personality characteristics; employment, occupation and work habits; appearance, grooming; emotional adjustment and mental composition; residence in relation to the crime; socioeconomic status and sexual adjustment/perversion. Alison, Smith and Morgan (2003) highlight a shift in recent years from profilers providing an outline about the potential offender's characteristics as described above to focusing instead on a "more general behavioural perspective to the enquiry as it evolves" (2003, p. 179), for example giving advice about investigative strategies.

Who Are Profilers and What Do They Do?

Gudjonsson and Copson found that profilers can only really be defined as "Those who present themselves as having some kind of relevant experience" (1997, p. 68). This definition arose from one of the few studies up until that point that had investigated the value of profiling the "Coals to Newcastle" (CTN) project conducted by Copson (1995). The project investigated many aspects of those working as profilers in the UK. Before the CTN there were very few studies which investigated the value of profiling, and the majority of those that had been conducted were based on police officers' perceptions of the usefulness of profiles they had used (Britton, 1992; Jackson *et al.*, 1993). The CTN project found that profilers came from a range of backgrounds, and included forensic psychiatrists, academic psychologists, clinical psychologists, forensic psychologists, therapists and police officers. The profilers interviewed in the CTN project were divided into those who held police data for the purposes of profiling and those who did not (e.g. statistical vs. clinical profilers). The major disagreements amongst profilers in the UK emerge from debates about the relative value of statistical and clinical approaches (Gudjonsson & Copson, 1997).

The CTN project analysed 111 written profiles developed for the police and found huge variations in what was included in them. In order to be able to compare the profiles, the CTN project devised a coding frame within which the information in profiles could be categorised as falling into one of 10 variables:

1. features of the offence;
2. character of the offender;

3. origins of the offender;
4. present circumstances of the offender;
5. criminality of the offender;
6. geographical location of the offender;
7. predicted future behaviour of the offender;
8. interview strategy to be adopted;
9. threat assessment;
10. specific recommendations to the police.

It was found that the clinical profilers focused more on the personality and character of the offender and predictions for future behaviour, while statistical profilers offered more information concerning present circumstances, criminality and geography (Gudjonsson & Copson, 1997). It was also found that there were wide variations in the techniques used to explain the advice that was given in the profile. All of this meant that it would be very difficult to train officers in the interpretation and use of the advice offered in a profile because there are so many variations. This in turn could mean that there is a wide range in the effectiveness with which officers interpret and use the information.

It is difficult to find agreement on how the accuracy and value of a profile can be measured: there needs first to be agreement about how accurate something has to be to fit the criteria. Similarly, what is considered to be of value in a profile in a serial murder investigation may be completely different to what is found useful in a serial rape investigation. It must also be considered whether a profile is adding anything new to what the police already know or have been able to piece together themselves. Ainsworth (2001) argues that it is perhaps not important for a profile to offer anything new to investigators; it may simply help to focus their thinking and direct the police towards new lines of enquiry by providing a fresh perspective on the information available.

Since the CTN project was conducted there have been significant developments in the profiling profession in the UK. As previously mentioned, the use of BIAs is now included in national guidance manuals and promoted in senior detective training programmes (Rainbow, 2008). Further, steps have been taken to regulate the profession. New criteria have been introduced to make explicit the minimum requirements for people who would like to be included on the ACPO-approved list of BIAs (see Rainbow, 2008 for details). Now that a two-tier system operates, the only full-time accredited profilers are six BIAs employed by the NPIA. Most BIAs in the UK do their profiling as consultancy work in addition to their full-time employment and should be accredited by the ACPO Sub-Committee for Behavioural Science. The full-time BIAs are provided to investigations at no cost, but if they are not available or if specific skills are needed beyond their expertise, other approved BIAs will be used (at a cost to the investigation).

As a result of concerns expressed by the ACPO working group about the quality of advice being given in profiles, a new policy has been introduced which means all BIAs must sign up to a new set of working conditions (ACPO, 2000). This includes an annual audit of each accredited BIA (for further details see Almond *et al.*, 2007; Rainbow, 2008). In a series of recent papers, attempts have been made to evaluate the claims made in profiles and how accurately profiles are interpreted by police officers (Alison, Smith, Eastman & Rainbow, 2003; Alison, Smith & Morgan, 2003; Almond *et al.*, 2007). Comparison of profiles produced by independent profilers from a range of backgrounds (produced between 1992 and 2001) with those produced by the BIAs working at the NPIA found that

> the contemporary sample of profiles is less ambiguous, with more claims including backing, grounds, and warrant, resulting in the senior investigating officer being able to determine which claims are speculative statements and which are based on empirical findings.
>
> (Almond *et al.*, 2007, p. 82)

This suggests that the standard of profiling is improving, which is particularly important when the findings of Alison, Smith and Morgan (2003) are considered, they discovered that officers, when presented with an offender profile, were prepared to perceive ambiguous statements as relatively accurate descriptions of complete strangers.

SUMMARY

One of the major problems in evaluating profiling is that the majority of profilers write selectively about the cases they helped to solve. The omission of accounts of cases where profilers have been incorrect means that it is almost impossible to assess the accuracy rate of profiling, and future profilers do not have the opportunity to learn from their mistakes. The overall impact of this is that offender profiling is not sufficiently advancing and developing as a technique. In terms of the popular press, profiling is only presented in terms of success. Whilst this might make for good reading and create feelings of safety (or fear), it also promotes a false perception of the effectiveness of the technique. However, the British police are moving towards more use of general crime analysis and intelligence-led policing, which shows that profiling, or at least some of its principles, is becoming more widely used.

Profiling has a lot to offer in terms of the investigation of crime, but its potential must not be overstated. Ultimately it would probably be best if all of the different approaches to profiling were brought together and a hybrid form developed. A recent paper by Alison *et al.* (2004) presents useful analysis of these concerns and uses a case study to demonstrate how bringing together the different approaches to profiling should be a priority for the development of the technique. Unfortunately there are still people working in the field with the entrenched attitude that their approach to profiling is superior. There are still many challenges on the road to a combined approach to profiling.

NOTES

1. There is debate over the best definition of psychopathology – for an overview of this, see Bergner (1997). Bergner concludes that the best definition is that proposed by Ossorio (1985): "significant restriction in the ability of an individual to engage in deliberate action and equivalently, to participate in available social practices".
2. The term "modus operandi" has been used interchangeably with "method of operation" or "MO" to describe a certain criminal's way of operating (see Keppel, 2000 for a full discussion of the history and usage of the term). Modus operandi is not fixed and may change slightly from crime to crime.
3. Ted Bundy was an American serial killer who murdered dozens of women. Estimates of how many range from 29 to 100; he eventually confessed to 30. He committed the murders across at least four states, Washington, Utah, Colorado and Florida. He first went on trial in 1979 and was executed in Florida in 1989.
4. Multidimensional scaling is a set of related statistical techniques often used in data visualisation for exploring dissimilarities and similarities in data.
5. Facet theory is a systematic approach for co-ordinating theory and research.
6. Caroline Osborne was murdered after being repeatedly stabbed. Her feet and hands were bound, and a pentagram was found near her body. In 1986 Paul Bostock was convicted of the murders of Caroline Osborne and Amanda Weedon.
7. Stagg was acquitted in 1992 and cleared at the Old Bailey in 1994. In 2008 he received £706,000 compensation from a government scheme for victims of miscarriages of justice for the year he spent in jail. The case was reviewed and microscopic traces of DNA identified Robert Napper, who was charged in November 2007. When identified,

Napper was in Broadmoor secure mental hospital after being convicted of killing a young mother and her child in the mid-1990s. In December 2008, Napper pleaded guilty to Rachel Nickell's manslaughter; the judge sent Napper back to Broadmoor telling him it was "highly unlikely" he would ever be released. The officer who was "Lizzie James" resigned from the police, citing trauma, and was awarded damages in 2001.

8. John Duffy raped and murdered numerous women at railway stations in the south of England in the 1980s. Duffy was convicted of two murders and four rapes in 1988. After his conviction he confessed that he had not attacked alone (as was always suspected), but did not reveal who his accomplice was until 1997, when he implicated his friend David Mulcahy. In 2000 Duffy gave evidence against Mulcahy, who was convicted of three murders and seven rapes, and Duffy was convicted of a further 17 rapes.

REVIEW QUESTIONS

1. Compare and contrast any two of the four identified approaches to profiling discussed in this chapter.
2. Identify five ways that profiling can assist in the investigation of serious crime.
3. Outline the strengths and weaknesses of the FBI approach (crime scene analysis) to profiling.
4. Describe the main difficulties in forming profiles.

QUESTIONS FOR FURTHER RESEARCH AND ANALYSIS

1. What lessons can traditional policing techniques and profiling learn from each other?
2. What experience/expertise should a profiler possess in order to be used on police investigations?
3. How could (and should) profiling be incorporated more into everyday policing?
4. What are the new directions/developments for offender profiling?

RECOMMENDED READING

Ainsworth, P.B. (2001). *Offender profiling and crime analysis*. Cullompton: Willan Publishing.

Britton, P. (1997). *The Jigsaw Man*. London: Bantam Press.

Canter, D. (1995). *Criminal shadows: Inside the mind of the serial killer*. London: HarperCollins

Canter, D.V. & Alison, L.J. (eds.) (1999). *Profiling in policy and practice: Offender profiling series* (Vol. 2). Aldershot: Ashgate.

Canter, D. & Youngs, D. (eds.) (2008). *Principles of geographical offender profiling*. Aldershot: Ashgate.

Copson, G. (1995). Coals to Newcastle? *Part 1:* A study of offender profiling *(Paper 7)*. London: Police Research Group Special Interest Series, Home Office.

Douglas, J.E. & Olshaker, M. (1996). *Mindhunter*. London: Heinemann.

Douglas, J.E., Ressler, R.K., Burgess, A.W. & Hartman, C.R. (1986). Criminal profiling from crime scene analysis. *Behavioral Sciences and the Law, 4*, 401–421.

Holmes, R.M. & Holmes, S.T. (2002). *Profiling violent crimes* (2nd edn.). Thousand Oaks: Sage Publications.

Homant, R.J. & Kennedy, D.B. (1998). Psychological aspects of crime scene profiling: Validity research. *Criminal Justice and Behaviour, 25*(3), 319–343.

Jackson, J.L. &. Bekerian, D.A. (eds.) (1997). *Offender profiling: Theory, research and practice*. New York: John Wiley & Sons.

Kocsis, R.N. (2003). An empirical assessment of the content in criminal psychological profiles. *International Journal of Offender Therapy and Comparative Criminology, 47*(1), 37–46.

Pinizzotto, A.J. & Finkel, N.J. (1990). Criminal personality profiling: An outcome and process study. *Law and Human Behavior, 14*(3), 215–233.

Rainbow, L. (2008). Taming the beast: The UK approach to the management of behavioural investigative advice. *Journal of Police and Criminal Psychology, 23*, 90–97.

Ressler, R.K., & Shachtman, T. (1992). *Whoever fights monsters*. London: Pocket Books.

Rossmo, D.K. (2000). *Geographic profiling*. Boca Raton, FL: CRC Press.

CHAPTER 5

Eyewitness Evidence

MIRANDA A. H. HORVATH

INTRODUCTION

Varying estimates suggest that in the USA approximately 77,000 people per year are charged with crimes solely on the basis of eyewitness testimony (Goldstein *et al.*, 1989; Wells *et al.*, 1998). Studies conducted in the UK have found that eyewitnesses usually provide major leads for investigations (Kebbell & Milne, 1998), and in interpersonal violent crime victim descriptions are even more important (Phillips & Brown, 1998). Smith *et al.* state that "more innocent citizens are wrongfully tried and convicted on the basis of eyewitness evidence in Great Britain and North America than by any other factor within the legal system" (2004, p. 146). Almost every paper on eyewitness research highlights the increasing evidence for the numerous wrongful convictions that occur as a result of inaccurate eyewitness identification and testimony (e.g. Scheck *et al.*, 2000; Wells *et al*, 2000). In the USA, in 2007 the Innocence Project stated that 75% of studied wrongful convictions are a result of faulty eyewitness identification and testimony (see www.innocenceproject.org). In fact, eyewitness misidentification is thought to be the single most important factor leading to wrongful conviction in the USA and UK (Huff, 2003). There is a substantial body of evidence that supports the conclusion that eyewitnesses frequently make mistakes (e.g. Connors *et al.*, 1996; Goldstein *et al.*, 1989; Pynoos & Eth, 1984).

However, numerous authors have also identified that eyewitness evidence continues to hold an important place within the criminal justice system (CJS) (e.g. Cutler & Penrod, 1995; Kebbell & Milne, 1998; Rand Corporation, 1975; Sanders, 1986). In fact Wakefield and Underwager (1998) say its evidential power is second only to confession. Despite its importance, unfortunately the empirical data (almost without exception) indicate that eyewitness identification evidence does not perform very well (e.g. Penrod, 2005). The focus of this chapter will be on identifying the reasons why this is the case and how police procedures can be modified to improve eyewitness evidence.

There is a small group of researchers who contest the power and importance of eyewitness testimony. They do this on the basis of research which shows that the majority of criminal defendants plead guilty (Willis, 1995); therefore eyewitness testimony is not required as the facts are not in dispute. Furthermore, the majority of cases are not decided by a jury (making jury perceptions of eyewitness testimony irrelevant), hence eyewitness testimony can be argued to play only a small role in crime detection (Kapardis, 1997). A study by Farrington and Lambert (1993) reports that eyewitness descriptions (whether by victims or not) of offenders in cases of burglary and violence in England led to arrests in only 2% to 14.7% of cases.

One of the most common misperceptions within the CJS is that memory operates like a video recorder, allowing eyewitnesses to recall exactly what they saw irrespective of any other influences. Decades of research on human attention, perception and memory have consistently demonstrated that this is not the case, suggesting instead that these are active constructive processes influenced by multiple factors both within and outside the person (Clifford & Bull, 1978). Limits of space preclude an explanation of the fundamental principles of how attention, perception and memory work. The interested reader should consult Ainsworth (2002) and Kapardis (1997) for detailed introductions to these processes and how they relate to eyewitness evidence.

Like many areas of psychological research, eyewitness research has not been short of controversy and debate. Much of this has emerged from conflicting opinions about the generalisability of experimental laboratory-based research as opposed to realistic field studies (Kapardis, 1997). Both have strengths and weaknesses and passionate supporters who champion the methods with which they work (for arguments for experimental laboratory-based work, see Cutler & Penrod, 1995 and Wells 1993; for arguments for realistic field studies, see Yuille, 1986), and of course there are a few detractors who think that both approaches are so flawed that their findings are virtually useless (McCloskey & Egeth, 1983). This chapter reviews research from both perspectives, and supports the position taken by Davies: "problems need to be addressed from a number of perspectives... Only by pooling the results of these different varieties of study is a reliable psychology of the eyewitness likely to emerge" (1992, p. 265).

THE STATUS OF EYEWITNESS EVIDENCE AND PROCEDURES IN ENGLAND AND WALES

In 1976 the Devlin Report (produced by the British government) highlighted that in numerous cases other evidence undermined eyewitness identification. The report tried to explain why eyewitnesses could be mistaken even if they believed they were being honest (Clifford & Bull, 1978), and looked at pre-trial identification procedures and the role of identification evidence at trial. Recommendations were made based on scientific data. One key recommendation was that the police should tell witnesses that the perpetrator might not be in the identity parade (or line-up as it is referred to in the USA; the terms will be used interchangeably in this chapter). The report also encouraged co-operation between the police and scientists. However none of the report's recommendations became law. It was not until the Police and Criminal Evidence Act 1984 (PACE), which came into force in April 1985, that there were any statutory changes to identification procedures, including the introduction of codes of practice, in England and Wales.

More recently, in 2004 there was a shift in police procedure from live identity parades to video parades, which allowed eyewitness identification to take place sooner. The parades, typically using video files of the suspect and eight or more fillers, take place in specialised suites with suspects and foils being presented sequentially (Valentine *et al.*, 2003). The witness is asked to give a decision at the end once they have seen each face twice. The identity parade is not run blind (if it were, the officer running the parade would not know who the suspect was), but the person conducting it must not be part of the team conducting the investigation (see Davies & Valentine, 1999). Valentine and Heaton's 1999 paper describes the video procedures in some detail, and their research shows that video parades are fairer than traditional ones. In the UK, the identification suites follow a code of practice outlined in PACE (Home Office, 2005).

Police procedures in the USA for conducting line-ups are not streamlined and vary from state to state. The Department of Justice has developed National Guidelines for Preservation and Collection of Eyewitness Evidence (Technical Working Group for Eyewitness Evidence,

1999). However, as a result of conflicting research findings, there have been a number of high-profile debates and controversies about exactly what procedures the police should be following (see Spinney, 2008 for a concise summary).

Clifford and Davis (1989) identified the three stages of a police investigation that use eyewitness identification. First, in what they refer to as the descriptive phase, the eyewitness provides information (usually verbally) that can be used in a computer program or by a sketch artist to provide an image of the suspect or a description of other information related to the crime. In the second phase, police searching for the suspect will use a combination of the information provided by the eyewitnesses and searches of criminal records to identify potential suspects. In the final phase, the police will require the eyewitness to identify the perpetrator from the potential suspects they have, often using an identification parade. Depending on the jurisdiction they are operating within, slightly different procedures will be used by the police. However the influence on the quality of the information provided by the eyewitness remains fairly consistent, with only slight variations when different procedures are used.

There are two widely used ways of thinking about the variables that affect eyewitness identification, either as estimator and system variables or as stages in memory. Figure 5.1 shows how estimator variables map onto the first two stages of memory and how system variables occur at the third, retrieval, stage of memory.

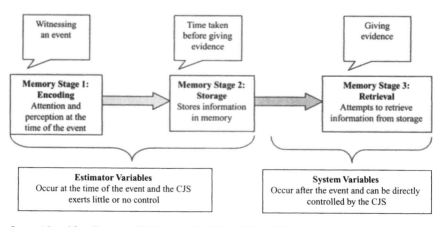

Source: Adapted from Kapardis, 1997; Sporer *et al.*, 1996, and Wells, 1978.

Figure 5.1 Stages in the eyewitness process, memory and variables involved in identification

More recently, Wells and Olson (2001) suggested that eyewitness identification variables could be distinguished according to suspect-bias variables and general impairment variables. Suspect-bias variables are those that explain why eyewitnesses presented with a line-up specifically select the innocent suspect rather than one of the fillers in the line-up. General impairment variables can only broadly account for poor eyewitness performance; they cannot explain why the eyewitness identified the person they did. For the sake of simplicity, this chapter will discuss the variables in two sections using Wells's (1978) distinction between estimator and system variables.

ESTIMATOR AND SYSTEM VARIABLES

Estimator Variables

Estimator variables occur at the time of the crime and cannot be manipulated post-event. As a result the CJS exerts little or no control over them and they cannot be controlled when the criminal event is taking place, but they can be easily manipulated in experimental research. Memon *et al.* (2003) classified estimator variables into seven categories: stable witness factors; malleable witness factors; style of presentation; consistency and confidence; stable target characteristics; malleable target characteristics; environmental conditions and post-event factors. These categories have been used as a basis for devising the three that are discussed here. It is not intended that this section will provide a comprehensive account of every possible factor; instead, it will draw attention to some of the most important ones and direct the reader to more in-depth literature.

Witness Factors[1]

Intelligence, gender and race: In their review of the literature, Memon *et al.* (2003) conclude that intelligence, gender and race are not useful predictors of accuracy in eyewitnesses. However, Kapardis points to a large body of work which concludes that "cross-racial identifications are more difficult, less accurate and thus less reliable than within-race identifications by adult witnesses" (1997, p. 56; see e.g. Brigham, 1986; Jalbert & Getting, 1992; Lindsay & Wells, 1983; Shapiro & Penrod, 1986). In relation to gender, Memon *et al.*'s conclusion appears more viable as there is a large amount of inconsistency in studies on the importance of gender. For example, some have reported greater accuracy of recall and better identification of a bystander by females than males, while other have found no gender differences for identification (see e.g. Lindsay, 1986; Lipton, 1977; Yarmey & Kent, 1980). Similarly, almost all the studies that have looked at intelligence and eyewitness identification accuracy have found no significant link (see e.g. Brown *et al.*, 1977; Feinman & Entwistle, 1976).

Alcohol intoxication: Police superintendents in the UK have advised that alcohol is present in half of all crimes committed (Crime and Society Foundation, 2004). Furthermore, in England and Wales approximately 70% of crime audits published in 1998 and 1999 identified alcohol as an issue (Home Office, 2001a). These figures suggest that alcohol plays a role in the majority of crime, which in turn suggests that a significant proportion of those who witness crime will be intoxicated. Very little research has been conducted into the effects of intoxication on eyewitnesses specifically. This is because of the numerous practical and ethical problems associated with conducting studies in which participants must be intoxicated and witness a potentially stressful event. The early studies investigating the impact of alcohol on the memory performance of witnesses have contradictory findings. Parker *et al.* (1980) compared participants who consumed alcohol during the retention period with those who did not and found better recognition and recall performance amongst those who had consumed alcohol. However, Read *et al.* (1992) found significant impairment of recall of peripheral information amongst intoxicated participants. Interference with the acquisition and encoding of information when alcohol had been consumed was found by Steele and Josephs (1990) and Yuille and Tollestrup (1990). In more recent research, Dysart *et al.* (2002) found that eyewitnesses with high blood alcohol levels were more likely to make false identifications in target-absent show-ups than those who had low blood alcohol levels. In light of the limited research in the field, Cutler and Penrod conclude that "at some level of intoxication, perception and storage can be expected to deteriorate. Further research is needed to determine the level" (1995, p. 89).

Stress: Yuille and Cutshall (1986) found that high levels of stress in eyewitnesses lead to more detailed recall than low levels of stress. However, stress level is dependent on the degree of involvement and on the proximity of the eyewitness to the event, as demonstrated by Yuille *et al.* (1994) who enlisted 120 Metropolitan Police probationers to experience a stressful or non-stressful "stop and search" as either participants or observers. Their recall of the event was tested after either one or 12 weeks. The results after one week showed that those in the stressful situation consistently provided less information than those in the non-stressful situation. However, when interviewed after 12 weeks, those who had been in the stressful situation were more accurate in their recall than those who had been in the non-stressful situation. Overall those probationers who were actively involved in the event recalled more details than those who just observed it. These findings present a complex picture of the role of stress and involvement in an event for eyewitnesses. Interestingly Christianson and Hubinette's (1993) study of witnesses to real-life bank robberies found that the bank tellers who were both victims and witnesses (and therefore more involved and in closer proximity to the event) were no more stressed than bystanders (who were less involved and proximate to the event). More recently, Hulse and Memon (2006) found that the more physiological activation an eyewitness experienced, the fewer correct details they remembered when they viewed violent scenarios compared to non-violent scenarios. Similarly Valentine and Mesout (2008) found that the higher an eyewitness's anxiety level, the fewer correct details they recalled. Ihlebaek *et al.* (2003) also found that eyewitnesses who were involved in the event recalled fewer details than those who just watched the event.

Suspect Characteristics

Face recognition: Accurate identification of the suspect does not seem to be influenced by the suspect's gender (Memon *et al.*, 2003), but the distinctiveness of the suspect's face does seem to have an effect. Brigham *et al.* (1999) found that the more distinctive a suspect's face, the more likely the witness was to recognise it; however, it is much more difficult to construct "fair" line-ups when the suspect has a distinctive face. In the same study, Brigham and colleagues report that in cases where suspects had very typical facial features, there was a much higher likelihood of the witness making a false identification. Another more consistent and well-replicated finding is that faces rated as highly unattractive or attractive are more easily identified than faces rated as neutral (Davies *et al.*, 1979; Light *et al.*, 1979).

Other research has highlighted that witnesses primarily rely on external characteristics such as hair when they are asked to identify an unfamiliar face (O'Donnell & Bruce, 1982). This creates numerous problems because external characteristics are fairly easy for a suspect to change, and other research has demonstrated that disguises and changes in facial appearance severely affect the accuracy of witnesses' facial recognition (Cutler *et al.*, 1987; Narby *et al.*, 1996; Read *et al.*, 1990).

Event Characteristics

Crime seriousness: Leippe *et al.* (1978) conducted one of the first studies in this area, and found that whether eyewitnesses were told an item was valuable or worthless and whether they were told this before or after they had witnessed a theft affected the likelihood of correct identification. Those eyewitnesses who were told before they witnessed a theft that the item was valuable were more likely to make a correct identification than any other group. Searcy, Bartlett and Siepel's (2000) study is noteworthy. Two groups consisting of participants from two distinct age groups (young adults, 18–30 years, older adults, 60–80 years) were shown a video of a man breaking into a house. One group was told that while in the house the man had committed a minor theft (they were also told he had no criminal history); the second group was told he had committed a murder (they were also told he had a criminal history). When they took part in a line-up task, those who were trying to identify a murderer were more likely to attempt an identification. Furthermore, the young adults had higher accuracy rates in the murder condition than the minor theft condition, while the older adults made more false identifications, particularly when they had viewed the murder. This suggests that crime seriousness affects eyewitnesses' propensity to choose. Unfortunately Searcy *et al.*'s study is let down by the confounded manipulation; it is not possible to identify whether eyewitnesses' increased accuracy is a result of the characteristics of the criminal or the crime.

Weapon focus: Weapon focus has been described as the best known but least understood error in eyewitness testimony (Wells & Olson, 2003). The classic study demonstrating the effect was conducted by Loftus *et al.* (1987). They showed participants slides of a customer in a fast food restaurant who approached a cashier and pulled out either a chequebook or a handgun. When tested, witnesses made more and longer eye fixations on the gun than on the chequebook. These findings were very strongly supported using both similar (e.g. Kramer *et al.*, 1990) and very different experimental designs (Maass & Köhnken, 1989). The two best-established explanations for the weapon focus effect are that when an eyewitness notices a weapon they experience increased levels of arousal, which focuses their attention on the weapon.

In a meta-analytic review of 12 studies which allowed 19 tests of the weapon focus effect, Steblay (1992) showed that, in relation to eyewitness line-up identification accuracy, the weapon focus effect was small (0.13), but it was stronger for accuracy of description of the suspect's features (0.55).

More recently the explanations for the weapon focus effect have been challenged by Pickel (1999), who proposed an alternative: that weapons surprise witnesses, and that because the weapon appears out of context their attention is drawn to it, which means they have fewer attentional resources left for other details. Pickel provided support for this explanation in a study in which witnesses saw the same man dressed either as a priest or a policeman and carrying either a gun or a mobile phone. When the witnesses saw the priest carrying the gun they provided poorer descriptions of him than when they saw him carrying a mobile phone or when they saw the policeman carrying either the gun or mobile phone. Pickel explains that the gun is inconsistent with the priest's occupation so the eyewitnesses were surprised. The weapon focus effect has also recently been found to occur in children (Davies et al., 2008; Pickel et al., 2008).

Despite the differing potential explanations for the weapon focus effect, it can be concluded, as Kapardis (1997) does, that "the empirical evidence involving witnesses as bystanders or victims strongly indicates they are more likely to remember details of the weapon itself and perhaps the essence of the situation (Tooley et al., 1987; Kramer, Kerr & Carroll, 1990)" (1997, p. 45). When a weapon is involved, eyewitnesses are not likely to remember the face or indeed other features of the suspect involved in the event.

Exposure duration: Exposure duration to the suspect's face is a relatively simple variable to record and vary in experimental laboratory research; despite this, very few studies have done so, even though they often report the event duration (Memon et al., 2003). This is surprising, as in a real crime situation it is relatively difficult to gauge the witnesses' duration of exposure to the suspect, making it a prime area for laboratory research. Memon et al. (2003) identify only two studies that have manipulated exposure duration systematically. Memon et al. (2002) and Read (1995) found that the longer exposure eyewitnesses have to a crime event, the more correct choices they make in suspect-present line-ups.

In a meta-analysis of face recognition studies, a positive linear relationship between exposure duration and correct identifications was found (Shapiro & Penrod, 1986). Exposure duration, whether to the crime or the suspect, is an important determinant of eyewitness accuracy for jurors. Lindsay (1994) demonstrated that, for potential jurors asked to rate 25 factors that determine eyewitness accuracy, the duration of the crime was the fourth most important.

Post-event factors: As the case an eyewitness is involved with moves through the CJS, they will be asked to describe what they saw to many different people (police officers, prosecutors, judges) and for many different purposes (e.g. to assist with the creation of a photo-fit, to provide a statement). On every occasion it is possible that their memory could be interfered with and altered as a result of the information they are exposed to, commonly referred to as post-event information.

Post-event information: The "misinformation effect" (Loftus & Hoffman, 1989) has been the subject of a plethora of research internationally. In one of the earliest studies, conducted by Loftus and Palmer (1974), participants were shown a film of a car accident and asked to estimate the speed at which the car was travelling at the moment of impact. Participants' estimates of the speed varied according to whether they were asked what speed the car was travelling at when it *smashed* (40.8 m.p.h.) or when it *contacted* (31.8 m.p.h.). Later, when they were asked if they had seen broken glass, those who had been in the *smash* condition were more likely to report that they had, even though there was no broken glass. This study demonstrated how simply asking questions using different verbs can alter what an eyewitness reports they have seen (there is some debate over whether the original memory is altered irrevocably or whether is could still be retrieved under appropriate circumstances; see e.g. Loftus & Ketcham, 1983; McCloskey & Zaragoza, 1985; Zaragoza & Koshmider, 1989). Since the original study, many other studies have confirmed that eyewitnesses exposed to post-event information are subsequently likely to report that information confidently when they are asked to recall what they saw (e.g. Lindsay, 1994; Loftus *et al.*, 1989; Weingardt *et al.*, 1994).

A witness's memory is most likely to be altered by post-event information that is introduced shortly before their memory is tested (Loftus *et al.*, 1978) and when the detail that is being altered is peripheral to the witnessed event rather than central (Dristas & Hamilton, 1977; Loftus, 1979).

SYSTEM VARIABLES

System variables are those which are controlled directly by the CJS. As a result they can be controlled and manipulated both by researchers and by practitioners working in the CJS. Before discussing system variables, in particular focusing on the line-up, consideration must be given to the processes used to extract information from witnesses. In the UK (and in fact in other parts of Europe, in the USA and in

Australia at different times) the cognitive interview (CI) was incorporated into the Home Office Investigative Interviewing package in 1992. This was a result of a number of studies both in the field and in the lab which found consistently that the CI improved eyewitness recall (see Köhnken *et al.*, 1999 for a meta-analysis of 42 studies). The CI was devised in the USA by Geiselman *et al.* (1984), and has been revised and developed since then (e.g. Fisher, Geiselman, Raymond, Jurkevitch & Warhaftig, 1987; Fisher & Geiselman, 1992), but the basic principles have remained the same. Here, we will provide only a brief overview of the cognitive interview, which is discussed more fully in Chapter 6 (for more detailed information also see Milne & Bull, 1999). The CI is made up of four memory-retrieval mnemonics and has its theoretical basis in two widely accepted cognitive principles of memory. The first principle is that memory trace is made up of several features (Bower, 1967; Underwood, 1969), and the second is that there may be several retrieval paths to the event in memory, so information can be accessed through a number of different routes (Tulving, 1974). From these basic principles, the four memory-retrieval mnemonics that help to improve eyewitness recall are:

1. reinstate the context;
2. report everything;
3. report events in different orders;
4. report events from a different perspective.

While there has been a large amount of research which has demonstrated that the CI is a superior technique for interviewing witnesses of crime (e.g. Clifford & George, 1995; Köhnken, 1992; Memon & Bull, 1991), it has not been without its critics; and there is a small body of work that has found that it does not significantly increase witnesses' accuracy or ability to resist misleading questions (e.g. Boon & Noon, 1994; Milne *et al.*, 1995).

In England and Wales there must be a police identification parade for the purpose of identification (R. v. Preston [1961], VR 762). Line-ups are either conducted live or, more commonly in the USA, using photos (Schuster, 2007), and in the UK using videoclips (Valentine & Heaton, 1999). Wells *et al.* (1994) recommend that line-ups should contain at least five other people (usually referred to as foils), as well as the suspect. In the UK and Australia, they usually consist of eight or more people (Kapardis, 1997). In the USA, simultaneous line-ups are most commonly used (Wells & Olson, 2003). The four most extensively researched system variables will now be briefly outlined. For more detailed discussion, see Cutler and Penrod (1995) and Memon *et al.* (2003).

Presentation Bias

There are a number of different procedures that can be used to ask an eyewitness to identify a suspect after the initial description has been given. The most commonly used and frequently researched are line-ups, dual line-ups, sequential procedures and show-ups. It should be noted that, regardless of which method is used (they are outlined below), they can either include all suspects, one suspect (either in a line-up with a number of other people who are not suspects or in the form of a show-up where the witness is just shown the one suspect) or no suspects. Yarmey *et al.* (1996) found that, in comparison to line-ups with one suspect and some foils, all-suspect line-ups and one-suspect show-ups lead to more false identifications of look-alike innocent suspects.

Wells *et al.* (1998) suggest that one reason the conduct of a line-up is so important is neatly summarised in relative judgement theory. This proposes that witnesses will choose the person in the line-up who looks most like the person they saw, relative to the other people in the line-up. This is particularly problematic for two reasons: firstly, the suspect is not always present in a line-up (known as a "target/suspect-absent line-up"); secondly, the eyewitness is not comparing the people they see in the line-up with their memory of the suspect (if they were doing this they would be making an "absolute judgement"). There is considerable empirical evidence that eyewitnesses tend to make relative judgements (Wells, 1984).

In traditional simultaneous line-ups the witness sees all of the potential suspects at the same time, either in person, in a photo or in a video clip. Line-ups can be thought of as a multi-person identification task. In a dual line-up, one line-up is created that only contains people who are known to be innocent of the offence, a "blank line-up". The witness is given the same instructions as they would be given in a single line-up – that the suspect may or may not be present. The blank line-up acts as a control, allowing the police to see if the witness will just select someone from any line-up, or whether they can resist and say that the suspect is not present in the blank line-up and then identify them from the normal line-up. Research in experimental conditions has shown that blank line-ups can help to filter out eyewitnesses who are prone to making mistakes (Wells, 1984).

In sequential line-up procedures the witness is shown each member of the line-up one at a time and must decide whether that person is the suspect before being shown the next person; they are not told how many people they will be shown. There is considerable empirical evidence that supports the use of sequential line-ups because witnesses must use a more absolute judgement process; even though they can think back to the face they saw before, they cannot be sure that the next face they are going to see will not be a far better likeness of the suspect (e.g. Lindsay *et al.*, 1991; Sporer, 1993). Steblay *et al.*'s (2001) meta-analysis found that sequential line-ups reduce false identifications when the suspect is not present and also reduces the number of correct identifications when the suspect is present. They also found that using a sequential line-up in comparison to a simultaneous one only results in a moderate loss in correct identifications and it increases the number of correct rejections. In summary, the evidence comparing sequential and simultaneous line-ups is contradictory. There is as much evidence that sequential line-ups increase correct identifications and reduce false identifications as there is of the reverse (Lindsay *et al.*, 1997; Memon & Bartlett, 2002; Memon *et al.*, 2003). Cutler and Penrod (1995) conclude that in both adults and children, sequential compared to simultaneous line-ups substantially reduce false identifications when the suspect is not in the line-up; reduce the separate and joint influences of instruction, clothing and foil biases; and are more effective when the witness does not know how many people they will be shown. Finally, and in contrast to all of the aforementioned procedures, show-ups are a one-person identification task. A photo or video of the suspect is shown to the witness and they are asked if that person is the one they saw.

In a recent paper Haw *et al.* (2007) draw attention to a limitation of much of the eyewitness research which has treated the different types of line-up identification procedures as distinct, mutually exclusive events. In fact police often use the show-up procedure and then at a later stage in the investigation get the witness to view a line-up containing the same suspect as was in the show-up (Behrman & Davey, 2001). There is a considerable body of evidence which demonstrates that using multiple identification procedures has a detrimental effect on eyewitness performance (e.g. Haw *et al.*, 2007; Hinz & Pezdek, 2001; Pezdek & Blandon-Gitlin, 2005).

Line-Up Instruction Bias

The effects of the instructions given to eyewitnesses have been researched extensively, and it has been consistently found that any kind of bias in the instructions given to eyewitnesses influences their identifications. For example, rather unrealistic and obvious instructions such as telling witnesses that officers believe the person responsible for committing the crime is present in the line-up; not giving witnesses the option of rejecting the line-up (i.e. saying that none of the people in it is the person they saw); and more subtle instructions such as asking witnesses to choose who in the line-up they believed was the robber (e.g. Buckhout et al., 1975; Cutler et al., 1987; Malpass & Devine, 1981b; O'Rourke et al., 1989). The research suggests that biased line-up instructions are especially problematic when the perpetrator is not present in the line-up, and they even have an effect when the witness is given the option of saying the suspect is not present in the line-up (Cutler & Penrod, 1995). Kapardis (1997) highlights, however, that in practice in the UK there is incredibly limited opportunity for the witness to be given biased instructions because the law "specifies how a witness should be instructed and what to be told" (1997, p. 253). But the extent to which police comply with the requirements of the law is unknown, so we cannot say with certainty that no effects of line-up instruction bias occur in the UK.

Foil and Clothing Bias

It is very important to create a line-up in which the suspect does not stand out from the foils (the other people in the line-up). There are a number of competing opinions about how to choose the foils that will be used in order to create an unbiased line-up. Wells et al. (1993) suggest that foils should be chosen on the basis of the witness's description of the suspect, not on the basis of their similarity to the suspect the police have arrested. This is based on Luus and Wells's (1991) proposal that if the foils are chosen to match the suspect the police have arrested then there will be unnecessary similarity between the suspect and the foils. Wells et al. (1993) compared line-ups constructed using the two methods and found those using the former (preferred) technique resulted in a high rate of correct identifications and a low rate of false identifications.

Lindsay et al. (1987) conducted a study looking at the influence of the clothing worn by the suspects on witness identifications and found that when the suspect was present in the line-up, clothing did not significantly affect identification performance. However clothing-biased line-ups (e.g. when the suspect was not present, an innocent foil was dressed in the same clothes that were worn by the perpetrator during the crime) significantly increased the likelihood of false identification compared to conditions where everyone in the line-up dressed differently and did not wear any clothes similar to those worn during the crime, or where everyone in the line-up wore identical clothes (whether identical to the perpetrator in the crime or not).

Investigator Bias

The main focus of research into investigator bias has been on the effect of the person administering the line-up knowing who the suspect is or not. The basic proposition is that, even if it is unintentional, the non-verbal behaviour of a line-up administrator who knows who the suspect is can bias the eyewitness, for example by smiling or nodding (Wells, 1993; Wells & Luus, 1990). Garrioch and Brimacombe (2001) showed that witnesses' confidence in their line-up choice is affected by the line-up administrator's belief about where the suspect is in the line-up. False identification rates were also found to be increased as a result of the line-up administrator's knowledge of the suspect's identity.

The Relationship between Confidence and Accuracy

The relationship between confidence and accuracy can be seen partly as an estimator and system variable. It is widely agreed that jurors rely on witnesses' confidence to infer how accurate their testimony is (Cutler et al., 1990). In fact Gary Wells and colleagues (1998) go so far as to suggest that confidence is the most powerful determinant of the judgement of accuracy. There is conflicting evidence about the link between confidence and accuracy. Loftus (1979) argued that the research rarely supported such a link, which was confirmed by a number of other researchers (e.g. Bothwell et al., 1987; Cutler & Penrod, 1989; Fruzzetti et al., 1992; Leippe, 1994; Smith et al., 1989; Wells, 1993). This position was challenged by researchers such as Sporer et al. (1995) and Weber and Brewer (2003), who found that the confidence–accuracy relationship is stronger for witnesses who make an identification from a line-up than for those who reject the line-up. Further, there have been numerous studies which have found a very robust positive relationship between confidence and accuracy (e.g. Kebbell et al., 1996; Perfect et al., 1993). Similarly Read et al. (1998) find support for the relationship in studies that use more real-world conditions.

Wells and Lindsay (1985) argued that often the findings of either a very positive or negative relationship between confidence and accuracy are a result of methodological issues with the studies, whereas Leippe (1980) suggested that the accuracy and confidence of witnesses are controlled by different mechanisms. Kebbell et al. (1996) proposed and tested an explanation for studies that have found little or no relationship between confidence and accuracy by suggesting that it might be a result of the difficulty or easiness of the question being asked. In their study they varied the difficulty of the open-ended questions they used and found that there was a higher correlation between accuracy and confidence with the easy questions than with the harder ones.

Despite the conflicting findings about the relationship between confidence and accuracy, there is fairly consistent evidence that eyewitness confidence is malleable. Repeated questioning (Shaw & McClure, 1996;

Turtle & Yuille, 1004); giving eyewitnesses the information that another witness has identified the same suspect (Luus & Wells, 1994); telling eyewitnesses after their identification that they have identified the suspect (Wells & Bradfield, 1998); and giving them prior warning about the kind of questions they might be asked (Wells *et al.*, 1981) all lead to increases in eyewitnesses confidence (Memon *et al.*, 2003).

Laboratory studies have shown that an eyewitness's confidence in their testimony can be affected by what other people say, commonly referred to as post-identification feedback (Bradfield *et al.*, 2002; Dixon & Memon, 2005; Wells & Bradfield, 1998). This post-identification feedback has been found, in a meta-analysis by Douglass and Steblay (2006), to be most powerful for measures of certainty rather than for the eyewitness's memory in general or their view of the culprit.

In a recent paper, Wright and Skagerberg (2007) propose that researchers should record confidence and other variables after eyewit-nesses make an identification but before they discover the outcome of the identification (a proposal previously made by Wells *et al.*, 1998; Wells & Olson, 2003). Their research found that eyewitnesses' judge-ments at this point were moderate predictors of accuracy and so have diagnostic value which could help police officers and jurors assess the reliability of the identification (Wright & Skagerberg, 2007).

Despite the conflicting evidence, the link between confidence and accuracy remains high on the research agenda and of practical interest because the general public (i.e. jurors) appear to be more persuaded by evidence from a confident witness (Lindsay, 1994).

Vulnerable Witnesses

Vulnerable witnesses traditionally include people with mental health problems, learning disabilities and physical and/or communication dif-ficulties. The case can be made, however, that children and older people also belong in this category: as Davies (1991) and Gudjonsson (1992) have identified, they are usually treated as second-class witnesses in the same way as people with the previously identified vulnerabilities. Furthermore, amongst the multitude of factors that influence eyewit-ness identification, it is becoming increasingly accepted that a witness's age reliably affects their accuracy (Kassin *et al.*, 2001). Below we give a brief overview of the issues surrounding witnesses with mental health problems or learning disabilities, and witnesses who are children or older adults.

Children/Young People

The performance of children as eyewitnesses is the most researched of the vulnerabilities considered in this section. A number of authors have noted the rapidly increasing focus on the eyewitness abilities of children (Peterson *et al.*, 1999; Ricci *et al.*, 1996; Melton & Thompson, 1987). Clifford (1993) identified that, prior to the early 1980s, the majority of research and textbooks on eyewitness testimony stated that children are poorer witnesses than adults (e.g. Wells & Loftus, 1984; Yarmey, 1979). Research that has compared identification accuracy across childhood has found that older children are more accurate than younger children and are less likely to make false identifications; in other words, identification accuracy seems to improve with age (Brigham *et al.*, 1986; Chance & Goldstein, 1984; Shapiro & Penrod, 1986). The most widely cited concerns about their abilities have been based largely on suggestions that children have less accurate memories and are more suggestible than adults (e.g. Brigham *et al.*, 1986; Goodman & Reed, 1986). However, the data are mixed (Goodman, 1984; Loftus & Davies, 1984): Brigham *et al.*'s 1986 study found no evidence to support this claim.

A body of work has emerged that suggests that in some circumstances children's eyewitness evidence can be as good as and sometimes even better than that of adults (e.g. Cashmore & Bussey, 1996; Gross & Hayne, 1996; King & Yuille, 1987; Parker *et al.*, 1986). Generally, however, research into children's memory compared to that of adults has yielded inconsistent results (Leippe *et al.*, 1993). Clifford (1993) reported that the findings are really dependent on the age of the children: in a series of studies, he found little difference between 11- and 12-year-olds and adults, but younger children's recall and identification were significantly worse than those of adults. It might be, however, that children's performance is not only dependent on their age but on the specific task they are asked to do. For example, in a review of studies concerning children's ability to make eyewitness identifications, Parker and Ryan (1993) highlighted that children of 6 and older have been found to perform at rates comparable to adults with regard to the number of correct identifications. This was supported by Gross and Haynes's (1996) work in presenting suspect-present line-ups. Conversely, numerous studies have found an effect of age (with younger children making far fewer rejections than older children) in suspect-absent line-ups (e.g. Davies *et al.*, 1988; Pozzulo & Lindsay, 1997), Further, Pozzulo and Lindsay (1998) found that children were less likely to make correct rejections, and the difference in the rate of correct rejections increased between adults and children in sequential compared to simultaneous line-ups (Beal *et al.*, 1995).

Older Adults

Within the eyewitness research, older adults are usually defined as people over the age of 60, and that definition will be applied here (Memon *et al.*, 2004). There is a fairly strong emerging body of research which is consistently finding that older witnesses are less likely to be accurate on identification line-ups than young witnesses (Memon *et al.*, 2003: Rose *et al.*, 2003; Searcy *et al.*, 1999; Wilcock *et al.*, 2007). Specifically, there is an age-related increase in false identifications: the older witnesses are, the more false identifications they are likely to make, and older witnesses make fewer correct identifications (Memon & Bartlett, 2002; Memon & Gabbert, 2003; Memon *et al.*, 2002; Searcy, Bartlett, & Memon, 2000; Searcy, Bartlett, & Seipel, 2000; Searcy *et al.*, 2001). Older witnesses also provide fewer descriptions of the perpetrator (Brimacombe *et al.*, 1997); are more likely to misidentify a stranger's face (Searcy *et al.*, 1999); are more susceptible to misleading post-event information than younger adults (Cohen & Faulkner, 1989); and are more like to be less accurate in their recall of environmental details and details of actions and events (Yarmey & Kent, 1980; Yarmey *et al.*, 1984).

Some research has emerged which suggests that including everyone over the age of 60 in one "older people" group may be misleading. Memon *et al.* (2004) report that there were significant differences between older adults aged 60–68 and those over 69. Those aged over 69 were more likely to make incorrect choices in a suspect-absent line-up than the younger group. This leads the authors to the conclusion, previously made by Glisky *et al.* (2001), that by combining older adults into one group the differences between sub-groups of older adults who are ageing differently may be hidden. However, there is other work which has not found any differences between older adults' and other adults' recognition performance (Smith & Winograd, 1978; Yarmey & Kent, 1980).

Recent research that has looked at methods to improve older witnesses' performance suggests that, if they are given additional support such as the use of photographic context reinstatement, they could be brought up to a similar level to young adults (Wilcock *et al.*, 2007). For good reviews of the literature on older eyewitnesses see Memon *et al.* (2004) and Yarmey (2001).

Learning Disabilities and Mental Health Problems

Research has found that people with learning disabilities are poorer at aspects of encoding, storing and retrieving information compared to the general population (Kebbell & Wagstaff, 1999). However, there is considerable variation in their abilities. While their accounts are often less complete than those of the general population, they do usually include the most important information (Kebbell & Hatton, 1999; see

Gudjonsson & Gunn, 1982 for a useful case example). Kebbell *et al.* (2004) draw attention to the finding that the type of question asked is a key factor in determining the accuracy and completeness of eyewitness testimony generally (see also Fisher, Geiselman & Raymond, 1987) and this has even more influence on people with learning disabilities (Bull, 1995; Clare & Gudjonsson, 1993). Clare and Gudjonsson (1993) found that eyewitnesses with learning disabilities appear to be more suggestible to leading questions than the general population, but when asked open, free-recall questions they are able to provide accounts with accuracy rates broadly similar to those of the general population (Dent, 1986; Kebbell *et al.*, 2004).

There is very little research on the effects of mental health problems on eyewitnesses. In fact Kebbell and Wagstaff report that "although direct assessments of the influence of mental illness such as depression and schizophrenia on eyewitness memory are rare, research suggests that they can have an adverse effect" (1999, pp. 17–18).

EMERGING AREAS OF RESEARCH AND DEVELOPMENT

The media portrayal of eyewitnesses has become an increasingly popular area of research in recent years. Desmarais *et al.* (2008) identified that the prevalence of eyewitness issues in the media has approximately doubled since the 1980s, but the presentation of the information about eyewitness testimony remains very similar in its implications. This suggests that the developments in eyewitness research have not filtered through to the media; other studies suggest that they have not really reached professionals working in the CJS either. This is demonstrated in the emerging field of work investigating the factors affecting what professionals working in the CJS know about eyewitness testimony. In 2004 Wise and Safer surveyed 160 judges in the United States and found that they had limited knowledge about eyewitness testimony. Out of 14 statements the judges were asked to rate, they got only 55% correct on average, just over chance. The study was recently replicated in Norway, with similar patterns of responses to the statements emerging: the Norwegian judges had a marginally higher percentage of correct answers. However, it is not possible to determine whether this is because they were genuinely more knowledgeable about eyewitness testimony or just because there had been heightened attention to the issues in the years since the study in the USA (Magnussen *et al.*, 2008). Linked to this, there has also been renewed interest in evaluating jurors' understanding of eyewitness issues (see Alonzo & Lane, 2006; Benton *et al.*, 2006; Read & Desmarais, 2007; Schmechel *et al.*, 2000). Finally there continues to be debate about the information provided to the courts about eyewitness testimony; Cutler and Penrod (1995) have argued that they should be made aware of the difficulties faced when trying to evaluate the accuracy of eyewitness testimony.

SUMMARY

On the basis of the available scientific literature, Wells *et al.* (1998) made four recommendations about the procedures used in eyewitness identifications that, they argue, would reduce the number of incorrect identifications and could be easily introduced because they are in the control of the CJS. The recommendations are, firstly, that "the person who conducts the line-up or photospread should not be aware of which member of the line-up or photospread is the suspect" (1998, p. 21). Secondly, "eyewitness's should be told explicitly that the person in question might not be in the line-up or photospread and therefore should not feel that they must make an identification. They should also be told that the person administering the line-up does not know which person is the suspect in the case" (1998, p. 23). Thirdly, "the suspect should not stand out in the line-up or photospread as being different from the distractors based on the eyewitness's previous description of the culprit or based on other factors that would draw extra attention to the suspect" (1998, p. 23). Finally "a clear statement should be taken from the eyewitness at the time of the identification and prior to any feedback as to his or her confidence that the identified person is the actual culprit" (1998, p. 27). They also add that ideally they would like to add a fifth recommendation that sequential line-ups are used instead of simultaneous ones, given the wealth of empirical evidence that they are more effective.

This chapter has provided a brief overview of some of the many problems and pitfalls associated with eyewitness evidence alongside its strengths. The shooting of Jean Charles de Menezes at Stockwell underground station provides a timely reminder of the many factors that influence eyewitnesses and the constant need for the CJS to be changing and developing its procedures on the basis of the evidence from scientific research. Eyewitnesses in the de Menezes case provided detailed descriptions of a suspect who vaulted over a ticket barrier running away from the police wearing a bulky jacket that could have concealed either a bomb or other weapon. In fact it has since come to light that Mr Menezes walked through the barriers at the tube station having picked up a free newspaper and only began to run when he saw his train arriving. He was also only wearing a light denim shirt or jacket. One eyewitness who originally claimed he saw Mr Menezes vaulting the ticket barrier has since conceded that he must have seen a plainclothes police officer. Wells and Loftus (2003) suggest that the CJS should treat eyewitness testimony in the same way that it treats physical evidence, to acknowledge that both can be contaminated and both should be collected by following stringent procedures developed by experts. If this change were to happen it is possible that the reliability of eyewitness evidence could be greatly improved, maybe not to the standard of physical evidence but not far off. This would have benefits for all parties involved in the criminal justice process.

NOTE

1. Age will be discussed in the section on vulnerable witnesses.

REVIEW QUESTIONS

1. Describe the main difficulties for the police when using eyewitness evidence.
2. Outline the impact of system variables on eyewitness evidence.
3. Outline the impact of estimator variables on eyewitness evidence.
4. Identify five key challenges faced when extracting evidence from vulnerable witnesses.

QUESTIONS FOR FURTHER RESEARCH AND ANALYSIS

1. How can/should the police change their procedures to improve the use of eyewitness evidence?
2. What research needs to be conducted to provide practical recommendations to the police about eyewitness evidence?
3. How have trends in the make-up of the population and patterns of crime influenced the nature of eyewitness evidence, and how will they do so in future?
4. What are the new directions/developments for eyewitness evidence?

RECOMMENDED READING

Ainsworth, P.B. (2002). *Psychology and policing.* Cullompton: Willan Publishing.

Cutler, B.L. & Penrod, S.D. (1995). *Mistaken identification. The eyewitness, psychology and the law*. New York: Cambridge University Press.

Devlin, P.A. (1976). *Report to the Secretary of State for the Home Department of the Departmental Committee on Evidence on Identification in Criminal Cases*. London: HMSO.

Fisher, R. & Geiselman, R.E. (1992). *Memory enhancing techniques for investigative interviewing*. Springfield, IL: Charles. C. Thomas.

Fisher, R.P., Geiselman, R.E. & Raymond, D.S. (1987). Critical analysis of police interview techniques. *Journal of Police Science & Administration, 15*, 177–185.

Kapardis, A. (1997). *Psychology and law: A critical introduction*. Cambridge: Cambridge University Press.

Kebbell, M.R., & Milne, R. (1998). Police officers' perception of eyewitness factors in forensic investigations: A survey. *Journal of Social Psychology, 138*, 323–330.

Memon, A., Vrij, A. & Bull, R. (2003). *Psychology and law: Truthfulness, accuracy and credibility* (2nd edn.). Chichester: Wiley. See Chapter 6.

Ross, D.F., Read, J.D. & Toglia, M.P. (eds.) (1994) *Adult eyewitness testimony: Current trends and developments*, New York: Cambridge University Press.

Spinney, L. (2008) Line-ups on trial. *Nature, 453(7194)*, 442–444.

Steblay, N.M (1992) A meta-analytic review of the weapon focus effect. *Law and Human Behavior, 16*, 413–424.

Wells, G.L. (1978) Applied eyewitness-testimony research: System variables and estimator variables. *Journal of Personality and Social Psychology, 36*, 1546–1557.

Wells, G.L., Memon, A. & Penrod, S.D. (2006). Eyewitness evidence: Improving its probative value. *Psychological Science in the Public Interest, 7*, 45–75.

WEBSITE

Innocence Project: http://www.innocenceproject.org/

CHAPTER 6

Investigative Interviewing

Lynsey Gozna and Miranda A. H. Horvath

INTRODUCTION

Effective police interviewing of suspects is a crucial element within police investigations of high-volume and major crime offences. Interviewing suspects is one of the most challenging aspects of policing, because of the range of individuals involved and the complexity of the interactions. The purpose of the interview has altered substantially over time, moving from focusing on obtaining suspect confessions towards a need to establish the truth. Therefore gaining information from suspects about an alleged offence and their possible involvement in it enables a broader base for police decision-making which incorporates evidence-gathering and credibility assessment. After setting the scene with a brief consideration of witness or victim interviewing, this chapter will focus on suspect interviewing. Although the interviewing of all three groups plays a fundamental role in the criminal justice process, there are differences between them which make it very difficult to consider them simultaneously.

Witness or Victim Interviewing

Table 6.1 shows the most salient differences between suspect, victim and witness interviews, although it should be acknowledged that their accounts are inextricably linked. The quality and quantity of information gained from witness or victim interviews can have a direct

Table 6.1 Differences between suspect, victim and witness interviews

Suspect interviews	Victim/witness interviews
Must be tape-recorded	Do not have to be tape-recorded but it is recommended as good practice.
All suspects have the right to legal advice	Do not have the right to legal advice
Must be cautioned against self-incrimination	Are not cautioned against self-incrimination
In England and Wales, if they are under 18 or mentally disordered they are entitled to have an "appropriate adult" present	It is recommended, but they are not entitled to have an "appropriate adult" present if they are under 18 or mentally disordered
They are asked to recall the crime but also to explain their intentions and actions	They are asked to recall the crime they observed or were involved in

Source: Adapted from Gudjonsson, 2007.

effect on which suspect is arrested and which strategies are used when interviewing them (Gudjonsson, 2003). The treatment of victims and witnesses in the interview room hit the headlines in 1982 as the result of the documentary *A Complaint of Rape* by Roger Graef. The film showed police officers interviewing a woman who claimed to have just been raped by two men she met in a pub.

> *First policeman.* I've been sitting 20 or 30 minutes, listening to you. Some of it's the biggest lot of bollocks I've ever heard. I can get very annoyed... What happened? I'm sick of the ups and downs, ins and outs. Some of this is better fairy tales than bloody Gretel can do. Stop mucking us about.
> *Complainant.* I'm not mucking you about.
> *First policeman.* I'm not saying you're lying. Get rid of the fruitiness, the beauty about it, and let's get down to facts and figures.
> *Complainant.* It's not beautiful at all, is it?
> *First policeman.* Some of it is. All this crap about bus stops, and "tea towels to wipe myself down with". What the hell's gone on? If nothing's gone on, let's go home. If something's gone [but] you think, that's just an experience; that's life, then all right.
> *Complainant.* That's what I do think.
> *First policeman (shouting).* This is the biggest bollocks I've ever heard.
>
> (extract of dialogue retrieved from Hill, 2006)

The impact of the film was extensive and wide-ranging (including questions in parliament and calls in the media for a major change of policy towards rape victims). As a result, police officers are now told to treat victims of rape with respect and an initial presumption of belief. The extract above shows the officer giving no consideration to the situation the victim is in and the other factors affecting her. It is crucial that officers take into consideration the multiple factors that may influence witnesses and victims as they will be directly impacting on their behaviour and presentation in interview, for example intimidation (perceived or real), fear, distress, indifference, work or family circumstances (for a detailed discussion see Fyfe & Smith, 2007).

Below we outline historical elements of interviewing suspects and how these have informed the current procedures that are implemented as standard in policing today. The discussion will continue by focusing on the practicalities of interviewing and the considerations for police and other practitioners involved in this process.

A LEGACY OF PROBLEMS

Historically the police interview occurred in isolation from wider scrutiny, and little priority was given to the experience of the suspect throughout the process of police custody, from initial arrest through to dispersal. In essence, the general secrecy surrounding the procedures and actions within the interview enabled the interaction between police and suspects to be unimpeded, and free from external monitoring. Research focusing on the interactions within the police interview setting commenced in the early 1980s (McConville & Baldwin, 1982). The lack of external monitoring created potential problems with the treatment of suspects and the ensuing admissibility of any evidence derived from the interview. Miscarriages of justice can take place for a number of reasons, not least as a result of any situation that may occur in police custody. Many of the events that lead to a miscarriage of justice appear to occur during the police investigation; they include biases held by investigating officers; the withholding or destruction of evidence; the fabrication or contamination of evidence; and false confessions obtained as a result of police processes or the psychological vulnerability of the suspect.

Criminal cases that are particularly important in understanding how police procedures did not assist in the correct conviction of suspects include the those of the "Guildford Four", the "Birmingham Six" and the "Maguire Seven" (see Gudjonsson, 1999 for detailed overviews and discussions of these cases). Such cases occurred during the height of an IRA bombing campaign on the UK mainland. Other cases have involved particularly horrendous offences where the need to secure a conviction might have overridden the need to ensure justice was achieved. The case of Stefan Kiszko was an example of this, when in 1975 he was arrested and later convicted of the sexual assault and murder of 11-year-old Lesley Molseed.

The Royal Commission on Criminal Procedure (RCCP) funded research resulting in a greater understanding of the processes occurring within the police interview (Irving, 1980; Softley, 1980). Observers were present during suspect interviews and identified five strategies that police officers employed during questioning to gain a confession:

1. police discretion in relation to charging and releasing suspects on bail;
2. providing expert knowledge regarding sentencing as a result of suspect co-operation;
3. having an influence on the assessment a suspect made as a result of confessing to an offence;
4. informing the suspect they have no decision to make; and
5. the use of custodial setting until a suspect confessed (Irving, 1980).

A further concern raised by the research was that some of the suspects exhibited "an abnormal state" prior to interview: this included intoxication, active symptoms of mental illness, and appearing mentally handicapped/vulnerable or physically frightened. As a result, Irving stated that it was "impossible to judge whether the state of a suspect would have constituted sufficient grounds for excluding the statements which ensued either on the basis of involuntariness or oppression" (1980, p. 136). The myriad behaviours exhibited by suspects present a huge challenge for interviewing officers in identifying the underlying cause and its implications for an investigation.

THE POLICE AND CRIMINAL EVIDENCE ACT

The Police and Criminal Evidence Act 1984 was initially developed as a code of practice for procedures during police investigations. Of particular relevance to police interviewing is Code C, which concerns the detention, treatment and questioning of suspects, and Code E, which focuses on the tape/video recording of interviews in custody. The development of PACE is considered to have discouraged the use of oppressive questioning and offers of inducements (Brown, 1997). It has, however, been suggested that, as a result of the codes of practice being implemented, "covert interrogations" now occur prior to the formal interview taking place (Brown, 1997; Moston & Stephenson, 1993). Essentially opportunities can present themselves that enable police officers to exploit the process and potentially display the coercive or manipulative behaviours towards suspects that PACE was designed to eradicate. However, the evidence for this is lacking, and has been gained more from anecdotal stories than research observations. Irving and McKenzie (1989) observed interviews and found little evidence of such covert activity, although the study used a relatively small sample based at one police station (Dixon, 1992). Ultimately the likelihood of such negative tactics will depend on the level of integrity displayed by individual officers. However, with a move in current police interviewing to incorporate wider considerations (such as personality, offence motivation and interactions) and to create an interview situation in which their ability to elicit truthful information from a suspect is enhanced, the use of negative tactics is likely to be a rare occurrence.

In addition to coercive police interrogation tactics, a wider focus on the general skills of police officers who conduct interviews with suspects was introduced to identify the main limitations (Baldwin, 1993; Moston & Stephenson, 1993; Williamson, 1993). To explore the inherent problems within police interviewing, Baldwin (1993) analysed a sample of 600 recordings (audio and video) of police interviews across three police forces in different areas of the UK. Few tactics were identified as being used; instead police interviewers were reported as often being unprepared, nervous and lacking in confidence. Furthermore, interviewing officers made assumptions of guilt and attempted to exert undue pressure on suspects in order to secure a confession. The questioning tactics used were problematic in that the interviewers asked many leading questions (i.e. questions that lead the suspect to respond in a specific manner) and rapport was difficult for police officers to build. Baldwin (1993) found that in 40% of the interviews where a suspect denied an offence, no challenge was made by interviewing officers to question this. However, Baldwin acknowledged that "the tapes can provide only a limited insight into the processes of detention and questioning ... [and] ... can never reveal everything that has happened while a suspect is in custody" (1993, p. 328). The findings of this research emphasised the need for police interviewing to receive some input in order to improve procedures and enhance the effectiveness of the interaction between suspect and interviewer.

Historically, the majority of training received by police officers was "on the job", via their observation of peers (Griffiths & Milne, 2006; Milne & Bull, 1999) or drawn from evidence contained in interrogation manuals such as *Criminal Interrogation and Confessions* (Inbau *et al.*, 2001). The manuals tend to be written by American retired or experienced police officers who have extensive knowledge of interview practice. The downside for the UK is that some elements of such police manuals may lead to an admission of guilt being rejected by the court as inadmissible under PACE guidelines (Williamson, 1993). The distinction between interrogation and interviewing divides the focus of questioning in the US and UK. Whereas in the US the objective of the interaction with a suspect is to secure a confession, in the UK the main emphasis for police officers has been on gaining information that can be incorporated into the wider investigation of an alleged offence and, if appropriate, to gain an admission from a suspect. This should be achieved through focused and planned questioning which is tailored to the suspect being interviewed.

Persuasive police interview tactics were identified as present following the implementation of PACE, and this weakness was exacerbated by a lack of skill identified in interviews. Hence in 1992 the Home Office and ACPO brought about a change in the ethos of police interviewing. The use of the term "interrogation" was considered inappropriate and was replaced with "investigative interviewing". This altered the purpose of questioning suspects from obtaining a confession to the gathering of information in relation to the alleged offence (Milne & Bull, 1999; Williamson, 1993).

PEACE INTERVIEW TRAINING

The requirement to enhance the effectiveness of police interviewing was addressed with the introduction in 1992 of a programme named PEACE, an acronym identifying five stages of the interview structure: **P**lanning and preparation, **E**ngage and explain, **A**ccount, **C**losure, and **E**valuation (Milne & Bull, 1999). The process outlined in PEACE incorporated the main factors that interviewing officers should consider when questioning suspects. However, as will be discussed below, PEACE is just one consideration when engaging with suspects, and can be used as a base from which to consider the interaction.

Planning and Preparation

This ensures that the interviewer/s can be fully prepared for the interview, understanding its purpose and defining its aims and objectives. This includes awareness of legal points to prove, assessing the evidence available and ensuring an understanding of PACE and associated codes of practice (McGurk *et al.*, 1993; Milne & Bull, 1999). In addition, this should incorporate a full understanding and ability to explain the police caution – "You do not have to say anything but it may harm your defence if you do not mention, when questioned, something which you later rely on in court. Anything you do say may be given in evidence" – to suspects during the interview. This process works in parallel with the requirement for an interpreter, legal adviser, or appropriate adult to be present. Prior to the interview commencing with a suspect, the requirement for an interpreter will alter the focus of the interview and will impede the flow of conversation. This should be incorporated into the planning phases of the procedure.

Engage and Explain

This section emphasises the need to use rapport-building techniques in order to shift the interaction with a suspect more towards investigative interviewing rather than interrogation. The assumption tends to be that rapport-building will occur during the interview with the suspect once all parties are present. The reality and perhaps requirement, though, is that rapport-building commences at the initial meeting between the interviewing officer and the suspect. The opportunity for this can be created when visiting the suspect in the cell, escorting the suspect to the interview room and in the informal section of the interview prior to the recording.

A wider factor that must be considered here is the welfare of the suspect (McGurk *et al.*, 1993) during their time in police custody, which relates to their basic needs and also the identification of vulnerability, which can include mental health problems, and issues of suggestibility and compliance within interviews (see Gudjonsson, 2003 for a detailed discussion of these factors). The interviewer must also explain legal requirements such as the caution, the provision of free legal advice (Milne & Bull, 1999), the reason for the interview, and what will happen after the interview. It is at this stage that any problems with comprehension of information should be identified by interviewing officers to ensure that suspects can answer questions appropriately.

Account

The use of two methods of interviewing – the cognitive interview (CI) (Fisher & Geiselman, 1992) and conversation management (CM) (Shepherd, 1993) – can assist in eliciting the maximum amount of information from the suspect (Milne & Bull, 1999). These are excellent devices to consider, but need to be tailored to the particular suspect

being interviewed in order to maximise the interaction. McGurk et al.
differentiate the two techniques: "The cognitive method provides the
interviewee with greater control over the way the interview develops,
whereas conversation management attributes more authority to
the interviewer" (1993, p. 8). These techniques will be beneficial
in certain interviews, although it will be apparent to some police
officers that the personality of certain suspects will mean that wider
considerations need to be taken into account, such as dealing with "no
comment" interviews. While both CI and CM approaches can be used
for suspects, it appears that CI is used more frequently with witnesses
and victims and CM with suspects (Milne & Bull, 1999), perhaps for
the reasons outlined by McGurk et al. (1993).

Closure

This section of the process was developed to ensure a suspect has
every opportunity to give their version of events and be provided with a
copy of the recording of the interview. The suspect is further told what
will occur as a result of the interview, which in the first instance tends
to require them to return to a cell while discussion occurs within the
investigative team. In some instances, the decision will be to conduct
further interviews and to request a longer period to hold a suspect in
custody, or discussion with the Crown Prosecution Service relating to
charging a suspect.

Evaluation

Reflection on the interview is a form of self-evaluation and/or feedback from colleagues or supervisors. However, Milne and Bull (1999)
suggest that police culture may prevent interviewers from admitting
deficiencies. The time spent in reflective practice is unfortunately limited within many professions, and this should be considered a vital
element of skill development in interviewing.

Initial piloting of the PEACE training course was carried out in 1992
and the trained officers' subsequent performance, as measured by a
number of performance indicators, was compared to a control group
of untrained officers in both simulated and real-life interviews. Overall the training course was evaluated as successful, with participants
exhibiting increased knowledge and enhanced interview skills. However, there were limitations in the knowledge of legal points to prove
and the ability of interviewing officers to effectively close the interview
(McGurk et al., 1993). These real-life interviews were analysed by lis-
tening to audiotapes, and as a result suffered from the same limitations

as the Baldwin (1993) study where only the interaction formally recorded was considered. It is difficult to gauge the impartiality of the research owing to a lack of information pertaining to whether the researchers rated audiotapes and simulated interviews blind (i.e. they were unaware whether the police interviewer was trained or not). Furthermore, having made their audio recordings available for analysis, less than half of each group (trained and untrained) was included in the follow-up study. It is possible that participation in the evaluation was motivated because officers perceived they had significantly improved as a result of the training.

Following the implementation of PEACE, Pearse and Gudjonsson (1996) analysed 161 audiotapes at two police stations in south London, and their findings were similar to those of Baldwin's (1993) study. While few coercive or manipulative tactics were identified, they found little evidence of any other tactics being used. The most commonly used tactic was the introduction of evidence; challenging a lie or inconsistency was the next most common, though it was employed in only one-fifth of cases. It appeared that the information being provided by suspects was in the main being accepted and not challenged. The questioning did not tend to gain clarity in the accounts provided, leading the authors to recommend that the "C" in PEACE could also represent "Challenge" to encourage the interviewer to test the veracity of the account given by the suspect (Pearse & Gudjonsson, 1996).

Clarke and Milne (2001) conducted an evaluation of PEACE training by asking police officers to assess 177 audiotaped interviews using a specially constructed rating scale based on previous research. It was identified that overall an improvement had occurred in officers' interviewing practices compared to earlier studies, although the elements of PEACE were not being implemented to the full. Furthermore, the police officers assessing the recordings identified 10% of the interviews as possible breaches of PACE due to oppression, mental health problems, legal requirements, background noise and the use of leading questions. Although two-thirds of the interviewers had received training, no distinction was identified by the raters in the exhibited interview skills. One of the drawbacks of the ratings was that the phases of planning and preparation which would usually occur prior to a formal interview commencing were only recorded within the interview itself. Little evidence of rapport-building was identified, but this is difficult to evaluate when audio recordings are analysed in isolation from the entire custody procedure. It appears that, post-PACE and PEACE, there is still a limited awareness of what constitutes oppressive interviewing – there appears to be no definitive answer (Cherryman & Bull, 2000; Cherryman et al., 2000).

THE RIGHT TO SILENCE

One of the rights of suspects is to remain silent. This is initially introduced in the police caution "You do not have to say anything", and is especially a consideration for interviewing officers when a suspect has access to legal advice (Moston *et al.*, 1992). Solicitors and legal advisers will often recommend exercising the right to silence if the suspect has admitted to the offence and is likely to incriminate themselves during the interview. Ultimately though the decision to give a "no comment" interview is the suspect's rather than a requirement of his or her legal advisers. The implementation of a "special warning" that can be issued to a suspect by an interviewing officer can remind a suspect that the courts are permitted to draw adverse inferences from a person's use of the right to silence (Bucke & Brown, 1997). Bucke and Brown (1997) found that 39% of suspects exercising the right to silence were given the warning, but this only led to a small number of suspects then providing a satisfactory account, thus calling into question the effectiveness of the special warning. The "no comment" interview is one of the most challenging to conduct because the cognitive load of the questioning rests with the interviewing officer, who thus needs to prepare a fully developed plan to account for the potential response. There is currently little understanding of the ways in which police officers can encourage a suspect to provide an account of events rather than remaining silent. An account is more beneficial to the police in weighing up the evidence of the likely involvement of a suspect in any given offence. Milne and Bull (2003) argue that research needs to start examining ways to help interviewers gain a truthful account from uncooperative suspects and the strategies required to achieve this.

INTERVIEWER STRATEGIES

While much of the research in this area has had the purpose of evaluating police interviewers' use of PEACE, there has been some research that has looked more broadly at the use of tactics which may or may not fall within the PEACE framework, as well as assessing how the use of these tactics impacts on interaction during the interview. Recently, research has identified that coercive tactics are used less frequently than tactics employed to obtain information (Alison & Howard, 2007; Soukara *et al.*, 2007). Soukara *et al.* coded 80 audiotaped police interviews for the presence or absence of 17 commonly used tactics, gathered from previously published literature on police interviewing and from relevant training documents. No relationships were found between the use of certain tactics and the suspect's behaviour during interview, although the research focused solely on suspect denial or admission and did not consider other suspect behaviours, for example compliance or aggressiveness, remorse, or external blame. As previously mentioned, the use of audio recording of police interviews has some limitations; however, research using real-life interview data is crucial for understanding the true nature of interactions within police interviews.

Tailoring the Approach

The understanding of PACE and PEACE underpins the process of formally conducting a police interview and optimising the interaction from an evidential perspective. It is, however, crucial to further understand a range of issues that will also influence the interviewing of suspects, whether dealing with high-volume or major crime offences. The first assumption that has to be quashed is that the suspect is guilty; in fact police officers are presented with a number of potential scenarios of individuals who are arrested or appear at a police station. Therefore credibility assessment and understanding the personality of the suspect become important, particularly in the range of situations that police officers are exposed to.

There are four helpful distinctions that can be drawn and used as a starting point to understand the suspect and tailor the interview accordingly, and these concern guilt and honesty (Gozna, 2008). Commencing with the least complex type of suspect, it is helpful to consider the individual who is innocent of the alleged offence and makes the decision to tell the truth in police custody.

"Honest – I ain't done nothing": The general consensus is that if a person finds themselves in police custody, they must have some involvement in offending – the "no smoke without fire" adage. It must be borne in mind, though, that in certain circumstances individuals are arrested and interviewed who have nothing to do with the particular offence. High-profile cases, such as R v. Stagg in the murder of Rachel Nickell, R v. George in the murder of Jill Dando, and the initial arrest of the suspect in the Ipswich murder case of five prostitutes, highlight the ease with which this can occur when people appear to tick many boxes that fit the "profile" of a suspect but are not the guilty party. It is therefore important that interviewing officers maintain an open mind and ensure they do not fit the evidence around the suspect to the exclusion of wider considerations.

One challenging interview for police to conduct is with individuals arrested following a false allegation that is made by a third party. Such cases tend to relate to interpersonal situations, including violent and sexual offences. The experience of police custody for a suspect who is falsely accused of committing an offence can be especially difficult when there is wider evidence from another person or persons stating that they have committed particular acts. It is common for the weight of credibility to be assigned to the victim in such cases, especially when some offences initially appear to be invasive and traumatic. In these circumstances, the worst case might involve a suspect not being believed by the police or the Crown Prosecution Service, resulting in them being charged and remanded in custody. In domestic or sexual offences when it is a case of one person's word against another, the presence of wider evidence will often be considered. In rape cases, such evidence is the proof of consent and reasonable belief (Sexual Offences Act 2003): the responsibility is on the suspect to show that they took steps to ensure consent was given and that they reasonably believed that the "victim" consented. While sexual intercourse might have occurred, cases of a false allegation will involve one party alleging there was no consent, and police officers need to identify who is the truthful party. Such incidents begin to illustrate the challenge facing police officers and the need for a broader range of knowledge and expertise than just the skills to question suspects.

"Yeah I did it": For various reasons, some guilty suspects will provide an admission during interview, although this outcome is perhaps less frequently expected because, in the main, suspects want to avoid being charged. In some circumstances, for example when an individual is arrested for the first time, being in custody is an extremely alien experience, and they find themselves in an environment where they are uncertain of the procedures and how they are expected to behave. Suspects are subjected to a search, and items that could lead to injury are confiscated; they are then moved to a cell, sometimes to stay there overnight, where their privacy and liberty are removed. Ultimately for a first-time offender, this can entail a loss of control and rights. For other suspects, the embarrassment of being arrested will be sufficient for them to provide a full and honest account of their behaviour to police officers in order to reduce any possible punishment and to avoid wider-ranging negative consequences. The knowledge that the police have sufficient evidence to charge them with an offence will result in compliance and co-operation with interviewing officers. It is also possible that some suspects who have extensive criminal histories will weigh up

the consequences of the current arrest, believe that the outcome is not likely to be especially serious, and therefore admit to their actions. In such cases, the knowledge that admission could speed up the likelihood of being released from custody and sent home could be enough to result in a helpful and compliant interaction with the interviewing officer.

This group of suspects needs to be considered individually as there are a variety of reasons why people will choose to admit their involvement in an offence to the police. However, suspects in such situations are compliant and responsive to police questioning, showing a willingness to engage in discussion of the offence. It is in such cases that there is also the potential to identify and ascertain more information pertaining to motivation for the offence, which can assist in future interviews and in understanding offending.

"It were me – NOT!": Individuals who are highly suggestible or compliant can falsely confess to involvement in offences they have not committed (Gudjonsson, 2003). The implementation of PACE procedures should have increased the likelihood of such vulnerability being identified, although it is still important to consider the three main types of false confession that occur: (1) voluntary; (2) coerced/internalized; and (3) coerced/compliant. There are thus different psychological factors – some of which might potentially co-occur – that cause a person to admit to an offence they have not committed. At worst, this can lead to conviction and a miscarriage of justice, therefore it is crucial that such false admissions are identified when such a "suspect" presents to the police. *Voluntary* confessions are regarded as fulfilling different needs, which include a morbid desire for notoriety, an unconscious need to expiate guilt, the inability to distinguish between fact and fantasy, or a desire to protect and aid the real offender (Kassin & Wrightsman, 1985). *Coerced-internalized* confessions appear to be caused by a belief in the suspect that they have committed the offence, although there is no actual memory of this occurring. This can be considered in the context of two sets of circumstances: first, the suspect who has no recollection of the offence due to amnesia or alcohol/drug intoxication but who comes to believe that they are responsible; second, the suspect who initially does not believe that they have any involvement in the crime they are accused of, but who, as a result of police interviewing and tactics, becomes convinced that they are guilty, and mistrusts their own recollection of events (Gudjonsson, 2003). *Coerced-compliant* confessions occur in response to particular instances within the police interview process where the suspect reacts to the demands and pressures placed on them. However, the suspect also perceives an

element of instrumental gain from complying and confessing to the police. There are four overarching reasons that have been identified as to why this can occur, and why suspects confess in such a situation: (1) being able to go home following a confession; (2) ending the interview; (3) enabling the suspect to cope with the demands of the situation; and (4) enabling the suspect to avoid remaining in police custody in the cells. The final reason applies to suspects who are claustrophobic and those with a habit of alcohol or substance misuse who need to get their "fix" (Gudjonsson, 2003). Overall, regardless of the underlying reasons, such suspects make a decision at some point during the interview process that it is more beneficial to them to admit to an offence than continue to deny it.

"What's all this got to do with me? – No comment": The expectation is that most guilty suspects in police custody will deny their involvement in an offence regardless of any incriminating evidence against them. One explanation is a general disregard for authority and in particular police officers. With individuals with extensive criminal careers, police officers should consider how elements of anti-social personality or, if the suspect is a juvenile, conduct disorder will influence the suspect's behaviour. It must be acknowledged that a high proportion of the offending population can exhibit characteristics of challenging personality disorders (DSM-IV, 1994), especially ones related to anti-social lifestyles and attitudes (Hare, 2005). This is manifested through: the inability to conform to social norms with respect to lawful behaviours through the repetition of acts that are grounds for arrest; deceitfulness indicated by repeated lying; the use of aliases or conning others; impulsiveness or failure to plan ahead; irritability and aggressiveness, evidenced by repeated physical fights or assaults; reckless disregard for the safety of self or others; consistent irresponsibility; and lack of remorse for one's actions (DSM-IV, 1994).

In observations of suspect behaviour in police interviews, it is apparent that some individuals will be extremely stubborn, aggressive and confrontational in their interactions with the police. Given the anti-authority beliefs held by many suspects, it is in these interviews that the emphasis for the police officers has to be much more on gaining appropriate evidence to enable the person to be charged and heard in court. However, it is important to distinguish between a suspect who is being uncooperative and non-compliant out of their own choice and individuals who are challenging because they have been advised by their legal representative to be so. In these interviews, the suspect will overtly deceive police officers when they are presented with evidence identifying them as the offender in a particular case.

Challenges

An approach to interviewing that has been termed the "Chameleon Offender" (Boon & Gozna, 2008a; Gozna & Boon, 2007) has been developed in order to respond to suspects who create a challenging interaction for professionals. The emphasis and critical aspects are to incorporate a proactive, holistic yet bespoke approach to suspect interviews. There are many situations in police interviews where the awareness of changes in the behaviour of the suspect is more instinctual on the part of the interviewing officers rather than considered and tailored; that is, the understanding of the mindset of the suspect is crucially neglected.

A range of factors need to be taken into consideration in parallel with the wider investigative process. The actions involved in each offence for which individuals are arrested are diverse, regardless of the legal definition of the offence; that is, the components of the offence vary. It is easy, and perhaps the route of least resistance, to consider that most domestic violence offenders commit the same crime, or that paedophiles only differ in the age or gender of the victims they choose. Therefore when a suspect is interviewed, police interviewers need to be aware of the idiosyncratic nature of offenders and their actions. While it is possible that generic themes will occur within legally defined offences, the number of factors (internal and external) that resulted in the specific crime and subsequent arrest will vary. This ultimately creates a situation where a categorical approach will increase practitioner vulnerability to the chameleon nature of some individuals being interviewed.

It is therefore important that police officers who are conducting investigative interviews consider that each suspect has the potential to:

1. be different from each other;
2. be different at different times;
3. behave differently with different interviewers;
4. behave differently across different offences committed;
5. behave differently across different interviews;
6. be different during each interview interaction; and
7. be different across different environments.

These considerations should be visualised as co-occurring as a composite "chameleon" presentation and require further explanation in order that the sheer challenge of such interactions is recognised and understood (Boon & Gozna, 2008a; Gozna & Boon, 2007).

Primarily, suspects will be *different from one another* across a multitude of demographics, life experiences, beliefs and attitudes, behaviours
and views of offending. Therefore different approaches are required
for interviews and interactions in police custody settings. It is vital to
acknowledge just how diverse suspects who present in an interview can
be, and how this can impact on the challenges for police interviewers.
Such diversity is illustrated by the following real-life cases:

1. a female with convictions for domestic violence and false imprisonment;
2. a male with convictions for sexual offences against boys aged 4–7 and
   a collection of 643,239 pornographic electronic images of children
   (Levels 3–5);
3. a male suspect (requiring an interpreter) arrested for a series of
   sexual offences against prostitutes;
4. a male with prior convictions for arson with intent and fraud.

These cases highlight the complex realities with which police officers
are faced. However, it is important that apparent similarities and subtle
differences are considered owing to the radical implications for tailoring
a bespoke approach. For example, in the case of an individual suspected
of viewing child pornography, the nature of the images of children will
correspondingly determine the approach that is taken.

Suspects will be *different at different times* in terms of current life
experiences, fluctuations in mood, and the influence of personality
(characteristics/disorders). The motivation to engage with practitioners
can be influenced by changes in affect and cognitions which are internal (e.g. hormones, bipolar disorder, drug dependency) or external in
causation (e.g. infidelity of a partner, arguments with other professionals). Therefore the desire to be obstructive, ambivalent or to conform
can be a product of diverse factors over time – and the better these are
identified and responded to, the more effective the police interaction
with the suspect will be.

Suspects will *behave differently with different interviewers* within
and across disciplines (e.g. uniform/plainclothes). Depending on the
environment in which the interaction is occurring, suspects will likely
identify those to whom they should display pseudo-compliance, and
who warrants less respect. Conversely, the range of behaviours towards
police officers and other practitioners could be the result of such extra-
interview factors as the suspect's need to portray a particular image,
mischief-making, or more malign motivations such as playing people off against each other. Therefore certain police officers may well

be identified, either on the basis of previous reputation or the way they present, as being targets who are amenable to manipulation and exploitation. Moreover particular officers might be assigned increased rapport, engendering heightened kudos which results in suspects partitioning their disclosures, for example, "I only want to be interviewed by DCI Tickle, he's the one who dealt with me last time I was arrested." It is therefore highly desirable for the lines of communication to remain open to keep abreast of the chameleon's unfolding manifestations, and necessary for pertinent information to be identified, recorded and continually updated for all professionals who are dealing with a particular suspect.

Suspects will *behave differently across different offences committed* and it is helpful to acknowledge that complex suspects are likely to have a number of previous convictions, engaging in offences that demonstrate similar acts and others where incredible versatility is exhibited. It is acknowledged that, across offences dealt with in major crime such as rape, arson or homicide, "signatures" can occur. However, each offence will have potentially different antecedents, behaviours and consequences. While there might be similar motivations for any given offence, the interactions during it and responses to victims can be diverse. This has implications for the way in which the suspect will want to present the events within the police interview and for the level of deceit or impression management they engage in.

Suspects will *behave differently across different interviews* and will *be different during each interview interaction*. These are distinct yet overlapping considerations for the interview and are therefore considered together here. Hence, whether an individual is to be interviewed extensively throughout a day or in shorter sessions over the course of several days, it is vital to understand the potential for behavioural change within and across interactions over time. For example it is likely that there will be differences between penetrative and non-penetrative questioning, direct and offence-focused questioning, the introduction of incontrovertible evidence and the challenge of cognitive distortions. In addition, fatigue can lead variously to non-compliance and the move towards exercising the right to silence, or if polarised, a suspect admitting to anything in order to be released from the situation. The gradual introduction of "no comment" responses can also be indicative of reactions to evidence as it is weighed up by the suspect. Overall there is the need to identify what the difference in mood or behaviour is and why it has occurred, whether from a need to impression-manage, a feeling of being over-scrutinized or threatened interpersonally, or as a result of the nature of the questioning.

Finally, suspects will *behave differently in different environments*, which takes account of their behaviour exhibited during the offence, the arrest, time spent in police custody, the interview and in court. Any evidence of changes in behaviour should be recorded and interpreted accordingly by the relevant professionals dealing with the case.

The challenge of incorporating the considerations of the "Chameleon" is vast but achievable. The need is for police officers to create layers of knowledge and expertise which correspond to their level of training and rank. Investigative interviewing is challenging, particularly for police officers who are relatively new to engaging with suspects in such interactions. Furthermore, the experienced detective might believe that their tried and tested methods of interviewing are sufficient. However the concept of the Chameleon requires current skills and expertise to be revisited. The continued research within the field, and particularly collaborative work between psychologists and police forces, allows for a more tailored approach to be taken that develops interviewers' ability to maintain a heightened awareness when questioning complex individuals.

FUTURE DIRECTIONS

Investigative interviewing has advanced at an incredible rate since the early 1970s, when police–suspect interactions were more akin to those shown by the character Gene Hunt in the TV series *Life on Mars*. But while it is appropriate to acknowledge the advances that have been made in the field of interviewing, there is more to achieve in terms of understanding and tailoring strategies for use with complex individuals. This is based on a fusion of the range of factors identified throughout this chapter.

REVIEW QUESTIONS

1. What are the key components of PACE and PEACE that have improved investigative interviewing?
2. Identify four approaches that may be taken by suspects in an interview.
3. Describe the changes to policy and procedure that have occurred in relation to investigative interviewing since the 1980s.
4. Outline the seven key elements of the "chameleon offender" approach.

QUESTIONS FOR FURTHER RESEARCH AND ANALYSIS

1. What are the optimum methods to use when interviewing the chameleon offender?
2. What are the most effective interpersonal strategies for police officers when interviewing high-volume crime suspects or major crime suspects?
3. What are the limitations of PEACE and in what way should they be tailored to interactions with suspects?
4. How should "no comment" interviews be dealt with by police officers?
5. In what way should suspect vulnerabilities be better identified prior to interview?
6. What are the new directions/developments for investigative interviewing?

RECOMMENDED READING

Baldwin, J. (1993). Police interview techniques: Establishing truth or proof? *British Journal of Criminology, 33*, 325–352.

Gudjonsson, G.H. (1999). *The psychology of interrogations, confessions and testimony*. Chichester: Wiley.

Gudjonsson, G.H. (2003). *The psychology of interrogations and confessions: A handbook*. Chichester: Wiley.

Irving, B. (1980). *Police interrogation: A case study of current practice*. Research Study No. 2. Royal Commission on Criminal Procedure. London: HMSO

Milne, R., & Bull, R. (1999). *Investigative interviewing: Psychology and practice*. Chichester: Wiley.

Milne, R., & Bull, R. (2003). Does the cognitive interview help children to resist the effects of suggestive questioning? *Legal and Criminological Psychology, 8*(1), 21–38.

CHAPTER 7

Assessing Performance: Quantity or Quality?

STEPHEN TONG

INTRODUCTION

Assessing performance has been controversial throughout the public sector, from school league tables to criminal justice agencies. The perception of ineffective public services, modelled by a welfare state, has seen the introduction of managerialism and new public management (NPM) determined to measure public service performance and reduce waste while increasing inefficiency (Beattie & Cockcroft, 2006; Long, 2003). Managerialism signalled a shift away from a commitment to the welfare state and concerns regarding the effectiveness of criminal justice agencies. This viewpoint influenced policy change in the mid-1980s, regulating the tightening of resources and the "construction" of performance indicators (Newburn, 2007, p. 13). Home Office Circular 114 (1983) indicated a clear intention to focus on "economy", "efficiency" and "effectiveness" through the measurement of quantitative "outputs" providing a "numeric" assessment of performance (Long, 2003, p. 631). Evolving policies encouraged the pursuit of private sector methods within public services. During the 1990s this pursuit of high efficiency, accountability, objective-setting and performance measurement became known as "new public management" (Newburn, 2007, p. 553). The political controversy attached to these changes has remained to this day, questioning the validity of private sector management methods within the public sector (Garland, 2001). The importance of law and order in modern politics cannot be overestimated, whether debates are used to attack government, or to promote proposed policies from opposition parties (Reiner, 2007). Viewers of Prime Minister's Questions or other political debates within the House of Commons would perhaps be forgiven for accepting interpretations of crime statistics as they are announced by confident politicians in support of their political perspective (Statistics Commission, 2006). It is these debates that discuss the effectiveness, economy and efficiency of the police and other criminal justice agencies on the basis of a variety of statistical measures. Statistics are open to manipulation to make political points, which inevitably has implications for public services (Coleman & Moynihan, 1996). Crime statistics are regularly used as a measure of effectiveness in criminal justice, to make decisions about the distribution of rewards and to provide the basis for assessing law and order policy (Maguire, 2007; Smith, 2006). However, with differing interpretations of statistics and the intensity of political debate on crime and disorder, there is no doubt that the public becomes confused and extracts little help from politicians to enable them to assess the performance of criminal justice agencies. The use of police-recorded figures[1] and the British Crime Survey (BCS) in the context of criminal investigation is particularly political, both in the simplistic manner in which they are presented and in the manner in which they are used to claim significant conclusions. These approaches to data collection reveal substantial differences in the levels of crime identified as well as limitations in the methodology used.

The difficulty in communicating authoritative data in political debates is inevitably coloured by party politics. Indeed criticisms published in the recent independent review of crimes statistics have led to recommendations that

> In order to build trust, the Home Office should ensure that the release and statistical commentary on national crime statistics are quite clearly separated from political judgements or ministerial comments and should ensure the accuracy of any statements made about the statistics, whether in press releases or ministerial comments.
>
> (Smith, 2006, p. 17)

However, the complex nature of the occurrence of crime, methods of measurement, police strategies, changes in legislation and the impact of factors outside the criminal justice system create considerable difficulties for policymakers attempting to compare crime statistics over time (Maguire, 2007). Added to these complexities are the changes in the rules for the recording and detecting of crimes, (see Figure 7.3), not to mention changes in society that create new opportunities for crime and additional pressures on the police, probation, prisons, courts and criminal prosecution service (Home Office, 2001a; Maguire, 2007). However, as researchers, politicians and policymakers are only too aware, research methodology is not without its limitations (Statistics Commission, 2006). There will always be problems associated with attempting to produce infallible data that in turn lead to challenges over accuracy or criticisms regarding the data-collection methods used. Rather, researchers seek to provide a "rigorous" research design that aims to excise unreliable or misleading data collection, but nevertheless research findings will be influenced by the methodological tools selected (May, 2001; Reiner, 2007). The epistemological questions in research methodology are as important and relevant as data collection in the context of crime statistics and performance measurement (Layder, 1998).

This chapter will begin by providing an overview of the two most prominent crime-measurement approaches, namely police-recorded figures and the British Crime Survey. As the chapter progresses, closer examination of the context of police performance, including efficiency and effectiveness, and a critical analysis of traditional measures of performance will be conducted.

MEASURING CRIME

Recording accurate crime figures provides an important basis for measuring risk, assessing public sector workloads, understanding changes in society and measuring the activities of a range of agencies (Maguire, 2007). Public distrust in crime figures can be generated by a variety of interpretations relating to performance, distribution of resources, selection of police strategies and policy implementation (Statistics Commission, 2006). However, the data can still be valuable if researchers, policymakers and practitioners have a clear understanding of the limitations of data and the presentation of statistics. The following sections will provide an overview of police-recorded figures and the British Crime Survey to identify the strengths and weaknesses of each approach.

POLICE-RECORDED CRIME FIGURES

The police have recorded crime since 1857, and this source of information has been used to inform policy and measure police performance

(Nicholas *et al.*, 2007; Reiner, 2007; Statistics Commission, 2006). Police-recorded crime figures (for all crimes as a yearly total) have risen from 545,562 in 1957 to 4,950,700 in 2008 (Kershaw *et al.*, 2008; Whitaker, 1964). To understand this change over time we cannot simply infer that the police are less effective than in 1957, but must analyse closely the changes that have occurred in measuring crime, police practice and society in general, e.g. demographic and population changes (Maguire, 2007).

The key weakness of police-recorded crime data is that, although arguably they measure some police activity, they do not record all crime: they require two elements to be satisfied for the actual level of crime to be adequately represented in them, namely, that the offences are reported to the police and secondly that the police actually record the crime (Nicholas *et al.*, 2007). So this might appear to be a straightforward process. However, when the hurdles to be surmounted in reporting and recording are revealed, a pattern of attrition can be identified (Coleman & Moynihan, 1996; Johnston & Shearing, 2003; Newburn, 2007). The police are likely to record a crime if they witness the crime (e.g. proactive policing) or if the crime is reported by a member of the public, but this is by no means certain to take place (Reiner, 2007). There are a number of reasons why crimes go unreported to the police, and the level of reporting/recording crime falls disproportionately across a range of offences (see Table 7.1). The reasons for the police not recording crime are also many, ranging from perception of victims through to the discretion of the police themselves (Newburn, 2007). The category of the crime and the context in which the offence was committed are strong factors in influencing recording (Maguire, 2007). Historically, lack of trust in the police or the belief that a satisfactory result is unlikely have influenced non-reporting in a variety of offences, including hate crime, rape and crimes associated with young people (HMCPSI & HMIC, 2007; Muncie, 1996). Fear, for personal safety or of retribution, can be an important factor in under-reporting in domestic violence, while in the case of a number of crimes (e.g. drugs consumption) it is not in the interests of the "victim" to report it (Reiner, 2007). Table 7.1 illustrates the reasons given in the BCS for respondents not reporting the offences of vandalism, burglary and theft to the police. It also illustrates variations between the reasons for not reporting crimes to the police with variations between different crimes (e.g. vandalism and violence). However, there are also examples of consensual crimes (not perceived as crimes – so-called "victimless crimes") which are therefore not reported, such as counterfeiting, prostitution and gambling (Muncie, 1996). The focus of police attention is arguably disproportionate, in that substantial resources are directed

Table 7.1 Reasons for not reporting crime to the police (%), (British Crime Survey, 2007/08)

	Vandalism	Burglary	Thefts from vehicles & attempts[1]	Other household theft	Other personal theft	BCS violence[2]	Comparable subset[3]	All BCS crime
Trivial/no loss/police would not/could not do anything[4]	85	68	88	84	71	52	75	76
Private/dealt with ourselves	9	22	7	10	10	35	16	15
Inconvenient to report	4	3	5	5	6	6	5	5
Reported to other authorities	2	1	2	1	12	6	3	4
Common occurrence	2	0	2	1	2	3	2	2
Fear of reprisal	2	5	0	2	0	5	2	2
Dislike or fear of the police/previous bad experience with the police or courts	2	3	2	1	0	2	2	2
Other[5]	3	5	3	4	6	10	6	6
Unweighted base	2446	339	1144	1326	565	801	5514	7405

Source: Jansson, K., Robb, P., Higgins, N. & Babb, P. (2008) in C. Kershaw & S. Nicholas, A. Walker (eds) *Crime in England and Wales 2007/08*, Home Office Statistical Bulletin, London: Home Office, p. 58.

[1] Thefts of vehicles not shown as very few incidents were not reported.

[2] All BCS violence includes wounding, assault with minor injury, assault with no injury and robbery (and is equivalent to comparable violence in previous publications).

[3] The comparable crime subset includes vandalism, burglary, vehicle theft, bicycle theft, wounding, assault with and without minor injury and robbery.

[4] Too trivial/no loss/would not have been interested/police could not do anything/attempt at offence was unsuccessful are merged due to the similarity in their definition, for example: a respondent who thinks the incident was too trivial may code the incident as "too trivial, no loss" or "the police would not be interested" as these two codes may be understood as meaning the same.

[5] This category includes: something that happens as part of job; partly my/friend's/relative's fault; offender not responsible for actions; thought someone else had reported incident/similar incidents; tried to report but was not able to contact the police/police not interested; other.

[6] Figures may add to more than 100 as more than one reason could be given.

towards crimes against property and people, with a relatively recent focus on anti-social behaviour, rather than white-collar crime, money-laundering, fraud or political crimes (Maguire, 2007). Furthermore, behaviour that could be interpreted as warranting criminal sanctions is dealt with by agencies other than the police, such as tax evasion, health and safety breaches, insider trading, and the mis-selling of pensions (Reiner, 2007). Therefore the "dark figure of crime"[2] and particular categories of offences are not reflected in the police-recorded figures.

Research into police activity began in earnest in the 1960s, and with this a more informed understanding of police practice developed (Banton, 1964; Waddington, 1999). It was assumed that the police implemented enforcement to the letter of the law, inevitably resulting in the arrest and charge of the offender. It was during the 1960s when the "discovery of discretion" in policing identified that police officers were resolving problems through informal means (Waddington, 1999). As Waddington argues:

> Police undoubtedly secure far greater compliance by the use of informal means of achieving their goals than the law would other-wise allow, but this still seems a more amicable way of doing business that it would otherwise be.
>
> (Waddington, 1999, p. 141)

This manner of working inevitably leads to fewer instances of reported crime; it also requires balanced judgement by police officers working within communities, as discretion is not necessarily delivered equally or universally and can be politically sensitive (Newburn, 2002). However, there are alternative perspectives on the use of police discretion, as Reiner argues:

> They [Police Property] are low status, powerless groups whom the dominant majority see as problematic or distasteful. The majority are prepared to let the police deal with "their property" and turn a blind eye to the manner in which this is done ... The prime function of the police has always been to control and segregate such groups, and they are armed with a battery of permissive and discretionary laws for this purpose.
>
> (Reiner, 2000, p. 93)

The policing of the "underclass" is complicated further "by police culture, the context of social environment ... social exclusion and crime and disorder" (Crowther, 2000, p. 222). Discretion is not just used in decisions to formally investigate crime, but also in recording practices that promote the perception of effectiveness, that can be manipulated inappropriately[3] and not in the spirit of measuring genuine police activity (Newburn, 2007; Young, 1991). It can be argued that although the police still retain significant discretion, their freedom in making decisions has been restricted when compared to the 1950s (Garland, 2001). Discretion is used when the police decide whether or not to register a crime, for example, or in their judgements on the level of evidence required to validate an offence or the perceived reliability of a complainant, or in their willingness or otherwise to conduct the investigation (Newburn, 2007). Although police discretion is a useful tool when used appropriately, conflicting values, political sensitivity and the impact of performance measurement regularly contribute to controversy in its use. The police-recorded figures are a useful indicator for measuring police activity and provide the basis for assessing outcomes. From an investigative perspective they can provide important information regarding trends in serious and resource-intensive investigations, as well as on the proportion of police time spent on volume crime investigations.

Along with police-recorded data, politicians and policymakers also draw important data from the British Crime Survey.

THE BRITISH CRIME SURVEY

The BCS is a national victim survey introduced to address the main weaknesses in police-recorded figures, namely estimating the level of unrecorded crime (Newburn, 2007). The BCS is a useful survey because it provides an estimate of the level of under-reporting that occurs throughout a range of offences. The BCS was first published in 1983 as a victimisation survey, with an original sample of 11,000 respondents across England and Wales (Jansson, 2007). Ironically, the current BCS only reflects crime in England and Wales, with Scotland and Northern Ireland having their own surveys (Newburn, 2007). The BCS was conducted in 1982, 1984, 1988, 1992, 1996, 1998 and 2000, and from 2001 on an annual basis, with a sample size of approximately 45,000 (Hough et al., 2007). It is considered one of the most authoritative surveys of its kind in the UK due to the sample size, the extensive range of questions and the fact that it targets members of the general population who may not be victims of crime. Some commentators point to its limitations:

"BCS crime", like recorded crime, is to some extent an arbitrarily constructed aggregation of disparate types of offence: both include some offences in the "count", and omit others. It is therefore a serious

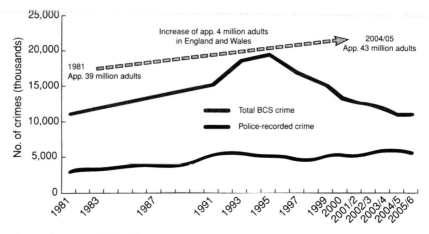

Source: Jansson, 2007, p. 8.

Figure 7.1   Trends in BCS and police-recorded crime, 1981–2005/06

misunderstanding to regard the BCS as offering a full picture...
it does not necessarily present a fuller picture than provided by
recorded statistics: it is "fuller" than the latter in some respects...
but narrower in others...

(Maguire, 2007, p. 269)

Maguire refers to the strengths and limitations in the methodology of
the BCS: the survey is "fuller" in terms of its attempts to acknowledge unrecorded crime but "narrower" in that it does not recognise
crimes against organisations, so-called "victimless crimes" and crimes
committed against children under 16. Clearly these limitations are an
important acknowledgement in any assessment attempting to establish
a "true" picture of crime.

The differences between police and BCS figures provide the basis for
analysis for the crimes that are not reported or investigated. For example, it is estimated that the police figures for burglary from a dwelling
(with loss) represent 72% of all crimes in this category when compared
to the BCS (Nicholas *et al.*, 2007). The same figure for burglary from
a dwelling (with no loss) is estimated at 19%. From an investigative
perspective, the potential for intelligence or forensic evidence to link a
series of crimes is lost because of substantial under-reporting. Other
offences that are poorly represented in the police statistics include robbery, child abuse, corporate crime, domestic violence, sexual offences,
international and transnational crime, crimes against business and
crimes within institutions (Maguire, 2007). However, Figure 7.1

illustrates how the extent of the estimated under-reporting of crime has reduced over time. It is important to examine this graph in close detail. If we compare Figure 7.1 to Table 7.2 we can see that there are two methods of calculating the extent of under-reporting. Figure 7.1 represents all crime recorded by the police (5,556,000) and reported by the BSC (10,912,000), estimating that the police record 50.9% of all crime. However, the criteria for registering crimes contained in police figures are restricted by legislation, whereas the BCS does not ask questions about all offences and does not measure crime using the same methodology (Maguire, 2007). Maguire has adapted Table 7.2 to compare similar crimes recorded by the police (2,551,000) and the BCS (8,558,000), and these figures estimate that the police record only 29.8% of all crime.

So although we can conclude that there is substantial under-reporting of crime, the extent to which this is occurring is subject to debate and depends upon the types of crime under analysis. Furthermore, there have been claims that the BCS significantly under-records crime using its own methodology. Local crime surveys have identified under-reporting, arguing that the reasons for not reporting crime differ from those given by the BCS, with Newburn (2007), using the example of the Islington Crime Surveys, arguing that the proportion of crime not reported because the victim perceived the offence as trivial is only 25% (compared to the BCS's 55%), while victims believing the police could not do anything was 38% (compared to the BCS's 16%). Consequently Young's (1988) conclusions point to a number of victimisations that fell within the "dark figure" of crime. Farrell and Pease point to methodological reasons for suppressing BCS crime estimates. They argue that,

> If the people who say they suffered 10 incidents really did, [and] it is capping the series at five[,] why is this? That distorts the rate... It is truly bizarre that the victimisation survey, based as it is on the assumption that people will by and large tell the truth about what happened to them... suddenly withdraws its trust in their honesty when what they are told does not chime with their own experience.
> (Farrell & Pease, 2007, p. 2)

Farrell and Pease estimate that crime is "understated" (by the BCS) by 29%.[4] They conclude:

> we believe that the worm in the BCS bud in 1981 has led to a blighted bloom ever since, one which misrepresents the extent and distribution of crime suffered. The unwillingness to believe the facts

Table 7.2 Estimated total offences in England and Wales, 2005/06, as derived from the British Crime Survey and offences recorded by the police

	BCS			Police[1]		
	N	(% of comparable offences)	(% of all BCS offences)	N	(% of comparable offences)	(% of all recorded offences)
Comparable offences						
Theft of/from vehicles	1,731,000	(20)	(16)	714,000	(28)	(13)
Vandalism private property	2,731,000	(33)	(25)	587,000	(23)	(11)
Burglary dwelling	733,000	(9)	(7)	307,000	(12)	(06)
Assault/wounding	2,038,000	(24)	(19)	652,000	(26)	(12)
Robbery	311,000	(4)	(3)	66,000	(3)	(1)
Theft from person	576,000	(7)	(5)	114,000	(4)	(2)
Bicycle theft	439,000	(5)	(4)	111,000	(4)	(2)
Subtotals	**8,558,000**	**(100)**	**(78)**	**2,551,000**	**(100)**	**(46)**
BCS offences not comparable with police data						
Other household theft	1,158,000		(11)	***		
Other personal theft	1,196,000		(11)	***		
Subtotals	**2,354,000**		**(22)**	***		

	Police-recorded offences not covered by/comparable with BCS			
Other theft	***		1,080,000	(19)
Other vandalism	***		1,597,000	(11)
Non-residential burglary	***		338,000	(6)
Fraud and forgery	***		233,000	(4)
Other violence/robbery[2]	***		439,000	(8)
Sexual offences	***		62,000	(1)
Drug offences	***		179,000	(3)
Other	***		76,000	(1)
Subtotals	***		**3,004,000**	**(54)**
Totals	**10,912,000**	**(100)**	**5,556,000**	**(100)**

Source: Maguire, M., Crime data and statistics. In Maguire, M., Morgan, R. and Reiner, R. (eds.) *Oxford Handbook of Criminology* (4th edn), pp. 270–1, adapted from Thorpe, K. and Robb, P. (2006) 'Extent and trends' in Walker, A., Kershaw, C. and Nicholas, S. (2006) *Crime in England and Wales 2005/06*, London: Home Office (Table 2.4); and Allen, J. and Ruparel, C. (2006) 'Reporting and recording crime' in Walker, A., *Crime in England and Wales 2005/06*, London: Home Office (Table 4.01).

Notes: 1. The figures shown in this column refers to offences recorded by the police in the financial year 2005/06. The totals of 'comparable' police-recorded offences reflect adjustments outlined by Walker *et al.* (2006: 49) which make reductions to allow for cases where the victim was either an organisation or institution, or was under 16 years old (i.e. types of offences not measured by the BCS).
2. Mainly assaults and robberies where the victim was under 16.

of chronic victimisation means that crime control, police training
and criminal justice action [are] now substantially misdirected.

(2007, p. 6)

It appears that, based on the BCS findings, in general terms the level
of crime is falling and the level of reporting offences to the police has
increased slightly since 1997. This discrepancy appears to have much to
do with recording practices (e.g. the introduction of the National Crime
Recording Standard (NCRS). However, changes in recording practices
and political debates switching between the police figures and the BCS
have resulted in the "gross misinterpretation" of the recorded figures by
politicians, as Hough argued in an article for the *Guardian* newspaper
in 2004, saying that "police statistics bear little relation to the reality". However, on the basis of Farrell and Pease's analysis the impact
of multi-victimisation has not been accurately measured. Clearly the
impact of extreme cases of re-victimisation since 1981 needs to be taken
into consideration to establish a fuller picture. However, it still remains
the case that the BCS represents a more comprehensive overview than
other sources.

As discussed earlier with respect to police-recorded crime figures,
it is necessary to recognise the limitation of the survey data and the
methodology used. It is important to acknowledge that the key strength
of the BCS is that it measures crime that is not reported or recorded
by the police, and provides a victim perspective on crime measurement
rather than relying upon police interpretations (Newburn, 2007). Any
exercise engaged with collecting information is dependent on the reliability of the testimony of the respondent; as with police interviews (see
Chapters 5 and 6 above), the precision of witness memories can impact
on the reliability of the accounts recorded for victim surveys (Newburn,
2007). The BCS does not measure crime from the perspective of the
homeless or those in institutions, such as prisoners, students on
campus, the mentally ill in temporary housing, people under the age
of 16 or those who live in short-term accommodation (Maguire, 2007).
Although the BCS still represents a comprehensive survey in the scale
of the information collected, there are still key areas of crime (e.g.
including the perspectives of under-16s and organisational crime) that
are not represented accurately in the findings. The complexity of crime
statistics requires an understanding of the data-collection methods
and the specific nature of the information collected. As Maguire (2007,
pp. 294–5) correctly concludes, crime statistics are not facts; they
do require interpretation and they are not free from the influence of
"political and social change". From an investigative perspective the
BCS provides useful information on changes in reporting patterns and

presents a more accurate picture of offending than police-recorded figures alone. This information provides the basis to make decisions on resources to measure attrition, as well as valuable information regarding victimisation and perceptions of victims regarding fear of crime and confidence in the police.

Although crime statistics are important to understanding the context of police work and criminal investigation, the process of crime investigation is also a valued indicator of police performance by politicians.

MEASURING INVESTIGATIVE PERFORMANCE: PROCESS, OUTPUT AND OUTCOME

Measuring performance does not rest solely on crime statistics but also focuses on measuring police activity. The measurement of police activities is perhaps best understood as "processes", "outputs" and "outcomes". Reiner reflects on the importance of assessing quality in policing: "Assessments of quality must rest on evaluations of the process, the way an encounter is handled, rather than its product or outcome" (1998, p. 60). In his comment, Reiner emphasises measurement of quality and identifies a product (or output) as the conclusion of a process and an outcome as a final result of all processes. The *process*, referring to "how the encounter was handled", assumes an individual assessment of the particular circumstances, decisions and interaction occurring that reflects the social reality of the incident (Pawson & Tilley, 1997). This represents characteristics that lend themselves to a qualitative method of measurement. An accurate reflection of the elements of a process cannot necessarily be encapsulated by quantitative techniques. The emphasis here is that the nature of police work is too complex for a quantitative form of assessment alone (Innes, 2003; Reiner, 1998). Therefore the idea of *process* is one that provides a wide and varied number of routes to a set of *outputs* resulting in an *outcome* reflecting the "impact on society as a whole" (e.g. lower crime rate) commonly measured in quantitative terms (Spottiswoode, 2000, p. 3).

Output measures refer to the end of a specific process (e.g. time spent on an investigation), the measurement of police "activities" (Bayley, 1996, p. 45). An output measure can often be used as a performance indicator. Examples of performance indicators that reflect outputs include the percentage of files that are proceeded with by CPS or the percentage of reported racial incidents where further investigative action is taken. Although this figure may be a useful indicator for the number of activities occurring, this category of measurement does not tell us anything about quality or how well these activities have been conducted.

The *outcome*-based measurement consists of the final numerical assessment referring to the completion of a number of processes that contribute to an absolute conclusion. Examples of an outcome-based measure include "clear-up", "detection" and "conviction" rates or "no crime" category. These figures do not contribute to a further series or process in crime investigation; they represent a collective final figure used to gauge the level of success or otherwise of investigation. These figures are often used to judge the efficiency and effectiveness of detectives on a local, regional or national basis. Outcome-based measures can also be used as performance indicators. An example of this category of measurement can be seen in the use of detection and conviction data for specific offences.

To illustrate these terms and to demonstrate the importance of acknowledging quality in assessing performance, the flow chart in Figure 7.2 details a criminal investigation that took place during observational research.[5] The chart shows two potential routes for a robbery investigation, where £4000 was stolen from a grocery store. Route A follows a line of enquiry that focuses on engaging with a range of investigative tasks; route B focuses on bringing the investigation to a close as swiftly as possible.

This case serves as an illustration of different approaches to investigating the same crime. Although other enquiries could also be completed (e.g. search for CCTV from other establishments in the high street, seek witness accounts from neighbouring shops), they have been left out in order to maintain clarity. This case provides two investigative approaches that initially lead to the same short-term conclusion in the robbery investigation (e.g. offender remains unidentified). On the one hand it could be assumed from the outset that the crime is not solvable and therefore little investigative effort should be applied to this investigation. However, a different perspective would argue that this is a serious crime and there are opportunities for prosecution even if this is not in the immediate future. Route B is clearly aimed at processing the crime quickly rather than engaging with a meaningful investigation. However, route A is using up significant resources in terms of the forensic investigator, crime prevention officer, victim support, the creation of the computer E-fit of the suspect, and the additional time spent on the investigation by the detective in the case. Even though the tasks in route A are more substantial than those in route B, the quality of those tasks cannot be adequately examined through quantitative means. A list of possible outputs and outcomes associated with the investigation are listed in Table 7.3.

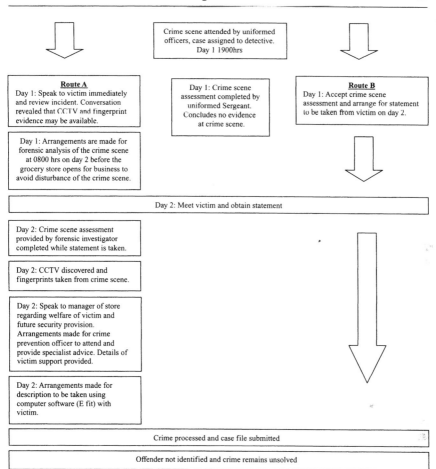

Figure 7.2 Investigative decision-making

The outcomes that can emerge from these investigative approaches are also different. While both routes have the potential for the offender to be caught later (e.g. through intelligence leads), only investigation A has the potential to identify the offender through the description circulated or the fingerprints taken from the crime scene. From a crime prevention perspective, only investigation A is likely to have the potential to reduce or eliminate future robberies from the grocery store (depending on the owners acting on crime prevention advice). From the additional investigative effort illustrated in route A, a conviction in the medium term or a reduction in the number of future robberies from the store are positive outcomes, and will not necessarily be

Table 7.3   Summary of outcomes/outputs.

Route A	Route B
Outputs 1 CCTV confirms offence has taken place (does not identify suspect) 2 Fingerprint evidence recorded 3 Crime prevention advice given 4 Victim support provided 5 Suspect description circulated 6 Crime processed 7 Statement obtained	Output 1 Statement obtained
Outcomes 1 Crime process 2 Evidence remains in storage to match up to future offences 3 Public confidence in handling the investigation	Outcomes 1 Crime processed 2 Minimal time spent on investigation, detective allocates time elsewhere

acknowledged within the performance measurement arrangements. These potentially positive outcomes will be dependent on the grocery store owner's willingness to follow police advice and the effectiveness of crime scene investigation in crimes where the criminal reoffends.

The detective concerned, given the context and the information available at the time, can make the appropriate decision in terms of which route to follow. However, a performance culture could encourage detectives to adopt route B routinely rather than route A, by spending more time on easy-to-solve cases at the expense of more complex enquiries. When we consider the broader concept of community safety or what counts as good-quality professional investigation, then route A would be the preferred option. This would be an easy decision if unlimited resources were available, but difficult decisions and assessments have to be made in terms of what gets thoroughly investigated and what does not. It also raises issues about the impact of performance measurement on police behaviour. This leads to debates, from discussions regarding performance to issues surrounding the function and role of the police in general. As David Bayley argues:

Although proving information about police performance is a critical task for chiefs, most evaluations of policing do not assess the institution's overall effectiveness... Judging the performance of a police force in general is more than a technical matter of choosing appropriate measurement criteria and methodologies; it involves controversial decisions about what the police should do and how they do it.

(Bayley, 1996, p. 37)

So when the measurement of performance is being considered, the more fundamental questions, such as the role of the police, are essential. Recently there have been a number of calls for police reform, and debate surrounding the role of the police service (Blair, 2005; Flanagan, 2008; HMIC, 2004; O'Connor, 2005). It appears that these relatively new calls for reappraisal of the role and function of the police in the UK need to be addressed before substantial investment and policy development in performance management and measurement take place.

DEFINING EFFICIENCY AND EFFECTIVENESS

Efficiency and effectiveness are often used synonymously when describing actual or proposed improvements in organisational performance. However, closer examination of these concepts reveals they are used to measure fundamentally different aspects of an organisation or practice (Collins, 1985; Pollard, 1983; Savage *et al.*, 2000). Effectiveness is about achieving goals concerned with maximising outputs of an organisation given a fixed level of resources (Froyland & Bell, 1996; Spottiswoode, 2000). So in theoretical terms, effectiveness can be achieved without efficiency, but efficiency still requires "satisfactory results" or "competent work". That is to say, an organisation would not be particularly useful if it was efficient (using a reasonable level of resources) without being effective (failure to have an impact) (Froyland & Bell, 1996; Pollard, 1983). For example, if a detective had completed all the tasks required in an investigation to an adequate standard but only achieved a small number of convictions, although the detective had been efficient in completing routine tasks, he or she has not made an impact. On the other hand, in an investigative context, a detective might achieve a "positive result" (in the form of a conviction) but use an undue amount of resources to achieve this outcome. An example of perceived efficiency without effectiveness can be seen in the declining detection and conviction rate in the context of a higher number of recorded crimes (Flynn, 2002; Whitaker, 1964). This is to say that although police officers are processing a higher number of cases than in the past,[6] the detection rate (see below) has been falling. So although efficiency may have improved, this has little impact on the perceived effectiveness of investigation, as clear-up, detection and conviction rates inform the perception of declining effectiveness (Home Office, 2001b; Maguire, 2002; Whitaker, 1964).

DETECTION RATES

The detection rate is recorded as a percentage and used to measure police efficiency and effectiveness. Traditionally known as the "clear-up rate", the "detection rate" is today being used more routinely as the Home Office measure of police effectiveness (Home Office, 2001b). This measure is aimed at quantifying the outcome of crime investigation. "Detections" are measured by the following criteria. An offence is "detected" when:

(A) A PERSON HAS BEEN CHARGED OR SUMMONSED FOR THE CRIME (irrespective of any subsequent acquittal at Court).
(B) THE OFFENDER HAS BEEN CAUTIONED BY THE POLICE (or given a reprimand or warning, under the Crime and Disorder Act 1998). The guidance under Home Office Circular 30/2005 must be followed, otherwise the detection cannot be claimed.
(C) THE OFFENDER ADMITS THE CRIME BY WAY OF A PACE COMPLIANT INTERVIEW AND ASKS FOR IT TO BE TAKEN INTO CONSIDERATION BY THE COURT ON FORM MG18.
(D) WHERE THE OFFENCE IS AN "INDICTABLE ONLY" OFFENCE AND a Crown Prosecutor is satisfied there is enough evidence to provide a realistic prospect of conviction but has decided not to proceed with the case, or the case cannot proceed because the offender has died.
(E) A PENALTY NOTICE FOR DISORDER (OR OTHER RELEVANT NOTIFIABLE OFFENCE) HAS BEEN LAWFULLY ISSUED UNDER S1-11 of the CRIMINAL JUSTICE AND POLICE ACT 2001.
(F) A WARNING FOR CANNABIS POSSESSION HAS BEEN ISSUED IN ACCORDANCE WITH ACPO GUIDANCE.
(Home Office, 2007, pp. 17–23)

Detections are divided into two "types", namely "sanction detections", reflecting the criteria above, and "non-sanction detections", when the offender, victim or essential witness is dead or too ill to give evidence, the victim refuses or is unable to give evidence, the offender is under the age of criminal responsibility, the police or Crown Prosecution Service (CPS) decide that no useful purpose would be served by proceeding, or the time limit of six months for commencing prosecution has been exceeded (Walker *et al.*, 2006, p. 138). Published figures referring to the detection rates (post-2003) in general reflect the "sanction detection" rate rather than a combination of the two. Detection rates are specifically outcome-based; these figures are based on the actual number of recorded crimes registered by the police and the disposal of the crime according to the counting rules above. There are specific rules applying to counting crimes and detections[7] that are aimed at providing consistency between the 43 police forces in the UK (Home Office, 2007). The NCRS is used to count crimes and detections for police services throughout the country. The rules provided to the police for recording crime changed in 1998/99 and 2002/03. These changes in recording practices and the introduction of new offence categories have influenced the number of crimes measured, and NCRS data cannot therefore be easily compared over time (Reiner, 2007). The Home Office has provided estimates on the impact of changes in the recording rules on detections rates.[8] Figure 7.3 details detection rates from 1988 to 2005/06.

The steady decline of the detection rate over time, from 50% in 1938, to 44% in 1960, to 23% in 2003/04, through to a slight increase to 26% in 2006/07, illustrates substantial change over time (Nicholas *et al.*, 2007; Whitaker, 1964). However, declining detection rates have been accompanied by increased reporting of crime, the introduction of PACE, increased levels of household insurance, huge rises in the number

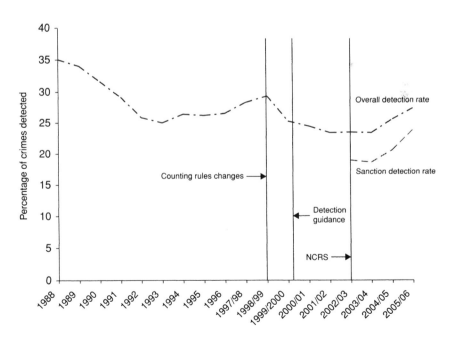

Figure 7.3   Crime detection rates, 1988–2005/06

of crimes recorded by the police, and more stealable possessions (e.g. CDs, DVDs and mobile phones) as social and economic conditions have improved (Maguire, 2007; Newburn, 2007; Reiner, 2007). This has had the impact of the police having to deal with an increasing level of crime. Although detection rates have been an important measure of police performance historically, Johnston and Shearing argue that "the public's willingness to report offences cannot be taken for granted; the police's capacity to detect offences is limited; and the court's ability to secure conviction is restricted" (2003, p. 67).

If the history of policing tells us anything about detection rates, it is that they are affected by changes in legislation, police procedure/discretion, and social and economic conditions, and should only be considered cautiously and alongside other data when used to assess police performance.

PERFORMANCE INDICATORS

Her Majesty's Inspectorate of Constabulary (HMIC) is responsible for examining and improving the efficiency of police services in England and Wales, and other agencies – including the Serious Organised Crime Agency (SOCA), British Transport Police (BTP), Ministry of Defence Police (MDP), Civil Nuclear Constabulary, and HM Revenue & Customs – in addition to supporting the Chief Inspector of Criminal Justice in Northern Ireland and conducting inspections by invitation in Jersey, Guernsey and the Isle of Man (HMIC, 2006). HMIC conducts Best Value inspections of police authorities, inspections of Basic Command Units (BCU) and thematic inspections using baseline assessments from quantitative data/performance indicators obtained from the Police Performance Assessment Framework (PPAF) (HMIC, 2006).

Performance indicators can incorporate a range of detection rates (for different crimes) as a method of measurement. However, the most commonly used is the output measure. Output measures are more specific than detection rates alone. There is a tendency for outputs to be action-based and measured in terms of their quantity. Measuring police work by numbers has revealed unethical practices (Rose, 1996; Young, 1991) where the focus is on achieving the performance targets, rather than making appropriate judgements and investigative decisions. Concern has been voiced over the influence of measuring police work using detection rates. An example includes the tactic of prioritising crimes that are easier to solve at the expense of those considered less solvable (Young, 1991). However, outputs do represent areas of significant importance to the investigative process, quantifying detective work and providing an indication of police activity. For example, one indicator measures the percentage of files proceeded with by the CPS. This indicator does not tell us anything about the quality of the case files, but can provide the basis for estimating workloads. Is the file lacking in investigative effort? Has every line of enquiry been followed up? Are statements sufficiently rigorous? These questions remain unanswered and will be dependent on local quality assurance and supervision, both of which have raised concerns in the past (Hobbs, 1988; Waddington, 1999; Young, 1991). Measures that are based on quantitative information alone can be used to support very narrow objectives set by central government; therefore measuring only the quantitative part of detective activity can potentially present misleading findings when quoted as a measure of performance (Reiner, 1988; Waters, 2000).

The origins of the current emphasis on performance management can be associated with the election of the Conservative government in 1979, which placed a clear emphasis on "value for money" in all public services (Loveday, 2000b). Concerns that the police were "poorly managed", "unaccountable" and "underperforming" led to the belief that "private sector management and principles" were required in order to reform public services (Mawby, 2002, pp. 28–29). Home Office Circular 114/83 reflected this ambition in policing, with directions to improve "manpower, efficiency and effectiveness" while setting clear priorities and encouragement in the recruitment of "civilian" staff, all with the intention of improving efficiency while reducing costs (Loveday, 2000b; Mawby, 2002; Weatheritt, 1986). The drive underpinning new public management (NPM) was a continued belief that encouragement of league tables would provide comparative and competitive performance, to achieve best value and the recognition of citizens as customers (e.g. the Citizens' Charter, 1991), legitimating benchmarking and performance regimes and providing increased accountability (Long, 2003; Senior *et al.*, 2007). The theme of "economy, efficiency and effectiveness" (the three Es) and "value for money" continued with the election of a Labour government in 1997 (Savage, 2007). The Local Government Act 1999 was evidence of the continued scrutiny of police performance, encouraging a performance culture. The Act introduced best value reviews, performance plans (compatible with government targets), consultation with service users, benchmarking, the creation of Best Value Performance Indicators (BVPI) (creating the basis for league tables) and emphasis on efficiency gains (Savage, 2007). The Home Office continued to develop the monitoring mechanisms for the police service and devised performance frameworks to address the difficulties of measuring police performance. The Policing Performance Assessment Framework, introduced in 2002, approaches performance measurement by recognising six "key" police functions, comparing similar-sized forces and key police priorities (referred to in policy documents as "domains") (Home Office, 2003). The aim of this framework is to combat geographical variations in performance through comparison, and encourage a balanced approach to a variety of police priorities. Police services are grouped together and compared on the basis of similar social and geographical characteristics (Home Office, 2003). The selection of group peers for comparison is based on geographical, demographic and social-economic information (Home Office, 2009). The only service not used in the group comparison is the City of London Police, owing to its unique nature (Home Office, 2009). The comparisons are made using an indicator calculated from a "group" average (Home Office, 2003).

This comparison, although crude and with immediately obvious inaccuracies (all police areas have unique characteristics), provides a useful mechanism for attempting to compare variations in performance figures. An illustration of the group comparison in the "performance monitor" framework is shown in Figure 7.4; the "domains" concept is shown in Figure 7.5.

Each domain attempts to focus on a particular aspect of policing, measured by a number of performance indicators. While arguably the police have little impact on the crime rate (Bayley, 1998; Bowling & Foster, 2002: table 27.4 (pp. 998–999); Coleman & Moynihan, 1996), one factor

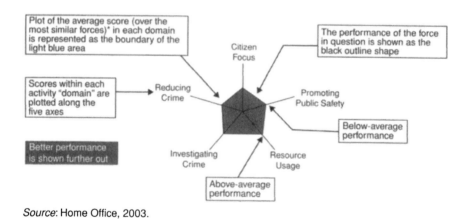

Source: Home Office, 2003.

Figure 7.4   Example of a performance monitor

**Providing Assistance
(Domain 4)**

This is also a reactive area, concerned with how the police deal with the public when the public come to them for assistance.

Citizen Focus (Domain A)

This is an area which is affected by all areas of police performance, i.e. whether the public are satisfied with the level of services they get from the police, be that as victims of crime or otherwise.

Both the local and national priorities will be reflected within the framework.

Reducing Crime (Domain 1)	**Investigating Crime (Domain 2)**	**Promoting Public Safety (Domain 3)**	**Providing Assistance (Domain 4)**
This is a proactive area, examining where policing activity helps to prevent and reduce crime.	This is a reactive area, i.e. how policing helps to solve crimes and bring offenders to justice	In this area, the police act to decrease the fear of crime and to ensure public safety.	This is also a reactive area, concerned with how the police deal with the public when the public come to them for assistance.

Resource Usage (Domain B)

The outcomes in the above activity are dependent on the level of resources available and how they are deployed.

Source: Home Office, 2003.

Figure 7.5 PPAF "domains" of policing

of PPAF criteria is nevertheless the focus on reducing crime. "Promoting public safety" and "citizen focus" indicators are reliant on public perceptions, and these are influenced by a range of factors (such as media coverage) over which the police have limited control. "Resource usage" indicators are limited to staffing issues rather than focusing on investment in a range of key areas (such as information technology). The "providing assistance" domain has yet to be developed. Finally, the indicator focused on crime investigation, to be discussed below, is not particularly representative of the broad investigative function. The framework that the PPAF provides for measuring police performance is an attempt to compare forces with similar characteristics and to ensure that the recording process is more consistent between forces. However, as Ashby and Longley argue:

Attempts to compare crime and policing statistics for regions with very different social-demographic compositions and urban-rural structures have been widely viewed as untenable, largely because it has proven impossible, in practice, to accommodate the diversity of policing needs across the country... Perhaps unsurprisingly, given their high profile and significance, each of these methodologies has generated criticism, debate and controversy.

(Ashby & Longley, 2005, p. 56)

This comment highlights one of the significant weaknesses in the PPAF approach and one that is particularly problematic in competitive performance culture.

Table 7.4 illustrates the changes in the number of indicators used to assess criminal investigation. Since the introduction of the PPAF in 2002 there has been continual change (in terms of a reduction) in the assessment tools used to measure police performance (within PPAF), creating difficulties for direct comparison with past performance. A consistent criticism of PPAF arrangements has been the substantial dependence on quantitative measures (Flanagan, 2008). More substantial changes to the performance framework were implemented in April 2008 with the Assessments of Policing and Community Safety (APACS) replacing the PPAF framework. These new arrangements are aimed at reflecting a greater emphasis on measuring quality and appear to be a work in progress, with some of the proposed indicators dropped and more indicators to be added in 2009/10 (Home Office, 2008). It appears that public confidence surveys are beginning to play a more important part in performance measurement regimes and will play a part in the first assessments from the APACS framework to be published in 2009.

It may be argued that police performance arrangements maintain traditional approaches to measurement, but Davidoff's (1993) claim that the crude nature of these approaches is easily hijacked by "political judgement" may be hard to sustain given the vicissitudes of political life at a national level. The weakness of these measures is that they seek to measure an organisational audit trail of the quantity of processes occurring within the organisation which can then be related to public spending (Flynn, 2002). This in turn can create considerable problems for measuring crime accurately. The Metropolitan Police Authority report examining "crime data recording" illustrates this point:

Detections are seen as a significant measure of performance... some officers feel that if they can't detect the crime, why should they record it? Detection targets can lead to concentrating on "quick wins" (e.g.

Table 7.4 Changes in PPAF performance indictors for criminal investigation

Indicators	2004	2005	2006
6	(a) Number of notifiable/recorded offences resulting in conviction, caution or taken into consideration at court.	(a) Number of offences brought to justice.	
	(b) Percentage of notifiable/recorded offences resulting in conviction, caution or taken into consideration at court.	(b) Percentage of offences brought to justice.	(b) Percentage of offences brought to justice.
	(c) Number of Class A drug supply offences brought to justice per 10,000 population; of these the percentage each for cocaine and heroin supply.		
7	(a) Percentage of notifiable/recorded offences resulting in charge, summons, caution or taken into consideration at court.	(a) Percentage of notifiable offences resulting in a sanctioned detection.	(a) Percentage of notifiable offences resulting in a sanctioned detection.
	(b) Percentage detected of domestic burglaries.		
	(c) Percentage detected of violent crime.		
	(d) Percentage detected of robberies.		
	(e) Percentage detected of vehicle crime.		
8	(a) Percentage of domestic violence incidents with a power of arrest where an arrest was made related to the incident.	(a) Percentage of domestic violence incidents with a power of arrest where an arrest was made related to the incident.	(a) Percentage of domestic violence incidents where an arrest was made related to the incident.
	(b) Of 8(a), the percentage of partner-on-partner violence.		(b) Value of cash forfeiture orders and confiscation orders per 1,000 population

cannabis warnings) or criminalising behaviour such as urinating in the street.

(MPA, 2008, p. 22)

Beattie and Cockcroft argue that this approach may be considered suitable for the private sector but that public criminal justice organisations work in a different context, and methods of measurement are not necessarily transferable:

> Unsophisticated performance indicators... fail to account for the diverse roles of the practitioners... Within criminal justice, however, there should be an acknowledgement of the role that discretion has traditionally played in police work. It does not necessarily follow that measurement leads to improvement in quality and, in fact, such changes may simply lead to unhelpful disturbances in the balance of role, function and expectation which simply intensify the bureaucratic burden.
>
> (Beattie & Cockcroft, 2006, p. 43)

While there are a number of challenges facing criminal justice agencies, it appears that the method of measuring performance can be misleading and not provide the level of accuracy required to justify the additional bureaucracy associated with performance management. As long as this is the case, it is possible that figures will continue to be manipulated and good "performance" claimed with little or no valid evidence. In summary, performance measurement informs policy but avoids measuring the quality of policing with any great degree of accuracy, running the risk of failing in its primary purpose.

CRITIQUE OF TRADITIONAL MEASURES OF EFFECTIVENESS

The lack of research into detective practice is in contrast to other roles in policing. It is for this reason that perhaps there is a lack of understanding of crime investigation and appropriate measures of performance in this context. Changes in criminal investigation discussed throughout this book present a clear picture of the dispersal of investigative tasks alongside the development of more specialist roles throughout the investigation process. This section aims to present some of the features that are not adequately recognised when evaluating detective performance.

The Impact of Other Agencies

Closer examination of detective practice preceding the disposal of criminal cases reveals a multitude of "public sector partners"[9] contributing to the outcome of investigations (Audit Commission, 1993; Butler, 2000; Gilling, 2000; Johnston, 2000). It is not just the processes of information-sharing, strategy selection and implementation associated with "public partners" as stipulated in the Crime and Disorder Act 1998 that impact upon detective performance. The move to legislate partnership has provided a more controlling form of governance, introducing "discipline and regulation" to activities in public, private and voluntary services in the "police, courts, correctional services, hospitals, universities, schools and local government" (Senior *et al.*, 2007, p. 30). But within this network of governance the complexity of inter-agency arrangements, multi-agency co-operation, differences in resources and regulation, conflicting goals and objectives, and spatial variations in the resistance and compliance to central government direction can provide substantial barriers to achieving meaningful social outcomes. The private policing sector is continually expanding, with security guards, electronic surveillance and private detectives contributing in a variety of ways to police investigation (Button 2002; Johnston, 2000). Groups including victims, witnesses, suspects, offenders and the jury all make a variety of positive and negative contributions to the outcome of an investigation (Cameron, 2001). It appears that the detection rates and performance indicators ignore these groups and place the sole responsibility of the outcome of the investigation on detectives. By measuring detective performance as a broad outcome, one cannot help but include the performance of other contributors (Cameron, 2001; Loader, 1999). This observation suggests that the outcome-based measures do not reflect police performance, but rather the cumulative sum of a significant group of contributors.

Investigative Practices that Are Ignored

Outcome and output measures reflect a narrow perspective in terms of what is considered effective detective performance. Indeed, what is recognised as "effectiveness achieved in one area may mean ineffectiveness in another" (Chatterton, 1987, p. 81). One example that illustrates this point concerns any performance indicator that targets police response time and the number of calls attended by uniformed officers. Measurement of response calls could mean that uniformed officers are so intent upon getting to a scene of crime quickly that the actual initial crime scene investigation becomes a hurried (and thus ineffective) affair. Placing such a heavy emphasis on the output of the investigation marginalises the key skills and knowledge required during the investigation process (Chatterton, 1987; MacDonald, 1999). There are many skills required of detectives, including interview technique, statement-taking, legal and forensic knowledge, IT skills, research skills, ability to identify lines of enquiry and interpersonal skills, to name a few (McGurk et al., 1994; NPT, 1999; Smith & Flanagan, 2000). There appears to be no direct incentive or substantive supervision that focuses on these areas to improve practice (Maguire & Norris, 1992; Stockdale 1993; Zander, 1994). This can lead to an approach where "what gets measured gets done" (MacDonald, 1999: 43; Rose, 1996), which could lead to poor investigation, resulting in unsafe convictions or an increase in the number of unsolved crimes because key components of the investigation process are given lower priority and easily solved crimes are targeted (Chatterton, 1987; MacDonald, 1999; Reiner, 1988).

The Impact of Performance Measurement on Motivational Factors

The focus upon the measurement of the outcomes or outputs rather than the means of criminal investigation suggests that performance measurement processes, rather than the quality of detective work, are the key motivation for practice (Maguire et al., 1992). If reward is recognised by a satisfactory conclusion, the means by which that conclusion is achieved can be open to a variety of manipulations (Rawlings, 2002). These manipulations can include working to the performance criteria guidelines and finding a loophole (against the spirit of good practice) to increase performance, such as the practice of prison write-offs[10] (Reiner, 2000; Walker, 1992). Bowling (1998) points to the redefining of the clear-up rate increasing "clear-ups" for racial incidents from 12.8% to 30.8% without any change in police performance. Alternatively, manipulation of suspects can result in forced confessions and false statements (Cox, 1975; Cox et al., 1977; Rose, 1996). The reward system for thief-takers in the eighteenth century (as discussed in Chapter 1) followed a similar system, with the focus on the ends rather than the means of investigation (Goddard, 1956; Pringle, 1958; Rawlings, 2002; Wright, 2000). The incentive for investigators to "perform" is highly questionable, not only in terms of the achievement of effective practice but also the effect on ethical behaviour.

Critique of Performance Criteria

Many critics and commentators have expressed the view that performance measurement can impact on ethical detective conduct and, more fundamentally, on the legitimacy of the public police institution itself.

In sum, performance assessment is a vital component of police accountability, but, at the end of the day, statistics have serious limitations and the judgements of police managers, HMICs and other outside groups concerned with monitoring the police, also have to take into account qualitative factors (the use of skills, the quality of relations with the public, the general "image" of the police, and so on) and, above all, to maintain vigilance against any tendency to believe that "the end justifies the means" and that civil rights can be sidestepped or ignored in the name of "effectiveness".

(Maguire *et al.*, 1992, 110)

This quotation identifies at least two key issues, namely the extent to which ethical police practice is recognised, and whether current measures of police performance ignore abuses of civil rights. Certainly, performance measurement has traditionally ignored this important feature of police behaviour.

The behaviour of the police in an investigative context has been influenced by performance measurement criteria (Maguire *et al.*, 1992; Young, 1991). The behaviour associated with performance measurement is rooted in values of crime control.[11] This view opposes some of the values pursued within the "search for the truth" (see Chapter 8) debate (Stevens, 2002), that is to say that an outcome of an investigation measured through traditional processes is not the same as one that may value the search for the truth. The identification of miscarriages of justice, suicide investigations, and investigations of suspicious deaths that yield comprehensive evidence and obtain the truth represent serious investigations that do not necessarily end in a conviction. Therefore traditional outcomes only provide a partial picture of the range of investigative tasks conducted by the police. In terms of effectiveness, acknowledging the quality of investigations in a variety of contexts may help towards improvements in investigative practice.

Such is the impact of performance measurement on police culture and practice that the criteria chosen to measure performance can have dramatic implications (Maguire *et al.*, 1992; Skolnick, 1994). Therefore it appears that outcome-based measures will provide the basis not only for policy-making, but also for the values that inform police practice itself. The continued focus upon "the ends rather than the means" does not necessarily provide an appropriate motivation for officers when considering the issue of the legitimacy of the police (Wright, 2000).

The Political Context

In the context of police performance, quantitative, outcome-based methods are routinely used. They are also routinely used in the media and

In the House of Commons 'There are particular political advantages to these methods. Davidoff argues that the weakness of performance indicators is that "absolute measures of effectiveness require political judgement" (1993, p. 14). This interpretation (using political judgement) can activate a number of controls through centrally formulated objectives (Loveday, 2000b; MacDonald, 1999; Neyroud & Beckley, 2001; Parkinson & Marsh, 2000). Outcome-based measures can also be used as evidence to introduce "hit squads", or set targets for dramatic short-term improvement (MacDonald, 1999). The use of league tables and the recognition of quartile performers reinforces competition within the performance culture context, encouraging the "celebration" of top performers while others "strive" to follow in the footsteps of identified centres of excellence (Long, 2003). This approach not only seeks to acknowledge the best performers but "names and shames" those languishing at the bottom of the league tables (Long, 2003). These control mechanisms allow the government to adopt a "crime control" approach to law and order (Reiner, 2000). Such an approach is popular with the electorate; slogans such as being "tough on crime" can be captivating (BBC Online, 2004). Despite the criticisms directed at outcome-based measurements, these methods are still used in politics as an adequate measure of police performance, despite the lack of recognition regarding the quality of police work (Audit Commission, 1993; Burrows, 1986; Reiner, 2000; Neyroud & Beckley, 2001). Nevertheless, these measures can be perceived as relatively consistent over time and therefore a major contributor to policy-making (Wilson, 1962). The advantages for a government using outcome-based measurement can be identified as the ability to provide control, and the provision of a simplistic measure that can be interpreted and manipulated by politicians to achieve political ends (Coleman & Moynihan, 1996; Ericson, 1993).

The Organisational Context

Police organisations are confronted with a multitude of performance indicators required from a number of government-sponsored bodies (Home Office, 1993). These "bodies" include the Audit Commission, HMIC, ACPO, the police authorities, and central government (Home Office, 1993; Neyroud & Beckley, 2001). Effective crime investigation does not just include detectives, but relies upon the police service and partnership agencies more broadly. However, performance indicators are created from the perspective of a particular police function, and this can result in performance indicators across different functions working against each other. The MPA reported:

the police service is assessed on its ability to maximize sanction detections, while the CPS is measured against the rate of ineffective trials. These two sets of targets are often in conflict as it is in the interests of police measured performance to ensure that as many cases as possible are prosecuted. However, CPS measured performance shows improvements by only taking forward those cases that are most likely to result in a conviction.

(MPA, 2008, p. 22)

As mentioned earlier in this chapter, achieving effectiveness for one performance indicator can create ineffectiveness in another (Chatterton, 1987). It is also important to acknowledge that performance indicator statistics are collected by the organisation and used to further organisational interests (Coleman & Moynihan, 1996). Data collection within the police has been a process systematically focused on enhancing the perception of performance through recording practices. However, police data are not recorded objectively (non-police interests) with crimes reported directly to the police (Coleman & Moynihan, 1996). The manipulation of data by police officers to present the police in a more favourable light has a comprehensive history (Young, 1991). The chief officer is in the position of having to respond to target-setting from a central agenda that defines effectiveness in the context of political, short-term and crime-control philosophies. This approach neglects the importance of local needs and the role of local people in contributing to managing crime and disorder. There is thus restricted room for manoeuvre in establishing new approaches to policing (Oliver, 1987). The dilemma of the chief officer becomes a measure of the ability to implement a central thesis to policing rather than an ability to identify local needs and respond appropriately. The balance of central control over police organisations imposes an approach to policing that restricts initiative and favours central government objectives over local needs (Neyroud & Beckley, 2001).

These tensions between competing perspectives do not appear to be approaching resolution, with government policy determined to improve detection and conviction rates (Home Office, 2001b). Fitzgerald *et al.* have argued that we need to understand much more how the investigative function is perceived, processed and enforced:

Whilst policing needs to remain outcome-focused, it does not make sense to deny the complexity of the police environment and to expect a simple relationship between policing effort and the achievement of crime targets. . .

Performance measurement will always be important, of course, but there is a need for new approaches. These need to capture quality as well as quantity and to strike a better balance between long-term and short-term goals. Simply refining quantitative performance indicators is not the solution. Those who actually deliver the service – and collate the performance statistics – will always be able to subvert the intentions of target-setters if the latter group does not share the former's appreciation of the reality and complexity of police work.

(Fitzgerald *et al.*, 2002, p. 141)

This analysis effectively sums up the tension relating to the police role, policing context and measurement. It is clear that the current outcome-focused measures do not necessarily achieve the aims of measuring or promoting the quality of police work.

SUMMARY

Measuring the true effectiveness of the investigative function is not straightforward. So far this book has identified the variety of tasks, methods and values used to measure and influence police performance. Criticisms have suggested that detective work should not be seen merely as a range of rigid tasks or targets. The weakness in traditional methods of measurement concerns not only what is measured but also what is neglected. As long as outcome- and output-based measures continue to reflect a narrow recognition of detective work, the means of investigation will be neglected in favour of the end result. This will not address the need to improve the quality of detective work; rather, it will "subvert" the process of performance measurement (Fitzgerald *et al.*, 2002; Maguire *et al.*, 1992).

While a focus on "quality" in policing represents a significant challenge to occupational culture and police professionalism, avoiding these challenges is likely to reinforce the perception of a spiral of deteriorating investigative practice. Public sector organisations have not been released from performance indicators that focus on financial control and quantify output. Political realities, whereby there is always an eye on the ballot box, do not bode well for the idea that there might need to be political support to implement important changes that will take time to produce results.

NOTES

1. Some senior officers do not receive an increment in their salary if they do not achieve their performance targets measured in outputs. This practice encourages the police organisation to become outcome-driven (BBC, 2005, 2007).
2. Coleman and Moynihan (1996) describe the "dark figure of crime" in broad terms as the proportion of crime that is "unseen" (or at least does not come to the attention of the authorities) and that many crimes and criminals go undetected. This creates substantial problems for criminologists and practitioners in estimating accurate levels and types of crime.
3. "Cuffing" refers to the disposal of crimes that are unlikely to be detected in order to achieve better performance statistics.
4. "As a sum of personal and household crime, total crime would have been understated by 29 percent" (Farrell & Pease, 2007, p. 3).
5. Some details have been changed to from the original case (Tong, 2005).
6. In the late 1930s there was a total of 238,220 recorded crimes in England and Wales. This figure had risen to over 5 million in 2006/07 (Whitaker, 1964; Nicholas *et al.*, 2007).
7. Further details of these specific rules can be obtained from the Home Office Counting Rules document (2007): http://www. homeoffice.gov.uk/rds/pdfs07/countgeneral07.pdf
8. *1998/99* Counting rule changes: the introduction of new offences had an estimated impact of increasing detections rates from 28% to 29%. *1999* Guidance on Detections brought the introduction of new rules requiring detections to have "sufficient evidence to charge" while detections obtained from prison visits no longer counted. The overall impact on the detection rates is estimated at a 1% decrease. *2002* The NCRS introduced rules aimed at promoting consistency between forces and a victim-focused approach to recording crime. Other changes impacting on detection rates included the Sexual Offences Act 2003, inclusion of British Transport Police data from 2002/03, use of Penalty Notices for Disorder (PND) for some notifiable offences in 2004/05 and guidance on recording of formal warnings for possession of cannabis from April 2004 (Walker *et al.*, 2006).
9. The Crime and Disorder Act 1998 s. 5 outlines the responsibilities of the local council, chief officer of police, the police authority and probation committee for crime and disorder strategies. In addition to these agencies, health authorities, police authorities,

voluntary groups, private sector agencies and community groups are all encouraged to work towards the goal of "community safety".

10. In the past, activities such as prison visits have contributed up to 50% to the clear-up rates (in one force). Today that figure is about 4% (Reiner, 2000; Walker, 1992). Prison write-offs involve obtaining admissions of offences from offenders in prison.

11. A crime-control perspective "stresses that the primary function is to punish offenders and, by doing so, to control crime" (Gelsthorpe, 2001a, p. 61).

REVIEW QUESTIONS

1. Outline the strengths and weaknesses of police-recorded figures.
2. Outline the strengths and weaknesses of the British Crime Survey.
3. Describe the current police performance arrangements.
4. Identify five key challenges to measuring police performance.

QUESTIONS FOR FURTHER RESEARCH AND ANALYSIS

1. What values should inform performance measurement?
2. Which aspects of detective work should be measured?
3. How can the desired objectives of the investigative function be consistent with other agencies and functions within criminal justice?

RECOMMENDED READING

Measuring Crime

Farrell, G. & Pease, K. (2007). The sting in the tail of the British Crime Survey: Multiple victimisations. In M. Hough & M. Maxfield (eds.), *Surveying crime in the 21st century* (pp. 33–54). Cullompton: Willan Publishing.

Hope, T. (2005). What do crime statistics tell us? In C. Hale, K. Hayward, A. Wahidin & E. Wincup (eds.), *Criminology* (pp. 39–60). Oxford: Oxford University Press.

Jansson, K. (2007). *British Crime Survey: Measuring crime for 25 years.* http://www.homeoffice.gov.uk/rds/pdfs07/bcs25.pdf

Maguire, M. (2007). Crime data and statistics. In M. Maguire, R. Morgan & R. Reiner (eds.), *Oxford handbook of criminology* (4th edn., pp. 241–301). Oxford: Oxford University Press.

Newburn, T. (2007). *Criminology* (ch. 3). Cullompton: Willan Publishing.

Nicholas, S., Kershaw, C. & Walker, A. (2007). *Crime in England and Wales 2006/07.* Home Office Statistical Bulletin. http://www.homeoffice.gov.uk/rds/pdfs07/hosb1107.pdf

Reiner, R. (2007). Law and order: An honest citizen's guide to crime and control *(chs. 3 and 4)*. Cambridge: Polity.

Smith, A. (2006). *Crime statistics: An independent review*. http://www. homeoffice.gov.uk/rds/pdfs06/crime-statistics-independent-review-06.pdf

Police performance measurement

Allen, J. (2007). Survey assessments of police performance in the British Crime Survey. In M. Hough, and M. Maxfield (eds.), *Surveying crime in the 21st century* (pp. 183–198). Cullompton: Willan Publishing.

Ashby, D.I. & Longley, P.A. (2005). Geocomputation, geodemographics and resource allocation for local policing. Transactions in GIS, *9*(1), 53–72. http://www.casa.ucl.ac.uk/ashby/downloads/01-geocomp-geodem.pdf

HMIC (2006). The role of Her Majesty's Inspectorate of Constabulary. http://inspectorates.homeoffice.gov.uk/hmic/docs/our-work/hmicrole.pdf? view=Binary

Home Office (2007). Home Office counting rules for recorded crime. http://www. homeoffice.gov.uk/rds/pdfs07/countgeneral07.pdf

Home Office (2008). *Improving performance: A practical guide to performance management*. http://police.homeoffice.gov.uk/news-and-publications/ publication/performance-and-measurement/Practical_Guide_to_Police_P1. pdf?view=Binary

Long, M. (2003). Leadership and performance management. In T. Newburn (ed.), *Handbook of policing* (pp. 628–655). Cullompton: Willan Publishing.

Savage, S. (2007). *Police reform: Forces for change* (ch. 3). Oxford: Oxford University Press.

WEBSITES

Crime statistics: http://www.crimestatistics.org.uk/output/Page1.asp

HMIC: http://inspectorates.homeoffice.gov.uk/hmic

National statistics: http://www.statistics.gov.uk

Performance and measurement: http://police.homeoffice.gov.uk/performance-and-measurement/

Police reform: http://police.homeoffice.gov.uk/police-reform/

CHAPTER 8

Criminal Investigation in Context

STEPHEN TONG, ROBIN P. BRYANT AND MIRANDA A. H. HORVATH

INTRODUCTION

There are many contributions to be made to the quality (or otherwise) of criminal investigation that aim to produce a satisfactory conclusion to an investigation. Many of these contributions have already been commented upon in a variety of contexts, from forms to reasoning (Chapter 3) to the use of psychology in identifying offenders (Chapter 4) and investigative interviewing (Chapter 6). This chapter selects some of the key issues in criminal investigation that continue to be raised in line with concerns around effectiveness, justice and truth. The chapter will begin with a brief debate considering the contribution of criminal justice principles and informal police practices to establishing "proof" or "truth" in criminal investigation, followed by a brief overview of the challenges and problems in the investigation of sexual offences, and finally an examination of the role of science in police investigation.

"PROOF" OR "TRUTH": CHALLENGES OF CRIMINAL INVESTIGATION

The principles underpinning the criminal justice system reflect the adversarial approach of a search for "proof" rather than "truth" (Sanders & Young, 2007). This claim is made on the basis that "at the final stage proof need not be absolute, but only 'beyond reasonable doubt'" (Sanders & Young, 2007, p. 954). The criminal justice process can be described using Herbert Packer's (1968) "due process" and "crime control" models, illustrating different approaches to achieving criminal justice goals. It is argued that commonly used methods, such as the detection rate, focus upon crime control values of the investigation and ignore those activities that reflect due process (Hepburn, 1981). A crime control perspective "stresses that the primary function is to punish offenders and, by doing so, to control crime" (Gelsthorpe, 2001a, p. 61). The idea of crime control is that if "social freedom" is to be achieved, the police must be free to interrogate and bring offenders to justice quickly and efficiently. This model represents a conveyor belt, in which quality control is the domain of the police. The deterrent factor is fundamental, and although a few mistakes (innocent people convicted) would be possible, this is a worthy sacrifice for the overall goal of repressing crime (Sanders & Young, 2007).

Alternatively a "due process" perspective has quite different ideals focusing on the need for justice to be done and be seen to be done; due process therefore "emphasises the need to administer justice according to legal rules and procedures that are publicly known, fair and seen to be just" (Gelsthorpe, 2001b, p. 104). Due process recognises that the police and witnesses make mistakes and that to ensure a safe and reliable criminal justice system the process of prosecution should resemble an obstacle course rather than a conveyor belt. The aim of this system is to prosecute the factually guilty and protect the factually innocent (Sanders & Young, 2007).

In practice the criminal justice system, in which investigation is a key process, does not conform to one particular model of justice. Rather, there are aspects of criminal justice that reflect both the crime control and the due process philosophies (Packer, 1968). Choongh (1997) argues that criminal justice is not just a process; instead, criminal justice, particularly from a policing perspective, operates in an informal way to achieve social discipline. This model of control begins with arrest and is concluded at the police station. Choongh argues that the procedures reflecting due process are rarely used, as the majority of defendants plead guilty to avoid trial and the possibility of greater penalties. Further to this, Choongh supports Packer in acknowledging the importance of police interviews: these important sources of evidence can be subject to physical and psychological coercion resulting in unreliable confessions that do not necessarily reflect the truth. It is from this perspective that a crime control approach can be challenged, in that assumptions regarding police "impartiality and neutrality" cannot be relied upon

(Choongh, 1997). These critical concerns contribute to the argument that the police play a major part in the process of case construction:

> The construction of a case is not confined to one aspect of the process, such as the creation of an internal record of compilation of evidence, but infuses every action and activity of official actors from the initial selection of the suspect to final case disposition. Case construction implicates the actors in a discourse with legal rules and guidelines and involves them in using rules, manipulating rules and interpreting rules.
>
> (McConville *et al.*, 1991, p. 12)

The informal and unseen practices of detectives contributing to case construction are under-researched. There are few studies[1] that reveal the operating style of the police detective, the use of informants, the selection of offences and suspects or the investigative effort applied (Ericson, 1993; Hobbs, 1988). These decisions that are made on the ground can determine if a case will be subject to a reasonable pursuit of the truth or prosecution. The work of Ericson (1993) and Hobbs (1988) examines crime investigation and reveals the nature of the craft of detective work.

Detective Craft

Hobbs's (1988) study focuses on the context of detective work and argues that the "policed" have an influence by "providing the occupational style for the police" as detectives mimic the cultural cues of the working class (Hobbs, 1988, p. 101). In his study of London's East End and its history, clues to the local working-class culture are set out; they are embedded in the casual labour markets, immigration, individualism, craft and entrepreneurial skills in which there was

> a fusion of communities; independence, internal solidarity, and pre-industrial cultural characteristics continuing to form a community that does not conform to either proletarian or bourgeois cultural stereotypes.
>
> (Hobbs, 1988, p. 101)

In Hobbs's view this historical evolution produced a continually developing economy of negotiation for trade in the form of entrepreneurship. He suggests that the impact on the "rookie"[2] detective is directly associated with being contained within a "cultural vacuum"[3] "absorbing a process of 'cultural photosynthesis'", the process of transgression To work effectively, the trainee detective must be able to exist not only by understanding the cultural dimensions of this world but also taking on some of its characteristics. The CID officer is presented as someone excluded from the uniformed branch, lacking direction from supervisors, but acquiring "stylistic devices of the policed" because of the autonomous nature of detective work and its cultural influences (Hobbs, 1991). The environment detectives work in has a fundamental impact on the development of the occupational culture, but also has implications for the effectiveness or otherwise of detective work.

Hobbs (1988) reveals that a relationship exists where detectives transgress the cultural characteristics of the policed, such as a "dealing" language and philosophy. This philosophy reflects the verbalisation of negotiation for trade within the specific locality of the East End to purchase and exchange goods. This physical and verbal expression of entrepreneurialism is not restricted to the traditional market arena but extends to the trade of information and favours between the "policed" and detectives. Detectives seek to target serious crimes and the "policed" aim to divert attention away from their trading activities. The dilemma of this "cultural photosynthesis" is the effect of the transgression. By transgressing into the world of the "policed", officers can operate in the environment where crime is planned, engage in proactive information-gathering and informant recruitment, and generally function in a world that requires bonds of trust and/or acceptance. This is not just in the use of language but in the adoption of "stylistic devices": by replicating gesture, rapport can be built, shared understandings developed, and information exchange can begin (Hobbs, 1988; Sanders, 1977). This can only occur by learning these skills in the very environment in which they are practised, but this inevitably brings with it significant risks of compromise and unethical practice (Cox et al., 1977). The absence of close supervision in guiding detectives reinforces the sense of isolation for the detective (Ericson, 1993; Maguire & Norris, 1992).

The informal and formal building of detective reputations rests on the basis of successful cases and detection rates, which serve as motivation for detectives to achieve results (Hobbs, 1988; Skolnick, 1994; Young, 1991). It is important to acknowledge at this point that "successful" cases are not identified as a "search for the truth" but by the categorisation of an outcome or through prosecution in the criminal court (McConville et al., 1991; Reiner, 2000). Evidence points to targets that have been achieved or exceeded through prison visits, "cuffing", persuasion, manipulation, deception and lying; these are important considerations when discussing issues surrounding the quality of justice and the search for the truth (Kleinig, 1996; Reiner, 2000; Skolnick, 1994; Young, 1991). These practices illustrate the vulnerability of suspects or the innocent to be subject to detective practices that reflect approaches such as "the end justifies the means", "corruption in a noble cause" and deceptive methods of investigation. This overall approach is the result of the detective's pursuit of justice through bypassing the procedures in place to protect suspects, in order to ensure that those who are believed to be "guilty" do not go free (Rose, 1996). Although this approach can include strong moral motivation in terms of detectives' determination to ensure the "guilty" are prosecuted, it also involves corruption (Kleinig, 1996). Therefore detective autonomy, particularly in the context of Hobbs's cultural characteristics that are learned from the "policed", suggests that informal practices can be detrimental to police integrity when investigation is seen as a search for the truth.

One task that detectives face, as with other police officers, is that of recording details of crime and of evidence. The presentation of information through paperwork creates a link between detective practice and the presentation of the case in court. As Hobbs states,

> The reality of detective work, and more specifically of detective–"criminal" encounters as they are manifested in court, is then a reality filtered through paperwork and marks the crucial link between the largely unsupervised autonomous activities of individual officers and the legally sanctified notion of due process as manifested in the wider criminal justice system.
>
> (Hobbs, 1988, p. 193)

This illustrates the importance of the transition from investigative practice through to presentation of case files in court. Although Hobbs observed detectives' dislike of paperwork, supervisors have recognised this process as vital to the smooth operation of the office. Hobbs argues that the paperwork is a "skilled and very precise process" requiring an "ordering of responses to management rules and directives" (Hobbs, 1988, p. 193). Hobbs compares this construction of a case with the entrepreneurial approach previously discussed; in this context, negotiation involves trading between officers to gain "documentary support for his paperwork without paying over the odds" (Hobbs, 1988, p. 194). Favours may be owed, but the overall aim is to present cases favourably in the interests of all concerned (except the criminal of course). Hobbs also observed that some documentation left detectives vulnerable to supervisors: for example, the officer's personal diary of daily events. The diary is not allowed to leave the office, but these diaries can disappear or, as Hobbs found, be stored at a detective's home. This tactic of removing the diary to prevent the detective sergeant from monitoring activities too closely has implications for constraining unethical behaviour. Monitoring detectives through the "paper chain" clearly has shortcomings in terms of ensuring adequate supervision and effective practice. Moreover, what is portrayed on paper (an official account) does not necessarily reflect the reality of practice. This shows that despite rigid organisational structures, detective discretion can have a fundamental impact on the outcome of criminal cases.

Hobbs (1988) argues that detectives are masters at manipulating paperwork to "fit" the official presentational requirements, ensuring that what actually happens is shaped and designed to fit into the requirements for court presentation. The same process could occur here by ensuring that operational practice "fits" the strategic instructions. Although the aim of providing a system of investigation that has consistency and achieves acceptable minimum standards has in the past sought to address some of the concerns of detective work, it does not bode well for the current context of the operational environment of investigative work. Not only has manipulation between practice and official records been a well-documented characteristic of detective work, but so too have a chronic lack of supervision and training in the skills of detective work (Hobbs, 1988; Tong 2005; Young, 1991). These characteristics do not necessarily serve the professional development of detective work, where current arrangements are argued to effectively deskill detectives, compromising their ability to investigate crime (Maguire, et al., 1992).

Ericson (1993) uses the phrase "covering one's ass" when referring to detectives processing cases in a particular way, to explain a variety of interpretations of organisational rules and procedures to manage workloads. This observation is consistent with Hobbs's (1988) findings of case presentation impacting on detectives' notions of crime and criminality. The difficulty of supervising through "paperwork" does not prevent supervisors from using discretion as a loose form of control. In his study, Ericson (1993) cites the discretion of supervisors to allow detectives on duty to spend time shopping and visiting friends (11% of detective time). This use of discretion illustrates supervisors' manipulation of organisational rules to manage workloads, but this control should not be exaggerated. Although supervisors did turn a blind eye to certain "unauthorised" practices, they could make substantial demands on detectives, such as working longer hours. However, Ericson (1993, pp. 56–57) concludes that the work of detectives was not closely monitored (with exception of high-profile cases) and supervisors were expected to "collaborate" in ensuring detectives enjoyed a "considerable degree" of autonomy. Despite this level of autonomy, Ericson (1993) argues that the decisions are still subject to structural frameworks and conditions that have a loose level of control on detectives' decisions and accounts.

Ericson states that "The rules detectives used were bound in with their accounts of their actions for official purposes. The rules which applied or could be applied were taken into the account, literally, as the detectives formulated a case outcome" (1993, p. 210). This process, Ericson argues, has seen the detective define crime, criminality, and the criminal in a context that is not accountable. The relationship between supervisors and detectives may suggest that organisational rules are not appropriate for operational needs. This problem is perpetuated further as the "slippery slope" explanation of corruption would suggest that the minor manipulation of rules may lead to more serious breaches (Delattre, 1996; Kleinig, 1996).

The analogy of criminal trials as games with two opposing teams pursuing conflicting objectives still rings true today for many of those involved in the process. The objective of the police and prosecution team is to prove the guilt of suspects "beyond reasonable doubt" while the defence team seeks to reveal weaknesses in the prosecution case; neither approach serves the pursuit of absolute truth. The bureaucracy of the criminal trial process, investigation and the impact of performance indicators are further barriers to this noble aim. However, although achievement of "absolute proof" may not be a realistic goal, attempts to identify barriers to a better quality of justice could lead to improved practice. There have been improvements to investigative practice since the work of Hobbs and Ericson: the introduction of PACE, rules surrounding disclosure, and improvements in the supervision and investigation of police complaints have all come about since this research was conducted. However, there remains a lack of research on the practice of investigative work and detective training while there still appears to be considerable autonomy and low levels of supervision. The roles of defence solicitors, barristers, witnesses and victims all play an important part in the pursuit of the truth. The detective is routinely associated with questions revolving around investigative effectiveness, but in truth the detective is only one participant among many. A meaningful attempt to reform the criminal justice system to pursue the truth would require a substantial review not only of the roles and contributions of detectives, lawyers, witnesses, victims and offenders but of the principles and motivations encouraging current practices.

INVESTIGATING SEXUAL OFFENCES

Sexual offences are some of the most difficult and challenging crimes to investigate. The difficulties they pose to investigators have, yet again, been thrust into the limelight by a number of recent reports and publications, for example *Without Consent* by Her Majesty's Crown Prosecution Service Inspectorate (HMCPSI & HMIC, 2007), *Investigating and Detecting Recorded Offences of Rape* by Feist *et al.* (2007) and *A Gap or a Chasm: Attrition in Reported Rape Cases* by Kelly *et al.* (2005). The issues these and many other reports raise are not new. As outlined in Chapter 6, the appalling treatment of rape victims hit the headlines in 1982 as a result of Roger Graef's documentary *A Complaint of Rape*. This section will provide a selective overview of the enduring key issues.

Sexual offences are under-reported (Walby & Allen, 2004); in fact current estimates suggest that between 75% and 95% of rapes are never reported to the police (HMCPSI & HMIC, 2007). Despite Home Office data showing there has been a steady increase in reporting in recent years, statistics also show a continuing decline in the conviction rate for rape over the last three decades (Kelly *et al.*, 2005). There are many reasons why women are reluctant to report rape, amongst them fear of being blamed and/or disbelieved and of living with the stigma of being a rape victim (Lees, 2002).

The focus of this section is the police investigation of allegations of rape, which is apt as research shows us that the majority of cases are lost at the early stages of the criminal justice process, i.e. the victim's decision to report it to the police and the initial police investigation (see Brown *et al.*, 2007; Harris & Grace, 1999; HMCPSI & HMIC, 2002, 2007; Kelly *et al.*, 2005; Lees & Gregory, 1993). Specifically, between a half and two-thirds of cases reported to the police do not proceed beyond the investigation stage (HMCPSI, 2007). For a detailed discussion of the reasons why, see Kelly *et al.* (2005).[4]

Factors Influencing Responses to Rape Victims

Perhaps the most problematic issue in rape and sexual assault is consent. In the HMCPSI (2007) report, 49% (n = 71) of the suspects in the cases they examined claimed "consent". Part of the reason consent is such a difficult issue is that in the majority of situations an explicit statement of consent is not given or indeed recorded by either or both parties or indeed witnessed by anyone else. Consent is often given and understood through unspoken behavioural cues but, as Susan Estrich outlines, in order to show non-consent the victim has to go to considerable lengths:

> Rape is most assuredly not the only crime in which consent is a defence; but it is the only crime that has required the victim to resist physically in order to establish non-consent.
>
> (Estrich, 1986, p. 1090)

The Sexual Offences Act 2003 defined consent in law for the first time, with the aim of making it easier for juries to make fair and balanced decisions and to place the onus on men that it is their responsibility to obtain consent. However, it is not yet clear whether this has had an impact on the conviction rate for rape and sexual assault.

Another stumbling block for many women[5] reporting rape is the consistent over-estimation of the number of false allegations of rape, particularly amongst the media, police officers and prosecutors (HMCPS & HMIC, 2007; Kelly *et al.*, 2005). This contradicts the research, which suggests that the rate of false allegations of rape is no higher than that for other crimes (Kelly *et al.*, 2005). Research estimates of false allegations vary from 3%–8% (Kelly *et al.*, 2005) to 41%–77% (Howard League, 1985; Kanin, 1994), with the former widely considered accurate. Kelly *et al.* (2005) suggest that this misperception of the scale of false allegations feeds a "culture of skepticism", which in turn prejudices those investigating cases and can result in victims having a lack of confidence in the police and communication between the two being negatively affected.

One of the most influential attitudinal problems that affects investigations is the existence of a "real rape" stereotype. The term was first used by Susan Estrich (1987) and refers to the belief held by many people that in order for a rape to be considered "real" it must fulfil certain criteria. These are that the rape occurred between strangers, in an outside location involving the use of physical force and weapons by the perpetrator and the victim being injured (Kelly, 2002). The impact of the "real rape" stereotype has many layers, for example if the victim's experience does not resemble that described above they may be less likely to report it to the police, and if they do report it then their account is likely to be judged as being less credible than if it resembled the "real rape" stereotype (Jordan, 2004). Further, if there are circumstances that can be interpreted as showing the victim was in some way culpable for their victimisation, the result can be that they receive less sympathetic treatment or are blamed for the assault when they report it to the police (Best *et al.*, 1992; Emmers-Sommer & Allen, 1999; Klippenstine *et al.*, 2007) – for example, if they were under the influence of alcohol when assaulted, or were assaulted by someone they knew whom they had invited into their own home. The HMCPSI report concluded, in relation to the victim's alcohol consumption:

> The extent to which alcohol use by victims may also be influencing police decision making, as suggested in the 2002 report, is not known, although the different findings within the advice and charged file samples suggest that it does play a part.
>
> (HMCPSI, 2007, p. 77)

Numerous national and international studies have found that police officers and other professionals involved in the criminal justice system are likely to be ill-informed and to hold stereotyped expectations about rape and sexual assault (such as the aforementioned "real rape" stereotype: see e.g. LaFree, 1981; Temkin, 1997; Ward, 1995). Furthermore, the delay between the assault occurring and the victim reporting to the police is a crucial factor in determining whether an allegation is likely to be perceived as genuine: the longer the delay, the less likely the victim is to be believed (Temkin & Krahé, 2008). However, there can be a multitude of reasons why a victim might not report rape immediately, for example shock, fear of being disbelieved or, if a victim was intoxicated when assaulted, she may have memory blanks that mean she does not remember what happened for some time after the assault. Feist et al. (2007) found that for adult victims, a quarter (26%) of rapes reported on the same day as they occurred resulted in detection, but when there was a delay in reporting of one or more days there was a statistically significant drop in detection rate to only 14%.

Studies have also shown that how victims present themselves is important. It has been found consistently that if victims do not conform to the expected "normal" emotional reaction of someone who has been raped, i.e. being visibly distraught, they are likely to be judged as more responsible for their assault and less credible than those who do conform to the stereotype (e.g. Buddie & Miller, 2001; Krulewitz, 1982; Rose et al., 2006).

The impact of judgements about victims and the circumstances of the rape itself have, as has been discussed here briefly, been shown to influence the outcome of investigations internationally (Brown et al., 2007; Jordan, 2004). Jordan (2004) found that cases categorised as "false" or "possibly false/true" contained more of the characteristics that do not fit the "real rape" template and contradict stereotypical notions about how victims should behave and react. Brown et al. (2007) support this: their research showed that cases that were put forward for prosecution were more likely to conform to the "real rape" stereotype. They speculate that police officers and prosecutors are trying to anticipate how juries will perceive cases, and in turn are perpetuating the "real rape" stereotype by being suspicious of and indeed dropping cases that in any way deviate from this template (Brown *et al.*, 2007; Temkin & Krahé, 2008).

New Developments

There have been many reforms and developments in recent years that should be helping to improve the investigation of sexual offences. It is not possible to include them all here, so just those judged to be most pertinent to police investigations are outlined (for more comprehensive overviews see Horvath & Brown, 2009, Kelly, 2008 and Temkin, 2002).

Sexual assault referral centres (SARCs) are one-stop shops where victims of rape and serious sexual assault can receive medical care and counselling and assist with police investigations by, for example, undergoing a forensic medical examination. There were 19 SARCs in operation in the UK in September 2007 (Coy *et al.*, 2007); in 2008 the Home Secretary announced additional funding to double the number of SARCs from 19 to 38 by 2011. This is a result of the identification of SARCs as good practice in a number of reports because they improve victim care, which in turn can lead to victims continuing to support an investigation and a better standard of forensic evidence being collected (HMIC & HMCPSI, 2002; HMCPSI, 2007; Lovett *et al.*, 2004). Gathering forensic evidence is of particular concern in rape cases, which often come down to "he said, she said". Ideally forensic evidence should be collected as soon as possible to avoid its deterioration; however, as has already been mentioned, victims often delay reporting which means this is not possible (Temkin & Krahé, 2008). Even if they do report quickly there can be delays before the forensic examination can take place (see Chambers & Millar, 1983). It is hoped, however, that the introduction of further SARCs will reduce the latter delays.

In 2005 the NPIA and ACPO published *Guidance on Investigating Serious Sexual Offences*. Amongst other useful information, it includes clear information and standards for investigations, from initial response to the investigation's conclusion, detailing each stage. HMCPSI (2007) highlights a number of examples of good practice in rape investigations, for example using a team approach to interview victims. A greater focus on developing lines of enquiry from an early stage has been found when the investigating officer (IO) and specially trained officer (STO) work together to develop a clear strategy for interviewing the victim. This in turn reinforces the importance of early links between the IO and STO which are crucial, and provide a strong basis on which to build successful cases.

It could be argued that some of the over-estimation of false allegations could arise from inconsistencies in victims' statements which are then misinterpreted by officers as lies when instead they are simply a result of the natural confusion that arises after experiencing a traumatic event. There are many reasons why there might be inconsistencies, and these need to be explored in a way that ensures that victims do not feel they are being disbelieved, and rather results in clarification of the situation. Dealing with such inconsistencies in a victim's statement at an early stage, and sensitively, is imperative as HMCPSI (2007) notes: if this is not done it can lead, at a later date, to the whole case being undermined.

Conclusion

This section has provided a very brief overview of some of the key issues facing officers investigating rape. While it has discussed many failings and difficulties affecting victims and investigators, it has also drawn together some recent developments that may offer solutions. As highlighted by Kelly (2008), while procedural and process changes within the criminal justice system are welcomed, and undoubtedly help, a more fundamental "change in culture – not just in the justice system, but across societies" (2008, p. 274) is needed.

CRIMINAL INVESTIGATION AND FORENSIC INVESTIGATION

Many textbooks on criminal investigation contain at least one chapter on what is variously termed "forensics", "scientific evidence", "physical evidence", "forensic science" or "forensic investigation". For example, the *Handbook of Criminal Investigation* (Newburn *et al.*, 2007b), a textbook described by its publisher as a comprehensive and authoritative source on the subject of criminal investigation, devotes a whole part of a total of five to "Forensic Techniques". Indeed, the largely US-derived term "criminalistics" is now almost completely synonymous with forensic science. In his introduction to his book on criminalistics, Richard Saferstein notes that "for all intents and purposes, the two terms ["criminalistics" and "forensic science"] are taken to be the same and will be used interchangeably in the text" (Saferstein, 2004, p. 2).

Similarly, detective fiction has often equated a subset of detective expertise with the effective use of forensic methods and technologies (which in shorthand is usually referred to as "forensic science") for, as Ronald Thomas noted, "the history of detective fiction is deeply implicated with the history of forensic technology" (Thomas, 2000, p. 3).

Other media portrayals, such as the popular US TV series *CSI*, reflect this association, but also often conflate investigative and forensic functions which are in practice kept apart. There is a sense in many of these fictional and media representations of criminal investigation of the particular hold that forensic science appears to have on objectivity and the truth. We have also seen elsewhere in this book the pragmatic importance of an understanding of forensic investigation techniques within the training of investigators.

It is therefore clear that both forensic investigation and forensic science bear some form of critical relationship with criminal investigation, and in particular that they that are both intimately connected with the search for the truth in an enquiry. However, "forensic science" and "forensic investigation" are not synonymous, and the distinction between the two is an important one for criminal investigation. As is often repeated in textbooks, the word "forensic" comes to us from the Latin word *forensis* meaning "forum" (not only a place of debate in ancient Rome but also a location for trials), and forensic science has long been associated with the application of science to legal contexts. So we have, for example, Jackson and Jackson's definition of forensic science as "any science that is used in the service of the justice system" (Jackson & Jackson, 2004, p. 1). There is some merit in such an all-encompassing but at the same time heavily restricted definition. However, it is also worth noting that the term "forensic science" may often (perhaps always) be essentially vacuous. As an example of this problematic vacuity, consider (in the UK at least) the classic archetypal "forensic scientist": the so-called "Home Office pathologist". Forensic pathology is a sub-speciality within the medical field of pathology. The Home Office maintains a list of pathologists who are deemed qualified to undertake autopsies in cases which might involve a criminal aspect. There are a number of routes towards qualifying as a "Home Office pathologist", but in most cases an individual would first need to complete a medical degree (five years in duration, usually after gaining entry on the basis of a high standard of school matriculation), followed immediately after graduation by a two-year postgraduate foundation programme. It is doubtful whether any significant "forensic" aspects would have occurred within training and education up until this point.[6] At this stage, after at least seven years' training, those intending to develop a specialism in forensic pathology would be expected to take first the histopathology specialism and then, some one or two years after, begin training in forensic pathology (Royal College of Pathologists, 2009). Hence it is at least 12 years before a highly trained and qualified medic is likely to begin to encounter the "forensic" aspects of their profession. It is clear that, in this case at least, "forensic scientist" means first and foremost a scientist, but one who finds the application of their specialism within the criminal justice system. They have certainly not become the "Home Office pathologist" through completing, for example, a degree in forensic science.

What, then, is "forensic investigation" if it is not "forensic science"? Fraser offers us the definition that forensic investigation "is the integration of a range of scientific and technological evidence and intelligence in support of a criminal investigation" (Frazer, 2008, p. 114), and this is much closer to the day-to-day experience of the criminal investigator.[7] However, we can perhaps extend this definition to conceptualise forensic investigation as being at the centre of a triangle of interrelated concerns, namely the application of a large number of scientific disciplines (such as pathology), in the context of both law enforcement (for example a criminal investigation conducted by the police) and the criminal justice system (for example, the decision-making of the Crown Prosecution Service, the burden of proof required in a criminal trial) and as depicted in Figure 8.1.

As an example, consider the recovery of the impression of a shoe print from soft soil at a crime scene—a scenario beloved in detective fiction. A cast is made of the impression of the shoe, traditionally using plaster of Paris. The fact that it appears to be a shoe (the so-called "class characteristics") is of limited interest; that it happens to be a particular

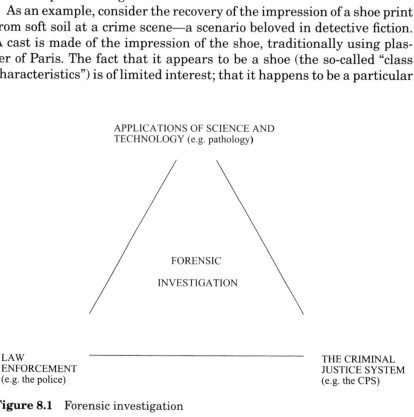

Figure 8.1   Forensic investigation

size and make (the "sub-class characteristics") is more so.[8] However, of potentially much greater importance are those individual characteristics of this particular shoe that transferred the impression: for example, areas of wear, the apparent presence of lodged stones, evidence of cuts to the surface and so on. Let us suppose that we have seized a shoe of the same make and size from a suspect and made a "test" impression of the shoe to compare with the impression from the crime scene. The print at the crime scene and the print of the suspect's shoe compare well, including individual aspects such as the wear marks. An obvious conclusion is that the seized shoe made the impression in the soil. However, what degree of certainty can be given to this? Is it possible, for example, that two or more shoes exist (but of the same make and size) that have quite independently ("randomly" is the word often used[9]) developed the particular pattern of wear, cuts, abrasions and so on that have been used to establish a match? And if so, with what likelihood? An answer to these important questions requires the application of the scientific disciplines of statistics, probability theory and empirical scientific experimentation (of shoe wear). The "forensic scientists" that the investigator consults on these issues may well provide a "likelihood ratio" which compares the probabilities of the match being due to the suspect's shoe making the impression to the match being due to another reason.[10]

Let us suppose the outcome is that there is only a very low chance the impression could have been made by any means other than by the shoe seized from our suspect. Does this suggest that we now have sufficient proof, to the degree required by the criminal justice system, of the guilt of the suspect? Obviously not. There may be other explanations, pointing away from guilt of the suspect, such as the simple possibility of another person wearing the shoe at the time the impression in the soil was made. Although the probability of match may be an important consideration in the investigation of this crime, it is an exclusively scientific matter; that is, it is forensic science as a component of forensic investigation. The match has, however, provided the police with an important link between the crime scene and the suspect[11] and could be used to help further an enquiry or decide between hypotheses; or it could be additionally "strengthened" in some way (as through circumstantial evidence that the suspect was wearing a shoe of the same type at around the time of the offence).

The example illustrates the dynamic interplay between the science (including scientific techniques and technological applications), law enforcement (primarily criminal investigation conducted by the police) and the demands of the criminal justice system, which together are the defining features of modern forensic investigation. Within this general description we can identify a number of features of forensic investigation—perhaps even principles—which guide its application within criminal investigation itself.

Firstly, there is the "Theory of Individualisation" as described, for example, by DeForest *et al.* (1983, p. 7): "Individualisation is unique to forensic science, it refers to the demonstration that a particular sample is unique, even among members of the same class." Some of these terms may require further explanation. A class is a set of objects sharing some common identity: i.e. we are all members of the class of humans. We can also consider the class of fingerprints, the class of blue cotton fibres and so. In this sense, all members of the same class are the "same". All fingerprints have the same kind of characteristics (for example, ridges). The Theory of Individualisation asserts that a single selection, or sample, from this class should be distinguishable from others in the same class *in some way*. For example, it is assumed that a single individual's fingerprint, taken from the class of all humans' fingerprints, will be distinguishable from any other. However, the theory applies equally well to the set of all Heckler and Koch USP handguns. In practice there are many ways of distinguishing between members of a class. For the purposes of forensic investigation, the challenge is to identify, and demonstrate beyond reasonable doubt their "claim" on uniqueness those characteristics that distinguish a member of a class but which are also likely to leave identifiable traces at the scene of a crime, or in other circumstances (see Locard's Principle below). Hence, for example, we are more interested in the unique characteristics of the barrels of Heckler and Koch USP handguns (as these can be linked with the marks made on rounds fired by the same handgun) then we are, say, in the exact shade of satin black or grey paint used as a finish.

Most writers on the history of forensic science trace the origins of the Theory of Individualisation to the work of the 19th-century statistician Adolph Quetelet, although it was subsequently elaborated by Bertillon, who used it as the basis of his system of "anthropometry". The history of the introduction of Bertillon's anthropometry, and its subsequent decline from use, is a good illustration of how certain characteristics, although unique to individuals, only become established fields of forensic investigation when they also support wider investigative needs.

Bertillon's technique consisted of photographing and measuring 11 physical characteristics of prisoners held in custody. For example, Bertillon measured the width of a prisoner's head, the length of the left middle finger and so on. A record of these measurements was kept on file. After release, if a prisoner was subsequently rearrested, the system would be able to identify the prisoner even if he or she were using an alias. Although never scientifically tested, it is likely that Bertillon's

11 measurements *did* provide the basis for a process of individualisation – it is highly unlikely that any two individuals would share all 11 characteristics. However, the system fell into disuse. Although it could link an individual to their record, it could not help provide evidence that a person had been in a particular place or had touched a particular object. The fingerprint, however, could perform both these functions, and this forms part of the explanation for why it replaced anthropometry.[12]

It is clear therefore that individualisation is intimately connected with the concept of uniqueness. However, within forensic investigation what is often the subject of discussion is not the uniqueness of the object itself but the uniqueness of its abstract representation produced for the purposes of comparison (and subsequent use in the criminal justice system). As an example, consider the use of recovered DNA material in a criminal investigation. There is much scientific evidence to suggest that our DNA is unique.[13] However, a DNA *profile* as generated for the purposes of a criminal investigation is not the same as the DNA itself. The profile is in effect a simplified representation of the uniqueness, and is in a form that can be readily compared for matches to known samples, from an individual or "speculatively" against entries in a database (e.g. in the UK, the National DNA Database). In the UK the method currently used for DNA profiling is SGM+. The technique looks for 10 markers known as Short Tandem Repeats (STRs) and a gender marker (male or female). STRs are short sequences of DNA that are repeated a number of times: it is the number of repeats that varies between people. A DNA profile consists of 20 numbers (two groups of 10 markers) and the gender indicator, and the probability of the DNA profiles of two unrelated individuals matching is claimed to be on average less than one in 1 billion (Parliamentary Office of Science and Technology, 2006).

Is the Theory of Individualisation scientifically justified? It would appear that this question is not one that currently concerns many practising forensic investigators – the theory seems to work well when applied as a guiding principle. However, the Theory of Individualisation would not appear to satisfy Popper's falsifiability criterion for a scientific law. Scientific theory should be *falsifiable* – that is, we should be able to make a logical deduction from the theory, devise some experiment which will potentially show the theory to be false, and carry out this experiment. What deductions can we make from the Theory of Individualisation? And what experiments could we use to test them? In this sense the theory appears to be a scientific "dead end". Put another way, the Theory of Individualisation is based in part upon inductive reasoning[14] – the facts that no two fingerprints have ever been found to be the same, or no two firearms have produced exactly the same markings on a bullet, are taken as supporting the theory. Despite these theoretical doubts, strong empirical evidence that physical entities exist in unique forms occurs within many other scientific fields, and this lends significant support to the practical application of the theory.

The Theory of Individualisation is used in practice by forensic investigators to derive a number of forms of intelligence or even evidence – for example, to demonstrate that a particular event occurred (e.g. a glass fragment from a particular window was transferred to the clothing of a particular person).

Locard's Principle – often summarised with the phrase "every contact leaves a trace" – is one of the best-known (and possibly clichéd) concepts in forensic investigation. Essentially it is a theory of exchange that states, for example, that whenever two objects come into contact there is a mutual exchange of material between them. Note the use of the word mutual: if objects A and B come into contact, then material originally present on A will be transferred to B and material from B will be transferred to A. The most famous example of the visible manifestation of Locard's Principle is probably the fingerprint: the transfer of oily deposits from the fingers of a person to another surface. However, note that Locard would also have observed that material passed between the surface and the fingers too. Furthermore, it is a theory of exchange in its widest sense. So, for example, impression evidence (for example footwear imprints, discussed above) is an example of Locard's Principle, although in these cases the investigator is usually as interested in the uniqueness of the pattern of impression (individualisation) as they are in the transfer of material.

Locard's Principle serves two main purposes in forensic investigation. Firstly, it produces intelligence and potential evidence of a likely interaction between two objects. Logically, this means that the two objects must have been present in the same place at the same time. Secondly, Locard's principle is an *imperative* to action – at some level or other (possibly the microscopic) there may be evidence of this exchange, and the forensic investigator could consider collecting this material.

In terms of the "admissibility" of Locard's Principle as a scientifically based theory, as with individualisation this has never been seriously challenged. However, the same observations concerning "falsifiability" made regarding individualisation apply equally to Locard's Principle. Perhaps a more serious problem may emerge with our greater understanding of so-called "small-world networks". Locard is essentially concerned with the interaction between two objects (e.g. a victim and offender). So for example, in the case of alleged rape we are interested in the transfer of DNA (e.g. in semen) from the suspect to the victim. It is highly unlikely, for obvious physical reasons, that this DNA-containing semen originates from a source other than the person (perhaps the suspect) with that particular DNA profile. However, as a result of rapid developments in technology, we are now able to analyse and establish individualisation for smaller and smaller samples. For example, skin flakes are now, in principle, able to be used to generate forms of DNA profile. The problem may be that, unlike relatively large amounts of semen, small-world network theory may provide an alternative explanation for the presence of the skin flake other than the interaction between the "owner" of the skin flake and its location.

In essence, small-world network theory attempts to model human society as a series of interlinked, relatively small collections of people known to one another. Most of us will know, at most, a few thousand people, a tiny proportion of the world's population. However, each of these associates will be members of other small networks. These connections between networks provide a theoretical means of linking any two people with a chain of linked associations. It was assumed, until relatively recently, that this chain would be thousands of links in length. However, in an interesting "thought experiment" in 1967, sociologist Stanley Milgram put forward the existence of "small world phenomena" – the idea that every person in the United States is connected by a chain of six people at most. The notion of "six degrees of separation" has entered popular consciousness with, for example, the invention of the "Six Degrees of Kevin Bacon" game. What has this to do with Locard's Principle? Consider fibre evidence. The evidential value of fibre evidence should be assessed by comparing two likelihoods: the probability that it was transferred from X to Y compared with the probability that it was present at Y "anyway". Potentially both these probabilities are affected by small-world network theory, as, for example, there may exist a chain between X and Z (involving transfer of the fibre) and where Z was present at Y, allowing for an "innocent" explanation of events. This chain need be no more than six links in length.

Based upon these two principles (the Theory of Individualisation and Locard's Principle) forensic investigation may aid a criminal investigation in a number of important ways. Firstly, there is the question of *corpus delicti* ("body of the crime"). Was a crime actually committed? Was a person responsible? For example, was a fatal fall from a height the result of an accidental slip, suicide or a push? Crime scene modelling, a branch of forensic investigation, might help to answer these questions. Secondly, given *corpus delicti*, what was the perpetrator's modus operandi (MO)? That is, how was the crime committed? What was the sequence of events (e.g. modelled through blood spatter analysis)? Thirdly, a forensic investigation may assist in either supporting or refuting a hypothesis. For example, if one hypothesis is that the offender entered the house through the front door, what evidence should be present to support this?[15] Fourthly, a suspect or witness's account of events may be either supported or refuted by a forensic investigation. For example, a suspect (with an eye to a manslaughter plea) may claim that the body of deceased was not moved after death, but hypostasis (or "post-mortem lividity") may indicate otherwise.

Finally, forensic investigation may provide opportunities for developing a criminal investigation by helping to develop the lines of an enquiry. An obvious example is a DNA profile obtained from material left behind at the scene of a crime linked to an existing profile on the National DNA Database.

Given that forensic investigation may reveal intelligence and evidence of invaluable use to a criminal investigation, and often of a scientific nature, there still remains the considerable challenge of interpreting the meaning of this information. Generic textbooks on forensic science normally offer little on the subject. For example, in Jackson and Jackson's popular undergraduate text on forensic science referred to earlier in this chapter, only five pages (from p. 395) are devoted explicitly to the subject. There are undoubtedly understandable reasons for this, not least of which is the complexity of ideas such as Bayes' Theorem[16] when complex situations involving chance elements are to be analysed. However, the interpretation of evidence is of central importance when the results of forensic investigation are scrutinised by the criminal justice system, and most notably in that small minority of criminal cases in the UK that reach the Crown Court. There are well-documented examples of errors of interpretation of scientifically based evidence leading to miscarriages of justice, for instance during the trial in 1975 (after a Provisional IRA bombing campaign in England during the previous year) of six Irishmen charged with murder and conspiracy to cause explosions (the "Birmingham Six"). A forensic scientist at the trial testified that, after performing the appropriate chemical tests, he was 99% certain that the test showed the presence of nitroglycerine in material found on the hands of some of the accused (Walker & Stockdale, 1995, p. 87).

The scientist concerned had used a presumptive test,[17] where a reagent changes colour in the presence of certain chemicals. In this case the reagent was chosen so that it would change colour in the presence of compounds containing nitrates, common ingredients of improvised explosive devices. However, the presumptive test used (as with all such tests) would occasionally not react even in the presence of nitrates, which accounted for why 99% was cited rather than 100%. The

Birmingham Six were found guilty and sentenced to life imprisonment.[18] Subsequent investigations in the mid-1980s revealed that the presumptive test used also gave positive results in the presence of many other types of sample other than explosives, including playing cards and cigarettes. Hence there was a plausible explanation for the positive tests on the accused other than that they had handled explosives.

In probability terms[19], the forensic scientist's claim at the trial can be expressed as follows:

P(explosive present | positive test) = 0.99

(Where the symbol | means "given that" or "assuming that")

The tests in the mid-1980s, however, indicated that this probability was very unlikely to be as high as 0.99 (99%). Indeed, at the time of the trial the value was probably unknown, even unknowable. Instead the scientist concerned had erroneously reversed the probabilities involved and in fact should have cited at the trial (if only it were relevant) the probability

P(positive test | explosive present) = 0.99

This is a very different statement from the previous conditional probability, but can appear beguilingly similar in the context of a criminal trial. It is essentially the statement that this particular test is 99% effective in identifying the presence of explosives if they are indeed present. It tells us nothing about the other substances (not involving explosives) which might also give a positive reaction. The error of reversing the probabilities, and assuming they are the same is usually referred to as the "Prosecutor's Fallacy".[20]

More recently there have been other damaging examples of the misinterpretation of scientific evidence. In 1999, Sally Clark was convicted of the murder of her two sons.[21] Both sons had died as infants, one at 11 weeks, the other at eight weeks. The prosecution of Sally Clark relied upon the evidence of Sir Roy Meadow, Emeritus Professor of Paediatrics and one of three such expert witnesses at the trail.

During questioning, Sir Roy Meadow was asked about the likelihood of two successive Sudden Infant Death Syndrome (SIDS) deaths in a family and explained[22] to the court that "you have to multiply 1 in 8,543 times 1 in 8,543 and I think it gives that in the penultimate paragraph. It points out that it's approximately a chance of 1 in 73 million",[23] adding that "in England, Wales and Scotland there are about say 700,000 live births a year, so it is saying by that happening will occur about once every hundred years". He later went on to draw an analogy with winning the Grand National[24] in three successive years by gambling on an "80 to 1" horse each year.

However, multiplying probabilities together in the way that Meadow did requires that each event (in this case a SIDS death) is independent of the other. If the events are not independent, perhaps because of some underlying genetic reason in the case of a SIDS death, then the probabilities cannot be simply multiplied together in this way. If a compound probability is required, alternative ways should be used to establish the likelihood of two successive SIDS deaths using Bayes' Theorem (see above) rather than simple multiplication. As the GMC subsequently observed, the problem lay in the fact that "Professor Meadow is not a statistician and had no relevant expertise which entitled him to use the statistics in the way he did" (GMC v Meadow, [2006] EWCA Civ 1390). The statistics quoted by Sir Roy Meadow, particularly his analogy with the "long shots" in the Grand National, may well have erroneously influenced the deliberations of the jury in the trial (GMC v Meadow, [2006] EWCA Civ 1390).

CONCLUSION

Both forensic science and forensic investigation have important contributions to make to a criminal investigation. There are, however, vital distinctions between forensic science and forensic investigation. The interpretation of scientifically derived information, intelligence and evidence is a particular challenge and errors made in the interpretation have led to a number of miscarriages of justice.

NOTES

1. Greenwood *et al.*, 1977; Innes, 2003; McGurk *et al.*, 1994; Smith & Flanagan, 2000, and other studies.
2. A "rookie" in this context is the new detective – a new recruit who has served a number of years in uniform but may just be starting out in detective work (Hobbs, 1988).
3. The cultural vacuum Hobbs refers to identifies both the isolation of the detective from his or her working colleagues and the detective's presence in the company of the community. It is this presence and isolation that result in the "cultural photosynthesis" where cultural cues, habits, speech and behaviour in witnesses are mimicked and finally become part of the detective's own cultural identity (Hobbs, 1988).

4. Reasons include insufficient evidence, perceived or actual false allegation and early victim withdrawal.
5. Throughout this section, rape will be considered in terms of its most frequently occurring dyad, male offender and female victim. Greenfield (1997, cited in Avakame, 1999) identifies that more than 91% of rape victims are female and nearly 99% of offenders are male. It is acknowledged that rape occurs between other dyads, but for the sake of clarity and consistency only the male offender–female victim dyad will be considered in this section.
6. One might even speculate that for most individuals concerned they may not even have considered a "forensic" career before this point of their training.
7. That is, forensic investigation will usually involve crime scene investigation.
8. Particularly if it happens to be somewhat unusual in some respect – for example, rarity.
9. As we saw in Chapter 3, the concept of randomness is a deep one.
10. In terms of DNA evidence, where similar questions occur, the probabilities of a "random match" are almost always calculated and may feature in a subsequent judicial process.
11. Indeed the suspect may have become a suspect precisely because their shoeprint matched a speculative search of a footwear database.
12. There were probably other reasons, such as the time-consuming nature of anthropometry.
13. This is even the case for identical (monozygotic) twins over time, as recent research (Bruder *et al.*, 2008) demonstrates that epigenetic factors result in changes in the copy number of genes and sequences of DNA. However, it remains the case that the DNA profiles of monozygotic twins are highly likely to be identical at any stage of their lives.
14. Discussed in Chapter 3.
15. Hypothesis testing is discussed more fully in Chapter 3.
16. Bayes' Theorem is a way of mathematically calculating combined events without assuming that one event is independent of the other. It is normally used in forensic investigation when the probabilities of separate pieces of evidence are combined.
17. Presumptive tests, as the name implies, are designed to test for the presence of a particular chemical substance (e.g. cocaine) and are used largely for the purposes of screening. A positive presumptive test is usually followed by a fuller chemical analysis of the substance, for example by using gas chromatography.
18. All six were subsequently cleared by the Court of Appeal in 1991.

19. See Chapter 3 for further explanation of conditional probability.
20. The term "Prosecutor's Fallacy" has also come to be used to describe any error of statistical argument that is employed by the prosecution, but is used here in its original sense.
21. Sally Clark was subsequently cleared by the Court of Appeal in 2003. She died in March 2007.
22. The record of Sir Roy Meadow's testimony during the trial of Sally Clark is taken from R v Clark [2003] EWCA Crim 1020 (11 April 2003).
23. 8543 x 8543 = 72,982,549, approximately 73 million.
24. The Grand National is a popular annual steeplechase in England. Odds of 80 to 1 indicate that the horse is highly unlikely to win the race. Winning the race three years in succession by backing an 80 to 1 outsider would therefore be very unlikely indeed.

REVIEW QUESTIONS

1. What are the key characteristics of the "due process" and "crime control" models?
2. What are the main weaknesses of detective practice as illustrated in the research?
3. What factors influence how rape victims are treated by the police?
4. What is the "real rape" stereotype?
5. What are the main distinctions between forensic science and forensic investigation?
6. What are the "Theory of Individualisation" and "Locard's Principle"?

QUESTIONS FOR FURTHER RESEARCH AND ANALYSIS

1. Is the achievement of "absolute truth" as opposed to "beyond reasonable doubt" a realistic objective?
2. What other new developments (not identified in this chapter) are being proposed or introduced to help improve the conviction rate for rape?
3. How are the random match probabilities calculated in the case of low copy number DNA profiles?

RECOMMENDED READING

"Proof" or "truth"

Choongh, S. (1997). *Policing as a social discipline*. Oxford: Clarendon Press.

Ericson, R.V. (1993). *Making crime: A study of detective work* (2nd edn.). Toronto: University of Toronto Press.

Gelsthorpe, L. (2001a). Crime control model. In E. McLaughlin & J. Muncie (eds.) *The Sage dictionary of criminology* (pp. 61–63). London: Sage Publications.

Gelsthorpe, L. (2001b). Due process model. In E. McLaughlin & J. Muncie (eds.), *The Sage dictionary of criminology* (pp. 104–106). London: Sage Publications.

Hobbs, D. (1988). *Doing the business: Entrepreneurship, detectives and the working class in the East End of London*. Oxford: Oxford University Press.

McConville, M., Sanders, A. & Leng, R. (1991). *The case for the prosecution: Police suspects and the construction of criminality*. London: Routledge.

Sanders, A. & Young, R. (2007). From suspect to trial. In M. Maguire, R. Morgan & R. Reiner (eds.). *The Oxford handbook of criminology* (4th edn., pp. 953–989). Oxford: Oxford University Press.

Smith, D.J. (1997). Case construction and the goals of criminal process. *British Journal of Criminology*, *37*(3), 319–346.

Stevens, J. (2002). *The search for the truth in the criminal justice system*. University of Leicester Convocation/Haldane Lecture, 6 March 2002. http://www.le.ac.uk/press/press/scalesofjustice2.html

Investigating sexual offences

Brown, J.M., Hamilton, C. & O'Neill, D. (2007). Characteristics associated with rape attrition and the role played by skepticism or legal rationality by investigators and prosecutors. *Psychology, Crime and Law*, *13*(4), 355–370.

Feist, A., Ashe, J., Lawrence, J., McPhee, D. & Wilson, R. (2007). *Investigating and detecting recorded offences of rape*. Home Office Online Report 18/07.

Harris, J. & Grace, S. (1999). *A question of evidence? Investigating and prosecuting rape in the 1990s*. London: Home Office.

HMCPSI (2007). *Without consent: A report on the joint review of the investigation and prosecution of rape offences*. http://inspectorates.homeoffice.gov.uk/hmic/inspections/thematic/wc-thematic/them07-wc.pdf?view=Binary (accessed 12 Sept. 2008).

Horvath, M.A.H. & Brown, J.M. (eds.) (2009). *Rape: Challenging contemporary thinking*. Cullompton: Willan Publishing.

Kelly, L., Lovett, J. & Regan, L. (2005). *A gap or a chasm? Attrition in reported rape cases*. Home Office Research Study 293. London: Home Office.

NPIA & ACPO (2005). *Guidance on investigating serious sexual offences*. Bedfordshire: ACPO/Centrex.

Sexual Offences Act (2003). http://www.legislation.hmso.gov.uk/acts/acts2003/30042-b.htm (accessed 6 June 2008).

Temkin, J. & Krahé, B. (2008). *Sexual assault and the justice gap: A question of attitude*. Oxford, Hart Publishing.

Criminal investigation and forensic investigation

Aitken, C. & Faroni, F. (2004). *Statistics and the evaluation of evidence for forensic scientists* (2nd edn.). Chichester: John Wiley & Sons.

Fraser, J. & Williams, R. (2009). *Handbook of forensic science.* Cullompton: Willan Publishing.

CHAPTER 9

Professionalising Investigation

STEPHEN TONG

INTRODUCTION

This chapter aims to outline the challenges to the professionalisation of the police service with specific reference to detective work. In order to do this, it is important to attempt to define what a professional police service would look like. With this in mind, the work of Niederhoffer and Kleinig is discussed, providing a platform for further examination of the issue, and from this basis we analyse some of the difficulties police training has faced in the past, followed by more specific commentary on the available evidence on detective training, and a brief description of attempts to improve detective work through the Professionalising Investigation Programme (PIP). The distinction between the role of education and training is discussed before outlining different approaches to education and training. Finally, we give a brief overview of two studies aimed at articulating the role of detectives to assist with the development of a curriculum designed for the education and training of detectives.

DEFINING PROFESSION

The label "profession" provides the basis of credibility, knowledge, expertise and status relating to work activities. Law and medicine are traditionally recognised as professions and are used as templates for the "ideal type" by other groups who wish to attain the same status (Erautt, 1994). However, Erautt argues that there are a number of other occupations that seek the full professional status of these traditional professions. The challenge for these aspiring professions is not only to wrestle with the definition of what it means to be a profession but to provide sufficient evidence of knowledge and expertise to be considered as such.

Arthur Niederhoffer (1967, p. 17) argued that policing in America was "ripe for professionalisation" with an increasingly complex society and advances in technology. This appealed to the middle-class college men who during the economic depression of the 1930s, joined the police service in larger numbers than in the past. However, the barriers to professionalisation in the United States included a poor public perception of police officers cultivated by the media, and resistance from less educated and more traditionally focused officers. It is clear that, in order to "professionalise", the police needed to change.

Niederhoffer (1967) identified a number of requirements for a job to become a profession, ranging from the achievement of high standards to public recognition of status. Kleinig (1996) agreed with Niederhoffer on some of these requirements, particularly a code of ethics, specialist knowledge and expertise, and self-regulation. It is these characteristics that have always been the most challenging for the police service to achieve.

The key requirement to achieve professionalisation appears to be specialist knowledge and expertise. Without this basis many of the other requirements cannot be achieved. In November 2005 Sir Ian Blair, commenting on the role of the police service and the need for public engagement, identifies the need to develop police knowledge:

> We have been a service which has always been separate and silent, which successive governments – until recently – ... have broadly left alone to get on with the job... For health, there is a King's Fund

Table 9.1 Characteristics of a profession

Kleinig (1996)	Niederhoffer (1967)
1. Provision of public service	1. High standards
2. Code of ethics	2. A special body of knowledge and theory
3. Special knowledge and expertise	3. Altruism and dedication to the service ideal
4. Higher education	4. A lengthy period of training for candidates
5. Autonomy and discretion	5. A code of ethics
6. Self-regulation	6. Licensing of members
	7. Autonomous control
	8. Pride of the members in their profession
	9. Publicly recognised status and prestige

and endless university departments for research, a National Institute of Clinical Excellence, an Agenda for Change. For education, there have been impassioned debates since Shirley Williams led comprehensivisation, since Kenneth Baker proposed grant-maintained schools, since Tony Blair said "Education, education, education" – and he's saying it again now, isn't he? Transport and the environment are the subject of think tanks and policy works. Even the BBC – blessed Auntie – is not immune: but not policing.

BBC (2005) Transcript of Sir Ian Blair's speech available from http://news.bbc.co.uk/1/hi/uk/4443386.stm

Blair argues that informed policing commentary is "piecemeal" and clearly illustrates the role of research and universities in contributing to professional status of health and education. So although professions require appropriate training and education for their members, there is also a need to develop knowledge generation through research, in order for the profession to maintain its status and remain informed despite changes that may affect practice.

Currently knowledge generation and research on policing-related matters are developed through the Home Office through the identification and implementation of key areas of research, and funding councils that offer the opportunity for organisations and universities to bid for money for research. The National Police Improvement Agency (NPIA) is engaged with doctrine development, providing manuals and guidelines for practitioners (see Chapter 2). Despite what appears to be substantial research and information generation, how this information is used and how effectively it is transferred to the workplace is unknown. This knowledge can be accessed internally through police sources (e.g. the ACPO *Murder Investigation Manual*), downloading off the internet (e.g. Home Office reports) and through education and training (delivery through direct teaching and independent research). However, as has been the case for many years, police recruits or trainee detectives have not been directed to broad areas of research but to legislation, cases, and policy sources of information that are focused on a narrow curriculum in order to reduce abstraction from operational duty (Morgan, 1990; Tong, 2005). Therefore the effectiveness or otherwise of the transfer of knowledge generation into professional practice requires further investigation.

POLICE TRAINING

In recent times, the focus on the need for the police to train and develop effective officers has intensified (HMIC, 1999a) because of criticisms of police performance and inadequate training (Bayley & Bittner,

1989; Fielding, 1988, HMIC, 1999b, HMIC, 2002; Macpherson, 1999; Stephens, 1988; UEA, 1987). Although there has been a lack of independent research into police training, there has been regular internal police evaluation. Unfortunately, most of the research and evaluation conducted on police training by training organisations or police services remains unavailable for independent analysis (Reiner, 1992). That is, the relationship between classroom-based training and practice has been under-researched.

The provision of an informed analysis of an apparent "cause-and-effect" relationship between training and the practice of police work is extremely difficult, and essentially requires a qualitative and quantitative approach (Bayley & Bittner, 1989). Unsurprisingly, it appears that such a relationship is complicated by the fact that people learn in different ways and at different speeds and that there are similar variations in the application of skills and knowledge to practical situations (HMIC, 1999a). Police trainees respond differently to teaching styles and curriculum content, while placing different values on what they learn (Fielding, 1988). Moreover, the police recruit a wide variety of personnel, including graduate entrants, those with little education, and those with considerable work experience from previous occupations. The implication of having such a diverse range of personnel is that the police are faced with particular challenges when attempting to develop officers with skills and knowledge that comply with minimum standards. The report *Training Matters* (HMIC, 2002, p. 56) identified key weaknesses in training, including inconsistent and inadequate training delivery and operational supervision resulting in probationers[1] completing their training with "significant development needs". The report argued that trainees were bypassing the assessment system, attaining skills that were described as "barely adequate" (HMIC, 2002, p. 24). These important findings point to fundamental concerns about how training is conducted, and this undoubtedly leads to concerns regarding the likely impact of inadequate training on police performance. Furthermore, with disagreement over performance measurement criteria (Reiner, 1998) and what counts as good police work, the development of a curriculum for police training becomes increasingly problematic.

As society has demanded a more sensitive police service aware of cultural diversity and civil rights, an increasing number of police training programmes have been introduced (Benyon, 1987; Lee & Punch, 2006; Macpherson, 1999; Wells, 1987). Despite public inquiries and political pressure in the 1980s, many of these programmes have not been effective (Macpherson, 1999). A move away from a dominant didactic mode of training delivery has been encouraged by HMIC, with the cautionary note that further research is required (HMIC, 1999b). Despite the need for more research being clearly identified, nearly a decade later there has been no significant independent research on police training (and nothing on detective training). While the focus of the available evidence has tended to be on probationary training, many of the lessons drawn are applicable to the specialist training police officers receive, including detective training. Moreover, the failures of probationary training can have a direct impact upon the development of police *officers* later in their careers when they pursue specialisation, particularly in the role of detective.

The introduction of the Initial Police Learning and Development Programme (IPLDP) in 2006 provided the basis for the reform of initial police training in response to the *Training Matters* report. However, there appears to be a broad range of delivery strategies, with some police services working in partnership with universities and others delivering "in-house" training with variations in the proportion of direct teaching and workplace learning. At the time of writing there has been no independent research examining the effectiveness or otherwise of these reforms and whether the shortcomings of the past have been addressed.

DETECTIVE TRAINING

The expectations of detectives fresh out of training school have been commented upon by a former Metropolitan Police Commander, R. Harvey:

> Nobody should expect that the satisfactory completion of the initial CID course or any other specialist course produces an investigator, but it does produce a good base on which to build and gives the young officer confidence. Regrettably, the pressures of today are such that all too often the embryo detective is launched into the CID after the course as a fully-fledged investigator. In an ideal world, he or she would serve their apprenticeship under strict supervision. Unfortunately, owing to the pressures of today those who should be supervising and giving advice and further training are themselves overburdened; and sometimes they also are lamentably short of experience.
>
> (1984, pp. 48–49)

A number of issues arise from these comments, namely the lack of supervision, training and experience. Maguire and Norris (1992) noted the lack of supervision of detectives' work, reinforcing Harvey's observations. It is apparent that these inadequacies in the process of learning detective work may have significant implications in the context of effectiveness. This point is particularly significant because of the craft model of learning that has dominated police training in general but also specifically detective training, where much of the learning is conducted "on the job" (Stelfox, 2007, p. 643). If detectives are inadequately prepared and supported, not only will they struggle to be competent in their duties but they may also have difficulty in keeping up to date with the continually changing legal and technological context in which they work. It seems that the problems experienced in terms of the lack of supervision and the early responsibilities thrust onto inexperienced detectives were still cause for concern almost 20 years after Maguire and Norris's research (Chatterton, 2008; Tong, 2005).

The commitment to highly structured, classroom-based approaches appears to have impacted upon the range of police training provisions. Traditionally police courses have adopted a "block" training approach to delivery. That is, rather than having an incremental approach to training where students develop their knowledge over time through distance learning, interactive learning and monitored experience, students are instead provided with a comparatively "short sharp shot" of training. For example, traditionally probationary training was usually one 15-week block of continuous training (or similar) at a District Training Centre. Similarly, detective training used to be 10 weeks of continuous training, reduced to six weeks in 1990s (Hufton & Buswell, 2000; Morgan, 1990). When detectives complete this initial training they become fully qualified detectives. This presents a picture of a small degree of training pressed into a short period of time. Rather than co-ordinated training reflecting trainees' needs, using a range of supporting learning methods over a reasonable period of time, training can be booked into one block where trainees are allocated a short period of training before returning to the workplace (Hufton & Buswell, 2000). Although this model minimises the need to take staff away from operational duties, it does not reflect a student-centred approach or indeed answer the long-term concerns about effective detective practice. Moreover, this model of training does not necessarily allow adequate reflection, as training is conducted over a compressed period of time (Hufton & Buswell, 2000).

More recently the NPIA has taken responsibility of PIP, an initiative with the remit to "Improve the professional competence of all police officers and staff who are tasked with conducting investigations" (NPIA,

2007). This new approach to investigative training aims to provide different levels (1–3) of competence for investigators. The PIP levels refer to Level 1 (patrol constable/police staff/supervisor), Level 2 (dedicated investigators, e.g. CID officers and specialist investigation such as child abuse investigation) and Level 3 (senior investigating officers) (Stelfox, 2007, p. 641). This is aimed at explicitly requiring levels of investigative competence to be achieved for a range of investigating officers. The introduction of registration for senior investigative officers appears to be an attempt to control the standards of lead detectives centrally (e.g. NPIA). Stelfox (2007) argues that the term "professionalising" in this context refers to attempts to improve investigation rather than reflecting the characteristics identified by Niederhoffer or Kleinig. This is perhaps not surprising given the challenges the PIP team faces in co-ordinating 43 different forces, the absence of one single professional body and the expense of commissioning research (Stelfox, 2007) aimed at advancing knowledge in the field of criminal investigation. The potential challenges for the new programme have already been highlighted in the Police Federation-sponsored report 'Losing the Detectives', in which the author comments:

The evidence from this study does not augur well for the new Professionalising Criminal Investigation Programme (PIP). Recruiting suitable TDCs (Trainee Detective Constables) is a problem. TDCs are not treated as trainees, are given a full crime-load immediately (sometimes before they start their course) and they are not mentored as well as they should be. This is a reflection of SMT's lack of commitment to the programme and their concern with achieving organisational outcomes at the expense of promoting professional practice.

(Chatterton, 2008, p. xii)

A comprehensive analysis of the strengths and weaknesses of PIP is difficult given the lack of independent evaluation. There is little publicly available material on PIP (see Chapter 2 above for further information) or internal evaluation of the programme, but it is evident that detective training in the past did require change to meet demands made on the modern detective. It is anticipated that the initial development of PIP will be completed in 2009, and perhaps at this point independent evaluation of the new arrangements may be forthcoming.

DISTINCTION BETWEEN POLICE TRAINING AND EDUCATION

The development and delivery of knowledge and expertise traditionally take place through training and education; within policing, training has traditionally been the dominant mode of learning and development. Although training and education can be delivered using similar techniques, the content and intention can be quite different. Building on the work of Timm and Christian (1991), who provide a list of contrasting strengths and weaknesses of both training and education in the context of policing, Haberfeld (2002) conducted his own analysis of the role of training and education in policing. He identifies training as the acquisition of skills, learning police procedure and performing tasks, in contrast to education, which focuses on research, categorising, evaluating and understanding, learning new facts and ideas, and communicating perspectives effectively both orally and in writing.

It is apparent from the lists in Table 9.2 that training aims to provide responses to fixed practical scenarios that can be delivered in a short time. Education, on the other hand, is less specific and requires a level of interpretation and application on the part of the student. In England and Wales, police training has conformed predominantly to a training model, which contains little opportunity for education. Training is considered to be a short-term intervention that is required for specialisation or new recruits. Indeed, the National Crime Faculty has raised concerns regarding the resistance of police culture to life-long learning, a concept that implies education rather than training (NPT, 1999). Although the need for both training (skills) and education (knowledge) is clear, the challenge for the police service is to deliver an appropriate balance of training and education to develop effective officers for the long and short term.

APPROACHES TO LEARNING

Workplace Learning

The academic literature points to evidence suggesting police officers believe that the best method of learning is in the workplace (learning through experience), learning a craft[2] from experienced officers in the operational environment (Bayley & Bittner, 1989; Chan, 2003; Fielding, 1988). This belief arises, in some cases, from a suspicion of academia, and proponents reject learning in training school or methods such as classroom-based lectures as irrelevant, in favour of the "real police work" to be learned on the streets (Bayley & Bittner, 1989; Fielding,

Table 9.2   Advantages and disadvantages of training and education

Training	Education
Advantages	
- Training prepares a person with a ready response in case of emergency - "Programmed" responses can be attained through intensive training - Research is used to determine the best response - Training makes people feel more confident - Training leads to quicker and more efficient responses - Training leads to more consistent responses that are in accordance with the authority - The training process is concentrated and inexpensive - Skills that require hands-on training are acquired efficiently - Training provides an alternative solution to people who do not have the interest or ability to find their own solution - Training decreases the likelihood of being sued because of the appropriate training for specific situations	- Skills can be applied to various situations - Education results in a wider range of knowledge, and more intelligent communication skills - Education provides knowledge of how to create good training programmes - Education may result in more worldly knowledge and thereby more tolerance of differences - Education takes the student through an extensive programme that prepares him or her for a wide range of occupations - Education provides greater awareness of contemporary and historical events - Education provides people with better logical solutions - Education provides problem-solving skills, critical thinking, and communication skills
Disadvantages	
- Training is situation-specific, and no two situations are the same - It can be difficult to improvise a solution if the problem differs from training - Correct responses tend to change more often than appropriate training - Training eliminates creativity in responses - Training may result in people who are unhappy with the responses the training provides	- Education is often expensive and has a diffuse focus - Education does not provide specific technical training - Programmes are long and people may not have the interest to complete them - Programmes offer no "pat" answers, which can be frustrating

1988; Young, 1991). The resistance of the occupational culture is a serious concern as organisations such as National Police Training (now known as NPIA) consider alternative approaches to training such as lifelong learning (NPT, 1999). The alternative nature of lifelong learning challenges traditional notions of a police culture that is resistant to learning and change; lifelong learning presents a learning model that embraces change through learning. Despite this perceived resistance, academics argue that police officers need reflection and rational analysis in order to develop professional practice, and to allow new recruits to learn policing skills more effectively and efficiently (Bayley & Bittner, 1989; Birzer, 2003; Fish & Coles, 1998; Foster, 1999; Neyroud & Beckley, 2001). While debates concerning the best method of learning have in the past involved criticisms directed at the police, it is also important to acknowledge that academics have a vested interest in "portraying policing as amenable to science"[3] (Bayley & Bittner, 1989, p. 87). The search continues for an appropriate solution to the training of police officers and facilitating an effective outcome in the practice of police work. A key question is "What works?" in both training and practice (Hayley, 1992).

Mentoring

The research available on mentoring in a police context is focused on tutor constables during the field training of probationer officers. There are a number of studies that have considered the usefulness or otherwise of tutor constables in police training (Chan, 2003; Fielding, 1988; Haberfeld, 2002; Holdaway & Barron 1997; Stradling & Harper, 1988; UEA, 1987). Mentoring in a policing context represents an attempt by the police service to plug the gap between theory and practice (Chan, 2003; Fielding, 1988), to ensure that recruit learning in the classroom is of benefit when conducting police work. The structure of police recruit training generally follows a pattern whereby the recruit spends a period of time at a training school learning the law and police skills in the classroom, followed by training "on the job" with the guidance of a tutor constable (Chan, 2003; Fielding, 1988). The latter period of training is aimed at gently introducing the "rookie cop" to the realities of police work. It is during this period of mentoring that ultimately decisions are made on whether the recruit completes their probationary training (Holdaway & Barron, 1997).

The process of mentoring could be considered a challenging prospect for course designers. It represents a clash of cultures within policing when the new recruits leave training school. After learning theory in the classroom, the recruits meet and ultimately depend upon police officers on the streets to get through the remainder of their training.

There has been a well-documented history of police officers advising recruits to forget what they learned in formal classroom training in favour of what they can learn in practice (Bayley & Bittner, 1989; Chan, 2003). This negativity does not bode well for an objective process of learning and discredits any attempt to make a link between theory and practice. Rather than categorise mentoring as an ineffective method, it is arguable that increased attention could be focused on the selection of tutors; if tutors do not have the necessary knowledge and abilities then the chances of trainees receiving comprehensive guidance are reduced.

While, in theory, mentoring offers the potential to bridge the gap between theory and practice, there are a number of shortcomings that have been found in a policing context. In Chan's (2003) study there are criticisms consistent with other research, including the lack of communication between police stations and the academy (Fielding, 1988). However, Chan's research reveals that there is no quality assurance procedure for the appointment of field training officers (FTOs) (Fielding, 1988; Holdaway & Barron, 1997), and that field training is delivered in an ad hoc/unstructured manner (Fielding, 1988). The FTOs were also critical of the academic programme (Bayley & Bittner, 1989): they perceived field training as having a low priority in the organisation, while trainees did not believe that the FTOs provided honest feedback. So the research evidence continually points to failings in the use of mentoring in police training. From this it appears that shortcomings in the training system are not being addressed, and that there is a considerable gap between approaches in learning in the academy and "on the job" training. This disparity represents two different styles of learning: the academy assists recruits to understand through theory, and policing develops recruits "on the job" through practice.

Although these studies have identified some problems with mentoring, it is important to note that tutoring in the workplace can only be effective if the appropriate support structures are in place. Officers with experience in training would have the knowledge of the training process and the curriculum to be delivered. Officers who are not routinely involved with all aspects of investigation will not necessarily be up to date and therefore unable to provide the trainee with the appropriate support. The literature shows that mentoring is less effective if the selection of tutors and support mechanisms for trainees do not underpin the approach.

Pedagogical Approaches

Police training has been described as didactic and rooted in cognitive pedagogical approaches to learning. That is, the delivery of skills and knowledge is through instruction and lecture styles that imply a "one size fits all" approach[4] to delivering training. Birzer (2003) uses the analogy of two pails: one empty, the other full. Through instruction, the trainer is metaphorically pouring the full pail (representing the expert knowledge of the trainer) into the empty pail (the learner gaining a full pail of knowledge). However, as Birzer (2003) identifies, there are few advantages to this approach: the main criticism is that linear, orderly and planned approaches are not able to meet the needs of police officers engaged with problem-solving and uncertainty in the context of their work. The academic and professional literature has repeatedly pointed to the gulf between training and practice (Bayley & Bittner, 1989; Fielding, 1988; Home Office, 2002). Police attitudes that value experience rather than classroom-based approaches (Bayley & Bittner, 1989; Fielding, 1988), reflecting the "sink or swim" existence of police trainees, can be particularly problematic (Stephens, 1988). The relationships in the police training context between theory and practice, training and implementation are weak, polarised and do not work in partnership to allow the development of practice. Police culture can also play a negative part in occupational learning, in that it is resistant to change, and rejects book-learning or problem-solving approaches in favour of traditional approaches to policing and crime fighting (Beckley & Neyroud, 2001; Fielding, 1988; Wright, 2002).

Andragogical Approaches

Andragogy as a learning style is in direct opposition to pedagogical learning. Rather than the teacher instructing and passing on knowledge to students, the teacher's role is one of facilitator, with students embracing a self-directed approach to learning (Birzer, 2003). This approach places a responsibility for learning upon the student, with the organisation playing a supporting role. This requires a commitment from the organisation to ensure that learning resources are available to allow the teacher to facilitate the learning, and from the students to ensure the resources are used through self-directed study that exploits a range of learning techniques and opportunities. Recognising that different people learn in different ways and at different speeds requires flexibility in the approaches selected by the students to meet their learning needs. Birzer (2003) argues that pedagogical methods have their place in police training, but that andragogical approaches are better suited in the context of problem-solving, community-orientated police work. Although there is a range of policing styles, from community policing through to intelligence-led approaches, the emphasis on problem-solving and reflection on practice still remain critical (Gill, 2000; Goldstein, 1990). Indeed, patrol and investigation both encompass scenarios where problem-orientated approaches are required. While traditional police training methods have been associated with pedagogical instruction, particularly in the context of teaching law (Morgan, 1990), in practice flexibility and unfamiliar scenarios actually require interpretation, discretion and decision-making to solve problems and frame best practice. In order for police officers to ensure appropriate decisions are made from the information available, training and learning styles need to reflect the uncertainty of police work and the principles that should inform practice. However, although the andragogical style of learning provides some hope of improving the training of police officers, the resistance of police culture to such an approach is sure to have an impact on its success or otherwise.

Needless to say, this does not have to be an "either/or" debate: both pedagogical and andragogical approaches for training police officers may be appropriate. Haberfeld (2002) argues that there are some elements of police training that require instruction along the lines of pedagogical approaches, such as memorising the law. Although recalling and remembering training is important in terms of officers applying what they have learned, it is also important that they understand the principles of what they have learned and can apply this knowledge in a range of practical scenarios. So learning styles can include a mixture of strategies and techniques. However, these approaches must be applied in the context of student-centred learning, where the learner is responsible for managing their own development. It is also essential to such an approach that the facilitator has a range of methods and resources available from which students can manage their own development. Rather, the question central to police training is how the gulf between training and practice can be reduced and how the effectiveness of best practice through learning can be improved.

DETECTIVE PRACTICE: SUMMARY OF THE LITERATURE

In order to provide the appropriate knowledge and expertise in any training or education curriculum, an understanding of detective work and learning needs is required. A detailed analysis of detective tasks can be found in "Detectives: A Job and Training Needs Analysis" (McGurk et al., 1994): this not only considers detectives' activities but the range, difficulty, importance and frequency of particular tasks required of detectives. Roles soon become associated with personal characteristics. McGurk et al. did not seek to design detective training courses but rather to provide a skills directory from which course designers could use their experience and judgement to formulate course content. Their findings, based on analysis of four police forces, can be summarised as follows:

1. Tasks that were both difficult and important but which were carried out less frequently were more suited to specialised training rather than a multi-disciplinary initial course.
2. A task that is not important but is frequently performed and easy to learn would not require the attention that should be given to an infrequently performed but critical task that is difficult to learn – this must be left to the judgement of those experienced in detective training.
3. No differences were identified between the four forces (Metropolitan, Greater Manchester, Hertfordshire and Cumbria police services) that took part in the study.
4. Results indicated that the work of a Metropolitan Police detective is essentially no different to the work of a detective in the other three forces.
5. Conclusion: the results of this job and training needs analysis provide a sound empirically derived basis for designing courses (and selection criteria) for detective training.

McGurk *et al.* argue that the information generated by this study needs to be applied by experienced course designers, selecting the important, less practised skills as key content for trainers. Since 1994 detective work has evolved, influenced by the National Intelligence Model, new public management, additional legislation and advances in new technology, as well as changes in society. So although the research may have been relevant in 1994, there have been substantial changes since this study was published.

McGurk *et al.* (1994) identified the most difficult and important tasks as interviewing prisoners, presenting evidence in court, interviewing witnesses, establishing rapport with suspects, arresting suspects, establishing a rapport with informants and preparing files. The difficulty of tasks is changing for detectives in some contexts. Establishing a rapport with informants is listed as one such task, yet with increasing reliance on intelligence and intelligence-led policing methods, the use of informants is likely to be a task conducted more frequently (Amey *et al.*, 1996). The frequency of interviewing prisoners, on the other hand, has decreased as there have been clampdowns on police tactics to improve clear-up rates (Loveday, 2000a). Nevertheless, a number of these difficult tasks remain a core aspect of detective work, such as interviewing witnesses, presenting evidence in court and arresting suspects.

So although this research is dated, there is still value that can be extracted that is relevant to modern-day detective training.

McGurk *et al.*'s research also identified the detective tasks that were most frequently carried out, including completing diaries/pocket books, taking statements, interviewing witnesses, preparing files, driving, giving advice to uniformed officers, reading documents (crime reports etc.) and typing tape transcripts. Again these results provide a snapshot of detective work at the time of the study. Developments of civilian roles in the police, proactive methods, increasing specialisation, and the fact that more investigations are being conducted at the end of a telephone have substantially changed the frequency and nature of the detective tasks identified in the research (Amey *et al.*, 1996; Ericson, 1993; Newburn, 2003). The development of DNA testing has increased the use of forensic science by detectives to solve crime rather than relying upon witnesses (Bayley, 2002). If McGurk *et al.* were to use a sample of detectives involved in a proactive unit, they may find that frequent activities include surveillance, searches and the analysis of intelligence. This research illustrates that while some detective tasks will be retained, new tasks will develop, and this change will create new training needs for modern detectives.

More recent research aimed at identifying the skills of an effective SIO by Smith and Flanagan (2000) perhaps provides another perspective in relation to the skills and abilities required of a detective. Smith and Flanagan take a different approach from McGurk *et al.* They selected a semi-structured interview approach using "repertory grid" and "critical incident" techniques to distinguish effective/less effective and good/bad practice. Forty police officers from different ranks were interviewed and their responses analysed. Unlike the previous studies, Smith and Flanagan (2000) organised the responses into 22 skills that were then categorised into three clusters: investigative ability, knowledge levels and management skills. Where McGurk *et al.* (1994) focused on personal characteristics or tasks, Smith and Flanagan (2000) attempted to identify investigative ability and knowledge specifically within the context of detective work. Although this study is focused on the skills of senior detectives rather than detective constables, most of the skills apply generically to the investigative role.

A summary of Smith and Flanagan's investigative ability and knowledge level requirements is given in Table 9.3, which illustrates SIO skill requirements in the chronological order of the development of an investigation. Thus Smith and Flanagan begin with "initial crime scene assessment" and move through to "assessment of incoming information", "selecting appropriate lines of enquiry", "case development" and finally "post-charge case management".

Table 9.3   Skills required of an effective SIO

Pre-charge Case Management: Principal Skill Requirements	
Initial Crime Scene Assessment	
Investigative Ability	**Knowledge Levels**
Investigative competence To start to formulate lines of enquiry **Appraisal of information** To create "slow time" To assimilate information from scene Not to make assumptions To begin to interpret crime scene information **Strategic awareness** To be aware of consequences of actions **Adaptation** To demonstrate flexibility	**Underpinning knowledge** Procedural Knowledge of roles Legal processes Ethical implications Domain knowledge of specific crime types
Assessment of Incoming Information	

Investigative competence
To formulate investigative strategies
To demonstrate ability to learn from
  experience
 	
Appraisal of information
To demonstrate ability to absorb incoming
  information
To establish the reliability and validity of
  information
To play "devil's advocate"
To verify expert advice
To display objectivity
 	
Adaptation
To remain reflexive
	Underpinning knowledge
	Awareness of strengths and weaknesses of
	  team
	Knowledge of roles
	Procedural
	Domain knowledge of specific crime types
	To be aware of specialist advisers that could
	  be approached

Selecting Appropriate Lines of Enquiry	

Investigative competence
To formulate a media strategy
To remain appropriately focused
To develop and test investigative hypotheses
To prioritise lines of enquiry
 	
Appraisal of incoming Information
To continue to display objectivity
To continue to evaluate incoming information
 	
Strategic awareness
To realise how the consequences of actions
  impact on both the force and the community
	Underpinning knowledge
	Procedural
	Knowledge of roles
	Domain knowledge of specific crime types
	Awareness of what resources are required
	  (both staff and finance)
	Knowledge of what resources are available
	Knowledge of how such resources are
	  obtained
	Awareness of specialist advisers that can be
	  approached

Table 9.3 *(Continued)*

Adaptation To remain open, particularly to expert advice To remain flexible	**Future developments** To be aware of current developments in the investigative field To be aware of changes in legislation, forensics and technology

Case Development

Investigative competence To investigate all feasible options **Appraisal of incoming information** To continue to review lines of enquiry To continue to validate incoming information To avoid speculation **Strategic awareness** To realise how the consequences of actions impact on both the force, the community, victim, witness etc. **Adaptation** To remain flexible To remain open-minded **Innovative style** To think laterally To incorporate new developments into the investigation	**Underpinning knowledge** Procedural Domain knowledge of specific crime types Awareness of specialist advisers that can be approached Awareness of what motivates team members **Future developments** To be aware of current developments in the investigative field To be aware of changes in legislation, forensics and technology

Post-charge Case Management

Investigative competence To be aware of possible defence arguments To ensure that all lines of enquiry are completed To demonstrate the ability to learn from experience **Appraisal of information** To question and challenge legal parties	**Underpinning knowledge** Legal processes Court "protocol" for presentation of evidence Rules of disclosure Knowledge concerning content and format of case file Knowledge of roles required **Future developments** To be aware of changes in legislation

Source: Smith & Flanagan, 2000, pp. 19, 21, 24, 27, 30.

These categories not only identify the skills required to complete key stages of the investigative process in the context of serious crime, but also relate more broadly to the demands on investigators. While "knowledge levels" are focused on the law, procedure and expert knowledge, "investigative ability" is focused on lines of enquiry, reflective and lateral thinking while remaining flexible and avoiding assumptions or speculation. Smith and Flanagan's findings suggest a wide range of characteristics that go beyond the findings of McGurk *et al.* Their findings also reflect attributes that are contained within the typologies of the detective as "artist", "craftsperson" or "scientist" (see Chapter 1), such as "lateral thinking", "awareness of consequences" and "developing hypothesis".

Smith and Flanagan (2000) provide a more detailed summary than the previous studies in terms of their conclusion of the skill requirements of a senior detective. There is a strong argument to suggest that the investigative ability and the knowledge levels listed within their summary of findings are also applicable to detective constables. It would be difficult to withdraw any of the criteria as not relevant to a detective's task. It could be argued that more detail is required to identify the particular legislation, occupational standards and theoretical/academic knowledge detectives should be attaining, but that was not the intention of Smith and Flanagan's research.

SUMMARY

This chapter has summarised a general history of police training while presenting some of the limited and dated evidence available to describe detective training. This is important as it provides a background to current developments in detective training and raises some of the key issues that need to be developed. The distinction between training and education has been examined, pointing to some of the strengths and weaknesses of each approach. Finally, two examples of research focused on the work of detectives (McGurk *et al.*, 1994; Smith & Flanagan, 2000) were discussed, drawing out the difficulties in terms of the changing nature of detective work and the intricate details required to develop detective learning.

NOTES

1. Police probationers serve two years learning their role through classroom-based teaching and on-the-job learning. At the end of these two years, if they are successful they will be appointed as a qualified police constable.
2. Skolnick provides a comprehensive description of the craft as practised by the craftsman: "the policeman tends to emphasize his own expertness and specialized abilities to make judgements about measures to be applied to apprehend 'criminals', as well as the ability to estimate accurately the guilt or innocence of suspects. He sees

himself as a craftsman, at his best, a master of his trade" (Skolnick, 1994, p. 197).
3. Universities are increasingly involved with teaching policing studies to police officers and conducting research in various aspects of police work.
4. One size fits all: one training approach for all students. This approach can be problematic because of the variety of learning needs within a group and the uniform standard in which training is delivered.

REVIEW QUESTIONS

1. Outline the strengths and weaknesses of traditional police training.
2. Outline the strengths and weaknesses of pedagogical and andragogical approaches to learning.
3. Identify four advantages/disadvantages in training and educational approaches.

QUESTIONS FOR FURTHER RESEARCH AND ANALYSIS

1. Does mentoring have a place in the professional development of detectives?
2. What are the key differences between PIP and the previous detective training arrangements?
3. How useful is Table 9.3 in identifying skills and abilities required of detectives?

RECOMMENDED READING

Erautt, M. (1994). *Developing professional knowledge and competence*. London: Falmer Press.
Haberfeld, M.R. (2002). *Critical issues in police training*. Upper Saddle River, NJ: Prentice Hall.
HMIC (2002). *Training matters*. London: HMIC.
Morgan, J.B. (1990). *The police function and the investigation of crime*. Aldershot: Avebury.
Newburn, T., Williamson, T. & Wright, A. (2007). The future of investigation. In T. Newburn, T. Williamson & A. Wright (eds.), *Handbook of criminal investigation* (pp. 652–656). Cullompton: Willan Publishing.
Palmiotto, M.J. (ed.) (2003). *Policing and training issues*. Upper Saddle River, NJ: Prentice Hall.

Stelfox, P. (2007). Professionalising criminal investigation. In T. Newburn, T. Williamson & A. Wright (eds.), *Handbook of criminal investigation* (pp. 628–651). Cullompton: Willan Publishing.

WEBSITES

HMIC, Personnel, Training and Diversity: http://www.inspectorates.homeoffice.gov.uk/hmic/ptd/

NPIA, Professionalising the Investigation Programme (PIP): http://www.npia.police.uk/en/10093.htm

NPIA: http://www.npia.police.uk/en/index.htm

Scottish Institute for Police Research: http://www.sipr.ac.uk/

Skills for Justice: http://www.skillsforjustice.com/default.asp?PageID=1

Morris inquiry: http://www.mpa.gov.uk/morrisinquiry/report/03.htm

National Centre for Applied Learning Technologies: http://www.ncalt.com/

CHAPTER 10

Conclusion: Future Challenges in Criminal Investigation

STEPHEN TONG, ROBIN P. BRYANT AND MIRANDA A. H. HORVATH

The history of criminal investigation reveals the continuing challenges facing investigators in their contribution to criminal justice. This book has illustrated that, despite a growing range of evidential sources and investigative methodology moving beyond a reliance on confessionary evidence, rather than a simplification of the investigative process more challenges have arisen. The complexities of investigative processes and the use of scientific techniques are far from providing a "silver bullet" solution to miscarriages of justice or offering foolproof investigations. Rather, the modern detective needs to command a broader range of knowledge and a more critical appreciation of the available evidence than in the past. The typologies of the art, craft and science of detecting provide a useful articulation of how detectives work in practice and potentially offer better understanding of the role of science in a criminal investigation context. The call for more effective detectives is not new, but in order to achieve a professional and effective detective, perhaps greater awareness of the factors influencing criminal investigation outside the control of detectives needs to be achieved.

Although we have critically engaged with the issues surrounding detective practice, there has also been important analysis of the challenges to the development of knowledge, specifically in the fields of criminal investigation; investigative reasoning; the strengths and weaknesses of offender/geographical profiling; the frailties of eyewitness testimony, the importance of carefully conducted inter views; the limitations and influences of the performance measurement regime; the challenges to "the search for the truth"; and the professional development of detectives. The police have had their discretion restricted (Garland, 2001), training and professional development are currently being reformed (Stelfox, 2007), performance is still recognised in quantitative terms (Flanagan, 2008), concerns over detective effectiveness still remain, and morale among detectives appears low (Chatterton, 2008). It would appear that the detective role has suffered since the Desborough Committee (1919) reported that detective training was not required as any learning needs would be met by "experience and practical work". Similarly the view that detectives do not need a high level of investigative skill appears to be still held in some quarters. Rather, the argument is made that crimes of the future will be solved through "docket squads"[1] who will match DNA collected from crime scenes with DNA profiles of people held in custody whose details are stored on a huge database. This perspective may suggest that detectives will no longer be required to investigate; "science", rather than investigative skill, will convict suspects.

The advantages of this approach are huge: savings on staff and training and potentially a more consistent approach to crime investigation. However, this perspective risks the deskilling of detectives and perhaps compromises aspirations to improve the quality of investigation (Maguire *et al.*, 1992). There have been clear problems with the application of science (see Chapter 8) in the cases of fingerprinting,[2] the use of DNA evidence[3] and expert testimony,[4] that illustrate some of the problems with the interpretation of scientific principles applied to investigation. The administration of criminal cases is also an important feature in the success or otherwise of crime investigation. Crimes and offenders are being linked not just through the use of science but through intelligence via the use of informants and from interaction between detectives, suspects, witnesses and offenders. As this book has illustrated through its discussion of theories on reasoning and the use of intelligence (Chapter 3), the challenges of identifying serial offenders (Chapter 4), the complexity of evidence taken from eyewitness accounts (Chapter 5) and the difficulties of suspect interviews (Chapter 6), the detective who truly wants to seek the truth needs to consider the complexities of investigating crimes in often unpredictable and changing circumstances. These chapters have illustrated that the role and professional development of detectives should be enhanced, and not reduced or simplified because of a desire to achieve efficiency gains.

The problems regarding professionalising the police are evident in the substantial differences between high-status professions and the semi-professional structure of the police service in the United Kingdom. There are no educational requirements for anyone wishing to join the police as a constable; the police provide all aspects of training and education to police officers as full-time paid employees, as opposed to professions where entrants usually have a degree in a relevant field before appointment. The craft model of learning (predominantly through experience) is still contributing substantially to the learning and development of detectives. Although this approach can be effective when delivered in a structured manner and aligned with appropriate learning objectives, there is no evidence to suggest that the training of detectives has reached similar levels of development as that of those working in other more established professions. This in part is due to the lack of independent research on detective learning and development. Although evaluation of PIP through the NPIA is currently under way and due to be reported back, an evaluation of the benefits of doctrine developments is also required. There appear to be substantial barriers to the professionalisation of the police in terms of cultural resistance to learning, the high costs attached to training officers on full-time wages (restricting time spent on development) and the lack of a single professional body providing clarity and consistency in terms of professional practice and standards. While there is a limited range of literature on the functions and practices of detective work, there is a lack of understanding and research on the effectiveness of new training regimes for uniformed officers and detectives. It would appear that, without such independent research, our understanding of the appropriate level of training and education for detectives will remain uncertain and any aspiration that police detectives should achieve professional status will be delayed (Wood & Tong, in press).

The arrival of the "new public management" philosophy focusing closely on the effective and efficient use of resources has had an increasing impact on public organisations. There has been a general obsession with measurement in order to improve productivity and performance, while attempting to minimise waste. The police service has not been immune to this obsession, and in many ways it has defined the practice of police work. Not only have the police been subjected to inadequate measurement criteria such as clear-up rates, but there has also been a lack of recognition of good-quality police work. The change in the structure of policing has seen a growing number of agencies becoming involved in the broad policing task (Crawford, 2003). This development causes problems when measuring true performance, as investigations can fail or become inefficient because of issues outside the control of the detective. Furthermore, as we have seen throughout history, the police and their predecessors have manipulated measurement procedures to present themselves in a positive light (Young, 1991). A measurement criterion therefore not only becomes a measure of achievement for policymakers, but also affects the behaviour of practitioners.

The task of recognising good detective work involves more than providing an appropriate method of measurement; it also implies an awareness of the impact of practice. Measurement criteria are focused on data that are widely agreed to misrepresent police work and, as history has shown, may encourage corrupt or inappropriate practice. While these methods have been criticised in this book, it is important to recognise that they do have a place, although it is arguable that they should have less prominence than they currently have. This book has illustrated a wide range of knowledge that contributes to a broader understanding of the influences on the criminal justice system, the use of science and the interpretation of the requirements for successful investigation. We do not claim that it is a complete reflection of all the knowledge requirements of the modern detective; rather, this book is a useful guide to some of the key issues prevalent in detective work. However, we do argue that the role of the detective is an expansive one requiring multidisciplinary knowledge in order to conduct comprehensive and appropriate investigations. It is from this perspective that we would argue that the task of the detective displays the characteristics of a profession, but that the infrastructure and knowledge generation in place for established professions are not yet in place for the modern-day detective.

NOTES

1. "Docket squads" is a term used to describe detective units that are responsible for checking case files that have a DNA sample. The "squads" are used to read the case notes, identify where the DNA sample was taken and then forward the case for further investigation if the DNA was taken in a place that would allow a straightforward prosecution. Other detectives see this task as low on investigative skill and high on administrative burden.
2. There have been cases of mistakes using fingerprint evidence. Most notably, Detective Constable McKie was charged with perjury after she denied having visited a house where Marion Ross was murdered. The court cleared McKie after the original fingerprint analysis had been judged to be wrong. Concerns over the reliability of fingerprint evidence have led to calls for urgent reform (BBC Online, 2000).
3. Inefficient and delayed DNA analysis by the FSS (Forensic Science Service) could result in criminals going free. DNA analysis only takes

36 hours, but delays could result in cases being dropped, and other lines of enquiry not being pursued (BBC Online, 2004b).

4. Concerns over evidence provided by experts. An example included Professor Sir Roy Meadow's evidence in five cases of baby death. Five people were convicted of killing babies, but these cases are now being reviewed after two convictions were quashed and one woman was acquitted in cases where Meadow gave evidence (BBC Online, 2004c).

References

ACPO (2000). *Murder investigation manual* (2nd edn.). Bramshill: ACPO/National Crime Faculty.

ACPO (2001). *ACPO investigation of volume crime manual*. London: HMSO.

ACPO (2006). *Murder investigation manual* (3rd edn.). Wyboston: National Centre for Policing Excellence.

ACPO Centrex (2005). *Practice advice on core investigative doctrine*. Camborne: National Centre for Policing Excellence.

Adhami, E. & Browne, D. (1996). *Major crime enquiries: Improving expert support for detectives*. Police Research Group Special Interest Series Paper 9. London: Home Office.

Ainsworth, P.B. (2001). *Offender profiling and crime analysis*. Cullompton: Willan Publishing.

Ainsworth, P.B. (2002). *Psychology and policing*, Cullompton: Willan Publishing.

Aitken, C., Connolly, T., Gammerman, A., Zhang, G. & Oldfield, D. (1995). *Predicting an offender's characteristics: An evaluation of statistical modelling*. Police Office Research Group Special Interest Series Paper 4. London: Home Office Police Department.

Alison, L. & Crego, J. (eds.) (2008). *Policing critical incidents: Leadership and critical incident management*. Cullompton: Willan Publishing.

Alison, L. & Howard, J. (2007). The interpersonal dynamics of police interviewing. In L. Alison (ed.), *The forensic psychologist's casebook: Psychological profiling and criminal investigation* (pp. 114–142). Cullompton: Willan Publishing.

Alison, L.J., Smith, M.D., Eastman, O. & Rainbow, L. (2003). Toulmin's philosophy of argument and its relevance to offender profiling. *Psychology, Crime and Law*, 9(2), 173–184.

Alison, L.J., Smith, M.D. & Morgan, K. (2003). Interpreting the accuracy of offender profiles. *Psychology, Crime and Law*, 9(2), 185–196.

Alison, L.J., West, A. & Goodwill, A. (2004). The academic and the practitioner: Pragmatists' views of offender profiling. *Psychology, Public Policy and Law*, 10(1/2), 71–101.

Allen, J. (2007). Survey assessments of police performance in the British Crime Survey. In M. Hough & M. Maxfield (eds.), *Surveying crime in the 21st century* (pp. 183–198). Cullompton: Willan Publishing.

Almond, L., Allson, L. & Porter, L. (2007). An evaluation and comparison of claims made in behavioural investigative advice reports compiled by the National Policing Improvements Agency in the United Kingdom. *Journal of Investigative Psychology and Offender Profiling*, 4(2), 71–83.

Alonzo, J. & Lane, S. (2006). *Saying versus judging: Assessing juror knowledge of eyewitness memory*. Paper presented at the meeting of the American Psychology-Law Society, St. Petersburg, Florida, March.

Amey, P., Hale, C. & Uglow, S. (1996). *Development and evaluation of a crime management model*. Police Research Series Paper 18. London: Home Office.

Ashby, D.I. & Longley, P.A. (2005). Geocomputation, geodemographics and resource allocation for local policing. *Transactions in GIS*, 9(1) 53–72. http://www.casa.ucl.ac.uk/ashby/downloads/01-geocomp-geodem.pdf

Audit Commission (1993). *Helping with enquiries: Tackling crime effectively*. London: Home Office.

Avakame, E.F. (1999). Females' labor force participation and rape: An empirical test of the backlash hypothesis. *Violence Against Women*, 5, 926–949.

Bailey, W. (ed.) (1995). *The encyclopedia of police science* (2nd edn.). New York: Taylor & Francis.

Baldwin, J. (1993). Police interview techniques: Establishing truth or proof? *British Journal of Criminology*, 33(3), 325–352.

Banton, M. (1964). *The policeman in the community*. London: Tavistock Publications.

Barrett, E. (2005). Psychological research and police investigations: Does the research meet the needs? In L. Alison (ed.), *The forensic psychologist's casebook: Psychological profiling and criminal investigation* (pp. 47–67). Cullompton: Willan Publishing.

Bayley, D.H. (1996). Measuring overall effectiveness. In L.T. Hoover (ed.), *Quantifying quality in policing* (pp. 37–54). Washington: Police Executive Research Forum.

Bayley, D.H. (1998). Criminal investigation: Introduction. In D.H. Bayley (ed.), *What works in policing* (pp. 71–74). Oxford: Oxford University Press.

Bayley, D. (2002). Law enforcement and the rule of law: Is there a trade off? *Criminology and Public Policy*, 2(1), 133–154.

Bayley, D. & Bittner, E. (1989). Learning the skills of policing. In R.G. Dunham & G.P. Alphert (eds.), *Critical issues in policing: Contemporary readings* (pp. 87–110). Illinois: Waveland Press.

BBC (2005). Panorama: Cops and robbers, Sunday 17 April. http://news.bbc.co.uk/nol/shared/spl/hi/programmes/panorama/transcripts/copsandrobbers.txt

BBC (2007). Targets destroy trust in police. http://news.bbc.co.uk/1/hi/uk/7145860.stm

BBC News (2002). "Cracker" misconduct charge dropped. http://news.bbc.co.uk/1/hi/england/2377235.stm

BBC Online (2000). Fingerprint experts "making mistakes". http://news.bbc.co.uk/1/hi/uk/986340.stm

BBC Online (2004a). In quotes: Blair's leadership. http://news.bbc.co.uk/1/hi/uk_politics/3750847.stm

BBC Online (2004b). Home Office's DNA labs criticised. http://news.bbc.co.uk/1/hi/uk_politics/3435487.stm

BBC Online (2004c). Five baby death verdicts "unsafe". http://news.bbc.co.uk/1/hi/health/3685957.stm

Beal, C., Schmitt, K. & Dekle, D.J. (1995). Eyewitness identification of children: Effects of absolute judgement, nonverbal response options and event encoding. *Law and Human Behavior, 19,* 197–216.

Beattie, I. & Cockcroft, T. (2006). Square pegs and round holes: Performance measurement in the police and prison services. *Prison Service Journal, 168,* 39–44.

Begg, P. & Skinner, K. (1992). *The Scotland Yard files.* London: Headline.

Behrman, B.W. & Davy, S.L. (2001). Eyewitness identification in actual criminal cases: An archival analysis. *Law and Human Behavior, 25,* 475–491.

Benton, T.R., Ross, D.F., Bradshaw, E., Thomas, W.N. & Bradshaw, G.S. (2006). Eyewitness memory is still not common sense: Comparing jurors, judges and law enforcement to eyewitness experts. *Applied Cognitive Psychology, 20,* 115–130.

Benyon, J. (1987). Interpretations of disorder. In J. Benyon & J. Solomos (eds.), *The roots of urban unrest* (pp. 23–41). Oxford: Pergamon Press.

Bergner, R. (1997). What is psychopathology? And so what? *Clinical Psychology: Science and Practice, 4*(3), 235–248.

Best, C.L., Dansky, B.S. & Kilpatrick, D.G. (1992). Medical students' attitudes about rape victims. *Journal of Interpersonal Violence, 7,* 175–188.

Birzer, M.L. (2003). Learning theory as it applies to police training. In M.J. Palimiotto (ed.), *Policing and training issues* (pp. 89–114). Upper Saddle River, NJ: Prentice Hall.

Blair, I. (2005). Jonathan Dimbleby lecture: Transcript of Sir Ian Blair's speech. http://news.bbc.co.uk/1/hi/uk/4443386.stm

Boon, J.C.W (1997). The contribution of personality theories to psychological profiling. In J.L. Jackson & D.A. Bekerian (eds.), *Offender profiling: Theory, research and practice* (pp. 43–60). New York: John Wiley & Sons.

Boon, J.C.W. & Gozna, L.F. (2008a). *New perspectives, new offences and the new approaches required to deal with the chameleon offender.* Paper presented at the British Psychological Society Division of Forensic Psychology Annual Conference, Edinburgh, 24–26 June.

Boon, J.C.W. & Gozna, L.F. (2008b). *The chameleon offender: A new look at our interactions with offenders.* Paper presented at the 18th Conference of the European Association of Psychology and Law, Maastricht, 2–5 July.

Boon, J. & Noon, E. (1994). Changing perspectives in cognitive interviewing. *Psychology, Crime and Law, 1,* 59–69.

Bothwell, R.K., Deffenbacher, K.A. & Brigham, J.C. (1987). Correlation of eyewitness accuracy and confidence: Optimality hypothesis revisited. *Journal of Applied Psychology, 72,* 691–695.

Bowell, T. & Kemp, G. (2005). *Critical thinking: A concise guide* (2nd edn.). London: Routledge.

Bower, G. (1967). A multicomponent theory of memory trace. In K.W. Spence & J.T. Spence (eds.), *The psychology of learning and motivation* (Vol. 1). New York: Academic Press.

Bowling, B. (1998). *Violent racism: Victimization, policing and social context.* Oxford: Oxford University Press.

Bowling, B. (2007). *Fair and effective policing methods: Towards "good enough" policing.* Stockholm Symposuim.

Bowling, B. & Foster, J. (2002). Policing and the police. In M. Maguire, R. Morgan & R. Reiner (eds.), *The Oxford handbook of criminology* (3rd edn., pp. 980–1033). Oxford: Oxford University Press.

Bradfield, A.L., Wells, G.L. & Olson, E.A. (2002). The damaging effect of confirming feedback on the relation between eyewitness certainty and identification accuracy. *Journal of Applied Psychology*, 87, 112–120.

Braine, M.D.S. & O'Brien, D.P. (1991). A theory of if: A lexical entry, reasoning program, and pragmatic principles, *Psychological Review*, 98, 182–203.

Brantingham, P.L. & Brantingham, P.J. (1998). Mapping crime for analytic purposes: Location quotients, counts, and rates. In D. Weisburd & D. McEwen (eds.), *Crime prevention studies* (Vol. 8, pp. 263–288). Monsey, NY: Criminal Justice Press.

Brigham, J.C. (1986). The influence of race on face recognition. In H.D. Ellis, M.A. Jeeves, F. Newcombe & A. Young (eds.), *Aspects of face processing* (pp. 170–177). Dordrecht: Martinus Nijhoff.

Brigham, J.C., Van Verst, M. & Bothwell, R.K. (1986). Accuracy of children's eyewitness identifications in a field setting. *Basic and Applied Social Psychology*, 7(4), 295–306.

Brigham, J.C., Wasserman, A. & Meissner, C.A. (1999). Disputed eyewitness identification evidence: Important legal and scientific issues. *Court Review*, 36, 12–27.

Brimacombe, C.A.E., Quinton, N., Nance, N. & Garrioch, L. (1997). Is age irrelevant? Perceptions of young and old adult eyewitnesses. *Law and Human Behavior*, 21, 619–634.

Britton, P. (1992). *Review of offender profiling*. London: Home Office.

Britton, P. (1997). *The Jigsaw Man*. London: Bantam Press.

Britton, P. (2000). *Picking up the pieces*. London: Bantam Press.

Brown, D. (1997). *PACE ten years on: A review of the research*. Home Office Research Study No. 155. London: HMSO.

Brown, E.L., Deffenbacher, K. & Sturgill, W. (1977). Memory for faces and the circumstances of the encounter. *Journal of Applied Psychology*, 62, 311–318.

Brown, H.G. (2006). Tips, traps and tropes: Catching thieves in post-revolutionary Paris. In C. Emsley & H. Shpayer-Makov (eds.), *Police detectives in history 1750–1950* (pp. 33–60). Aldershot: Ashgate.

Brown, J.M., Hamilton, C. & O'Neill, D. (2007). Characteristics associated with rape attrition and the role played by skepticism or legal rationality by investigators and prosecutors. *Psychology, Crime and Law*, 13(4), 355–370.

Brownlie, A. (ed.) (1982). *Crime investigation: Art or science? Patterns in a labyrinth*. London: Scottish Academic Press.

Bruder, C., Piotrowski, A., Gijsbers, A. Andersson, R., Erickson, S., *et al.* (2008). Phenotypically concordant and discordant monozygotic twins display different DNA Copy-number-variation profiles. *American Journal of Human Genetics*, 82(3), 763–771.

Bryant, R. (2008a) *Blackstone's student officer handbook 2009*. Oxford: Oxford University Press.

Bryant, R. (2008b) Geographic(al) profiling. In T. Newburn & P. Neyroud (eds.), *Dictionary of policing*. Cullompton: Willan Publishing.

Buck, C., Llopis, A., Najera, E. & Terris, M. (1988). *The challenge of epidemiology: Issues and selected readings*. Washington: Pan American Health Organization.

Bucke, T. & Brown, D. (1997). *In police custody: Police powers and suspects' rights under the revised PACE codes of practice*. Home Office Research Study 174. London: HMSO.

Buckhout, R., Figueroa, D. & Hoff, E. (1975). Eyewitness identification: Effects of suggestion and bias in identification from photographs. *Bulletin of the Psychonomic Society*, *6*, 71–74.

Buddie, A.M. & Miller, A.G. (2001). Beyond rape myths: A more complex view of perceptions of rape victims. *Sex Roles*, *45*, 139–160.

Bull, R. (1995). Interviewing children with learning disabilities. In R. Bull & D. Carson (eds.), *Handbook of psychology in legal contexts* (pp. 247–260). Chichester: Wiley.

Burrows, J. (1986). *Investigating burglary: The measurement of police performance*. Home Office Research Study 88. London: HMSO.

Burrows, J., Hopkins, M., Hubbard, R., Robinson, A., Speed, M. & Tilley, N. (2005). *Understanding the attrition process in volume crime investigations*. Home Office Research, Development and Statistics Directorate Home Office Research Study 295. London: HMSO.

Butler, T. (2000). Managing the future: A chief constable's view. In K. Leishman, B. Loveday & S. Savage (eds.), *Core issues in policing* (pp. 305–320). London: Longman.

Button, M. (2002). *Private policing*. Cullompton: Willan Publishing.

Cameron, I. (2001). The secret life of juries. *Metline* (Dec.), 18–19.

Canter, D. (1995). *Criminal shadows: Inside the mind of the serial killer*. London: HarperCollins.

Canter, D. (2000). Offender profiling and criminal differentiation. *Journal of Legal and Criminological Psychology*, *5*, 23–46.

Canter, D.V. (2004). Geographical profiling of criminals. *Medico-Legal Journal*, *72*, 53–66.

Canter, D.V. (2005). Confusing operational predicaments and cognitive explorations: Comments on Rossmo and Snook *et al. Applied Cognitive Psychology*, *19*(5), 663–668.

Canter, D.V. & Alison, L.J. (eds.) (1999). *Profiling in policy and practice: Offender profiling series* (Vol. 2). Aldershot: Ashgate.

Canter, D.V., Alison, L.J., Alison, E. & Wentink, N. (2004). The organized/disorganized typology of serial murder: Myth or model? *Psychology, Public Policy and Law*, *10*(3), 293–320.

Canter, D., Bennell, C., Alison, L. & Reddy, S. (2003). Differentiating sex offences: A behaviorally based thematic classification of stranger rapes. *Behavioural Sciences & the Law*, *21*, 157–174.

Canter, D., Coffey, T., Huntley, M. & Missen, C. (2000). Predicting serial killers' home base using a decision support system. *Journal of Quantitative Criminology*, *16*, 457–478.

Canter, D. & Gregory, A. (1994). Identifying the residential location of rapists. *Journal of the Forensic Science Society*, *34*, 169–175.

Canter, D. & Larkin, P. (1993). The environmental range of serial rapists. *Journal of Environmental Psychology*, *13*, 63–69.

Canter, D. & Youngs, D. (eds.) (2008a). *Principles of geographical offender profiling*. Aldershot: Ashgate.

Canter, D. & Youngs, D. (eds.) (2008b). *Applications of geographical offender profiling*. Aldershot: Ashgate.

Cashmore, J. & Bussey, K. (1996). Judicial views of child witness competence. *Law and Human Behavior*, special issue on children's capacities in legal contexts, 313–334.

Chakrabarti, S. (2007). Yet another step along a dangerous road. *Independent*, 15 Jan. 2007.

Chambers, G.A. & Millar, A. (1983). *Investigating sexual assault.* Edinburgh: Scottish Office Central Research Unit.

Chan, J. (2003). *Fair cop: Learning the art of policing.* Toronto: University of Toronto Press.

Chance, J.E. & Goldstein, A.G. (1984). The other race effect and eyewitness identification. In S.L. Sporer, R.S. Malpass & G. Köhnken (eds.), *Psychological issues in eyewitness identification.* Mahwah, NJ: Erlbaum.

Chatterton, M. (1987). Assessing police effectiveness: Future prospects. *British Journal of Criminology, 27*(1), 80–86.

Chatterton, M. (1995). The cultural craft of policing: Its past and future relevance. *Policing and Society, 5,* 97–107.

Chatterton, M. (2008). *Losing the detectives: Views from the front line.* Surbiton: Police Federation of England & Wales. http://www.polfed.org/8BCD53420D4D47BCAA9CFC6B5639A984.asp

Chenery, S., Henshaw, C. & Pease, K. (1999). *Illegal parking in disabled bays: A means of offender targeting* Policing & Reducing Crime Briefing Note 1/99. London: Home Office.

Cherryman, J. & Bull, R. (2000). Reflections on investigative interviewing. In F. Leishman, B. Loveday & S. Savage (eds.), *Core issues in policing* (2nd edn., pp. 194–212). London: Longman.

Cherryman, J., Bull, R. & Vrij, A. (2000). *How police officers view confessions: Is there still a confession culture?* Paper presented at the European Conference of Psychology and Law, Limassol, Cyprus, April 2000.

Choongh, S. (1997). *Policing as a social discipline.* Oxford: Clarendon Press.

Christianson, S.A. & Hubinette, B. (1993). Hands up! A study of witnesses' emotional reactions and memories associated with bank robberies. *Applied Cognitive Psychology, 7,* 365–379.

Clare, I.C.H. & Gudjonsson, G. (1993). Interrogative suggestibility, confabulations and acquiescence in people with mild learning disabilities (Mental handicap: Implications for reliability during police interrogations). *British Journal of Clinical Psychology, 32,* 295–301.

Clarke, C. & Milne, R. (2001). *National evaluation of the PEACE investigative interviewing course.* Police Research Award Scheme. London: Home Office.

Clarke, J. (2001). Crime and social order: Interrogating the detective story. In J. Muncie & E. McLaughlin (eds.), *The problem of crime* (pp. 65–100). London: Sage Publications.

Clarke, R.D. (1946). An application of the Poisson distribution. *Journal of the Institute of Actuaries, 72,* 481.

Clifford, B.R. (1993). Witnessing: A comparison of adults and children. *Issues in Criminological and Legal Psychology, 20,* 15–21.

Clifford, B.R. & Bull, R. (1978). *The psychology of person identifications.* London: Routledge.

Clifford, B.R. & Davis, G.M. (1989). Procedures for obtaining identification evidence. In D.C. Raskin (ed.), *Psychological methods in criminal investigation and evidence.* New York: Springer.

Clifford, B.R. & George, R. (1995). A field evaluation of training in three methods of witness/victim investigative interviewing. *Psychology, Crime & Law, 2,* 1–18.

Cohen, G. & Faulkner, D. (1989). Age-difference in source forgetting: Effects on reality monitoring and on eyewitness testimony. *Psychology and Ageing, 4,* 10–17.

Coleman, C. & Moynihan, J. (1996). *Understanding crime data: Haunted by the dark figure*. Buckingham: Open University Press.

Collins, K. (1985). Some issues in police effectiveness and efficiency. *Policing*, *1*(2), 70–77.

Connors, E., Lundregan, T., Miller, N. & McEwen, T. (1996). *Convicted by juries, exonerated by science: Case studies in the use of DNA evidence to establish innocence after trial*. Alexandria, VA: National Institute of Justice.

Cook, P.E. & Hinman, D.L. (1999). Serial murder. In H.V. Hall (ed.), *Lethal violence 2000: A sourcebook on fatal domestic, acquaintance, and stranger aggression*. Kamuela, Hawaii: Pacific Institute for the Study of Conflict and Aggression.

Cook, T. & Tattersall, A. (2008). *Blackstone's senior investigating officers' handbook*. Oxford: Oxford University Press.

Copi, I. & Cohen, C. (2004). *Introduction to logic*. Upper Saddle River, NJ: Prentice Hall.

Copson, G. (1995). *Coals to Newcastle? Part 1: A study of offender profiling* (Paper 7). London: Police Research Group Special Interest Series, Home Office.

Corsianos, M. (2001). Conceptualizing "justice" in detectives' decision making. *International Journal of the Sociology of Law*, *29*, 113–125.

Cox, B. (1975). *Civil liberties in Britain*. Harmondsworth: Penguin.

Cox, B., Shirley, J. & Short, M. (1977). *The fall of Scotland Yard*, Harmondsworth: Penguin.

Coy, M., Kelly, L. & Foord, J., with Balding, V. & Davenport, R. (2007). *Map of gaps: The postcode lottery of violence against women support services*. London: End Violence Against Women.

Crawford, A. (2003). The pattern of policing in the UK: policing beyond the police. In T. Newburn (ed.), *Handbook of policing* (pp. 136–168). Cullompton: Willan Publishing.

Crime and Society Foundation (2004). Report (Oct. 2004). Hosted by the Centre for Crime and Justice Studies, University of London, King's College.

Crowther, C. (2000). *Policing urban poverty*. Basingstoke: Macmillan.

Cutler, B.L. & Penrod, S.D. (1989). Forensically relevant moderators of the relation between eyewitness identification accuracy and confidence. *Journal of Applied Psychology*, *74*, 650–652.

Cutler, B.L. & Penrod, S.D. (1995). Mistaken identification: The eyewitness, psychology and the law. New York: Cambridge University Press.

Cutler, B.L., Penrod, S.D. & Dexter, H.R. (1990). Juror sensitivity to eyewitness identification cases. *Law and Human Behavior*, *14*, 185–191.

Cutler, B.L., Penrod, S.D. & Martens, T.K. (1987). The reliability of eyewitness identification: The role of system and estimator variables. *Law and Human Behavior*, *11*, 233–258.

Davidoff, L. (1993). Performance indicators for the police service. *Focus on Police Research & Development*, *3*(Dec.), 12–17.

Davies, G.M. (1991). Children on trial? Psychology, videotechnology and the law. *Howard Journal*, *30*, 177–191.

Davies, G.M. (1992). Influencing public policy on eyewitnessing: Problems and possibilities. In F. Lösel, D. Bender & T. Bleisener (eds.), *Psychology and law: International perspectives*. New York: Walter de Gruyter.

Davies, G., Shepherd, J. & Ellis, H. (1979). Effects of interpolated mugshot exposure prior to line-up identification: Interference, transference and commitment effects. *Journal of Applied Psychology*, *86*, 1280–1284.

Davies, G.M., Smith, S. & Blincoe, O. (2008). A "weapon focus" effect in children. *Psychology, Crime & Law, 14*(1), 19–28.

Davies, G., Stevenson-Robb, Y. & Flin, R. (1988). Tales out of school: Children's memory for an unexpected event. In M.M. Gruneberg, P.E. Morris & R.N. Sykes (eds.), *Practical aspects of memory: Current research and issues*, Vol. 1: *Memory in everyday life* (pp. 122–127). New York: John Wiley.

Davies, G.M. & Valentine, T. (1999). Codes of practice for identification. *Expert Evidence, 7*, 59–65.

Davies, N. (2003). *Fiddling the figures: Police cheats who distort force records.* http://www.guardian.co.uk/uk/2003/jul/11/ukcrime.prisonsandprobation1

DeForest, P., Gaensslen, R. Lee, H. (1983). *Forensic science: An introduction to criminalistics.* New York: McGraw-Hill.

Delattre, E.J. (1996). *Character and cops: Ethics in policing* (3rd edn.). Washington, DC: AEI Press.

Dent, H. (1986). An experimental study of the effectiveness of different techniques of questioning mentally handicapped child witnesses. *British Journal of Clinical Psychology, 25*, 13–17.

Desmarais, S.L., Price, H.L. & Read, J.D. (2008). Objection, your honor! Television is not the relevant authority: Crime drama portrayals of eyewitness issues. *Psychology, Crime and Law, 14*(3), 225–244.

Devlin, P.A. (1976). *Report to the Secretary of State for the Home Department of the Departmental Committee on Evidence on Identification in Criminal Cases.* London: HMSO.

Dixon, D. (1992). Legal regulation and policing practice. *Social & Legal Studies, 1*, 515–541.

Dixon, S. & Memon, A. (2005). The effect of post-identification feedback on the recall of crime and perpetrator details. *Applied Cognitive Psychology, 19*, 935–951.

Douglas, J.E. & Burgess, A.W. (1986). Criminal profiling: Available investigative tool against violent crime. *FBI Law Enforcement Bulletin, 55*(12), 9–13.

Douglas, J.E., Burgess, A.W., Burgess, A.G. & Ressler, R.K. (1992). *Crime classification manual.* New York: Lexington Books.

Douglas, J.E. & Olshaker, M. (1996). *Mindhunter.* London: Heinemann.

Douglas, J.E. & Olshaker, M. (1997). *Journey into darkness.* New York: Scribner.

Douglas, J.E., Ressler, R.K., Burgess, A.W. & Hartman, C.R. (1986). Criminal profiling from crime scene analysis. *Behavioral Sciences and the Law, 4*, 401–421.

Douglass, A.B. & Steblay, N.M. (2006). Memory distortion in eyewitnesses: A meta-analysis of the post-identification feedback effect. *Applied Cognitive Psychology, 20*, 859–869.

Dristas, W.J. & Hamilton, V.L. (1977). Evidence about evidence: Effect of presupposition, item salience, stress, and perceived set on accident recall. Unpublished manuscript, University of Michigan.

DSM-IV (1994). *Diagnostic and statistical manual of mental disorders* (4th edn.). Washington, DC: American Psychiatric Association.

Dysart, J.E., Lindsay, R.C.L., MacDonald, T.K. & Wicke, C. (2002). The intoxicated witness: Effects of alcohol on identification accuracy from showups. *Journal of Applied Psychology, 87*(1), 170–175.

Eck, J.E. (1999). Rethinking detective management: Why investigative reforms are seldom permanent or effective. In D.J. Kenney & R.P. McNamara (eds.), *Police and policing: Contemporary issues* (2nd edn., pp. 170–186). Westport, CT: Praeger.

Ede, R. & Shepherd, E. (2000). *Active defence*. London: Law Society.

Edwards, C.J. (1999). *Changing policing theories for 21st century societies*, Leichhardt, NSW: Federation Press.

Emmers-Sommer, T.M. & Allen, M. (1999). Variables related to sexual coercion: A path model. *Journal of Social and Personal Relationships, 16*, 659–678.

Emsley, C. (1996). *The English police* (2nd edn.). Harlow: Longman.

Emsley, C. (2002). The history of crime and crime control institutions. In M. Maguire, R. Morgan & R. Reiner (eds.), *The Oxford handbook of criminology* (3rd edn., pp. 203–30). Oxford: Oxford University Press.

Erautt, M. (1994). *Developing professional knowledge and competence*. London: Falmer Press.

Ericson, R.V. (1993). *Making crime: A study of detective work* (2nd edn.). Toronto: University of Toronto Press.

Estrich, S. (1986). *Rape. Yale Law Journal, 95*, 1087–1184.

Estrich, S. (1987). *Real rape: How the legal system victimizes women who say no*. Cambridge, MA: Harvard University Press.

Falvey, J, Bray, T. & Hebert, D. (2005). Case conceptualization and treatment planning: investigation of problem-solving and clinical judgment. *Journal of Mental Health Counselling* (Oct.), 292–303.

Farrell, G. & Pease, K. (2007). Crime in England and Wales: More violence and more chronic victims. *Civitas Review, 4*(2), 1–6.

Farrington, D.P. & Lambert, S. (1993). *Predicting violence and burglary offenders from victims', witnesses' and offence data*. Paper presented at the First Netherlands Institute for the Study of Criminality and Law Enforcement Workshop on criminality and Law Enforcement, The Hague, October.

Feinman, S. & Entwistle, D.R. (1976). Children's ability to recognise other children's faces. *Child Development, 47*, 506–510.

Feist, A., Ashe, J., Lawrence, J., McPhee, D. & Wilson, R. (2007). *Investigating and detecting recorded offences of rape*. Home Office Online Report 18/07.

Fido, M. & Skinner, K. (1999). *The official encyclopaedia of Scotland Yard: Behind the scenes at Scotland Yard*. London: Virgin.

Fielding, N.G. (1988). *Joining forces: Police training, socialization & occupational competence*. London: Routledge.

Fish, D. & Coles, C. (1998). *Developing professional judgement in health care: Learning through the critical appreciation of practice*. Oxford: Butterworth Heinemann.

Fisher, R. & Geiselman, R.E. (1992). *Memory enhancing techniques for investigative interviewing*. Springfield, IL: Charles C. Thomas.

Fisher, R.P., Geiselman, R.E. & Raymond, D.S. (1987). Critical analysis of police interview techniques. *Journal of Police Science & Administration, 15*, 177–185.

Fisher, R.P., Geiselman, R.E., Raymond, D.S., Jurkevitch, L.M. & Warhaftig, M.L. (1987). Enhancing enhanced eyewitness memory: refining the cognitive interview. *Journal of Police Science and Administration, 15*, 291–297.

Fitzgerald, M., Hough, M., Joseph, I. & Qureshi, T. (2002). *Policing for London*. Cullompton: Willan Publishing.

Flanagan, R. (2008). *Independent review of policing*. London: Home Office.

Flynn, N. (2002). *Public sector management* (4th edn.). London: Pearson Education.

Foster, J. (1999). Appendix 22: Memorandum by Dr Janet Foster, Institute of Criminology, University of Cambridge. In *Home Affairs Committee, Police training and recruitment* (Vol. 2, pp. 382–391). London: HMSO.

Pisani, J. (2000). Forensic investigation. In T. Newburn & P. Neyroud (eds.) *Dictionary of policing* (pp. 114–115). Cullompton: Willan Publishing.

Fritzon, K., Canter, D. & Wilton, Z. (2001). The application of an action systems model to destructive behaviour: The examples of arson and terrorism. *Behavioral Sciences and the Law, 19*(5–6), 657–690.

Froyland, I.D. & Bell, D. (1996). Making police more efficient? In D. Chappell & B. Wilson (eds.), *Australian policing: Contemporary issues* (2nd edn., pp. 71–84). Perth: Butterworth.

Fruzzetti, A.E., Toland, K., Teller, S.A. & Loftus, E.F. (1992). Memory and eyewitness testimony. In M. Gruneberg & P.E. Morris (eds.), *Aspects of memory* (pp. 18–50). London: Routledge.

Fyfe, N. & Smith, K. (2007). Victims and witnesses in criminal investigation. In T. Newburn, T. Williamson & A. Wright (eds.), *Handbook of criminal investigation* (pp. 450–465). Cullompton: Willan Publishing.

Gardiner, J. (2004). *Wartime Britain 1939–1945*. London: Headline.

Garland, D. (2001). *The culture of control: Crime and social order in contemporary society*. Oxford: Oxford University Press.

Garrioch, L. & Brimacombe, C.A.E. (2001). Lineup administrators' expectations: Their impact on eyewitness confidence. *Law and Human Behavior, 25*, 299–315.

Geiselman, R.E., Fisher, R.P., Firstenberg, I., Hutton, L.A., Sullivan, S., Artiscan, I. & Prosket, A. (1984). Enhancement of eyewitness memory: An empirical evaluation of the cognitive interview. *Journal of Police Science and Administration, 12*, 74–80.

Gelsthorpe, L. (2001a) Crime control model. In E. McLaughlin & J. Muncie (eds.), *The Sage dictionary of criminology* (pp. 61–63). London: Sage Publications.

Gelsthorpe, L. (2001b) Due process model. In E. McLaughlin & J. Muncie (eds.), *The Sage dictionary of criminology* (pp. 104–106). London: Sage Publications.

Gerberth, V.J. (1996). *Practical homicide investigation tactics, procedures, and forensic techniques*. Boca Raton, FL: CRC Press.

Gigerenzer, G. (2007). *Gut feelings: The intelligence of the unconscious*. Harmondsworth: Penguin.

Gigerenzer, G. & Goldstein, D.G. (1996). Reasoning the fast and frugal way: Models of bounded rationality. *Psychological Review, 103*(4), 650–669.

Gilbert, J.N. (1993). *Criminal investigation*. New York: Macmillan.

Gill, M. (2000). *Rounding up the usual suspects? Developments in contemporary law enforcement intelligence*. Aldershot: Ashgate.

Gilling, D. (2000). Policing, crime prevention and partnerships. In F. Leishman, B. Loveday & S. Savage (eds.), *Core issues in policing* (pp. 124–139). Harlow: Longman.

Glisky, E.L., Rubin, S.R. & Davidson, S.R. (2001). Source memory in older adults: An encoding or retrieval problem? *Journal of Experimental Psychology: Learning Memory and Cognition, 27*, 1131–1146.

GMC (2008). *Licensing and revalidation*. http://www.gmc-uk.org/about/reform/index.asp

Goddard, H. (1956). *The memoirs of a Bow Street Runner*. London: Museum Press.

Goldstein, A.G., Chance, J.E. & Schneller, G.R. (1989). Frequency of eyewitness identification in criminal cases. *Bulletin of the Psychonomic Society, 22*, 549–522.

Goldstein, H. (1990). *Problem-orientated policing*. New York: McGraw-Hill.

Goodman, G.S. (1984). Children's testimony in historical perspective. *Journal of Social Issues, 40*, 9–31.

Goodman, G.S. & Reed, R.S. (1986). Age differences in eyewitness testimony. *Law and Human Behavior, 10*, 317–332.

Goodwill, A. & Alison, L. (2005). Sequential angulation, spatial dispersion and consistency of distance attack patterns from home in serial murder, rape and burglary. *Psychology, Crime & Law, 11*, 161–176.

Gozna, L.F. (2008). Interviewing and deception techniques. In K. Fritzon & P. Wilson (eds.), *Forensic and criminal psychology: An Australian perspective* (pp. 151–164). New York: McGraw-Hill.

Gozna, L.F. & Boon, J.C.W. (2007). *The chameleon offender: The synergising of psychology and psychiatry to meet the challenge*. Paper presented at the Conference of Research in Forensic Psychiatry, Regensburg, Germany, 29–31 May.

Greenfield, L.A. (1997). *Sex offenses and offenders: An analysis of data on rape and sexual assault*. Washington, DC: Bureau of Justice Statistics.

Greenwood, P., Chaiken, J. & Petersilia, J. (1977). *The criminal investigation process*. Toronto: D.C. Heath.

Griffiths, A. & Milne, R. (2006). Will it all end in tears? Police interviews with suspects in Britain. In T. Williamson (ed.), *Investigative interviewing: Rights, research regulation* (pp. 167–189). Oregon: Willan Publishing.

Griffiths, T. & Tenenbaum, J. (2007). From mere coincidences to meaningful discoveries. *Cognition, 103*, 180–226.

Gross, J. & Haynes, H. (1996). Eyewitness identification by 5- to 6-year-old children. *Law and Human Behavior, 20*(3), 359–373.

Gudjonsson, G.H. (1992). *The psychology of interrogations, confessions and testimony*. Chichester: Wiley.

Gudjonsson, G. (1999). *The psychology of interrogations and confessions: A handbook*. Chichester: Wiley.

Gudjonsson, G.H. (2003). *The psychology of interrogations and confessions: A handbook*. Chichester: Wiley.

Gudjonsson, G.H. (2007). Investigative interviewing. In T. Newburn, T. Williamson & A. Wright (eds.), *Handbook of criminal investigation* (pp. 466–492). Cullompton: Willan Publishing.

Gudjonsson, G.H. & Copson, G. (1997). The role of the expert in criminal investigation. In J.L. Jackson & D.A. Bekerian (eds.), *Offender profiling: Theory, research and practice* (pp. 61–76). New York: John Wiley & Sons.

Gudjonsson G.H. & Gunn J. (1982). The competence and reliability of a witness in a criminal court. *British Journal of Psychiatry, 141*, 624–627.

Gudjonsson, G.H. & Haward, L.R.C. (1998). *Forensic psychology: A practitioner's guide*. London: Routledge.

Guyot, D. (1991). *Policing as though people matter*, Philadelphia: Temple University Press.

Haberfeld, M.R. (2002). *Critical issues in police training*. Upper Saddle River, NJ: Prentice Hall.

Hagan, M. (1992). Special issues in serial murder. In H. Strang & S. Gerull (eds.), *Homicides: Patterns, prevention and control*. Proceedings of a conference held 12–14 May 1992. Canberra: Australian Institute of Criminology.

Hare, R.D. (2005). Personal communication at PCL-R Training Course, Helsinki.

Harris, J. & Grace, S. (1999). *A question of evidence? Investigating and prosecuting rape in the 1990s*. London: Home Office.

Harvey, D.R. (1984). Can crime investigation be taught? In A.R. Brownlie (ed.), *Crime investigation: Art or science?* (pp. 47–54). Edinburgh: Scottish Academic Press.

Haw, R.M., Dickinson, J.J. & Meissner, C.A. (2007). The phenomenology of carryover effects between show-up and line-up identification. *Memory, 15*(1), 117–127.

Hayley, K.N. (1992). Training. In G.W. Cordner & D.C. Hale (eds.), *What works in policing? Operations and administration examined* (pp. 143–155). Cincinnati: Andersen Publishing.

Hepburn, J.R. (1981). The measurement of police performance. *Journal of Police Science and Administration, 9*(1), 88–98.

Heuer, R. (1999). *Psychology of intelligence analysis*. Washington, DC: Center for the Study of Intelligence, Central Intelligence Agency.

Hill, A. (2006). Damned by the law for saying "I can't remember". *Observer*, Sunday, 25 June. http://www.guardian.co.uk/uk/2006/jun/25/ukcrime.prisonsandprobation (accessed 15 Sept. 2008).

Hinz, T. & Pezdek, K. (2001). The effect of exposure to multiple lineups on face identification accuracy. *Law and Human Behavior, 25*, 185–198.

HMCPSI (2007). *Without consent: A report on the joint review of the investigation and prosecution of rape offences*. http://inspectorates.homeoffice.gov.uk/hmic/inspections/thematic/wc-thematic/them07-wc.pdf?view=Binary (accessed 12 Sept. 2008).

HMCPSI & HMIC (2002). *A report on the joint inspection onto the investigation and prosecution of cases involving allegations of rape*. London: HMCPSI.

HMCPSI & HMIC (2007). *Without consent*. London: HMCPSI/HMIC.

HMIC (1999a). *Managed learning: A study of police training*. London: HMIC.

HMIC (1999b). Appendix 7: Memorandum by HM Inspectorate of Constabulary. In *Home Affairs Committee*, Police training and recruitment (Vol. 2, pp. 239–261). London: HMSO.

HMIC (2002). *Training matters*. London: HMIC.

HMIC (2004). *A thematic inspection of workforce modernisation: The role, management and deployment of police staff in the police service of England and Wales*. http://inspectorates.homeoffice.gov.uk/hmic/inspections/thematic/mtps/

HMIC (2005). *Closing the gap: A review of the "fitness for purpose" of the current structure of policing in England & Wales*. http://inspectorates.homeoffice.gov.uk/hmic/inspections/thematic/ctg/

HMIC (2006). *The role of Her Majesty's Inspectorate of Constabulary*. http://inspectorates.homeoffice.gov.uk/hmic/docs/our-work/hmicrole.pdf?view=Binary

HMIC (2008). *HMIC Inspection Report, Derbyshire Constabulary Major Crime July 2008*. http://inspectorates.homeoffice.gov.uk/hmic/Inspections/major-serious-crime/Derbyshire_HMIC_Major_Crime1.pdf?view=Binary

Hobbs, D. (1988). *Doing the business: Entrepreneurship, detectives and the working class in the East End of London*. Oxford: Oxford University Press.

Hobbs, D. (1991). A piece of business: The moral economy of detective work in the East End of London. *British Journal of Sociology, 42*(4), 597–608.

Holdaway, S. & Barron, A. (1997). *Resigners? The experience of black and Asian police officers*. London: Macmillan Press.

Holmes, R.M. (1989). *Profiling violent crimes. An investigative tool.* Newbury Park: Sage Publications.

Holmes, R.M. & Holmes, S.T. (2002). *Profiling violent crimes* (2nd edn.). Thousand Oaks: Sage Publications.

Homant, R.J. & Kennedy, D.B. (1998). Psychological aspects of crime scene profiling: Validity research. *Criminal Justice and Behaviour, 25*(3), 319–343.

Home Office (1993). *Circular 17/93: Performance indicators for the police.* London: Home Office.

Home Office (2001a). *Policing a new century: A blueprint for reform.* London: Home Office.

Home Office (2001b). *Criminal justice: The way ahead.* London: Home Office.

Home Office (2002). *Police performance monitoring 2001/02.* London: Home Office.

Home Office (2003). *Police performance monitoring 2002/03.* London: Home Office.

Home Office (2005). *Police and Criminal Evidence Act 1984 (s.60(1)(a). s.60A(1) and S.66(1), Codes of Practice A–G.* London: HMSO.

Home Office (2006). *Police and Criminal Evidence Act 1984* (s.66(1). London: TSO.

Home Office (2007). *Home Office counting rules for recorded crime.* www.homeoffice.gov.uk/rds/countrules.html

Home Office (2008). *Improving performance: A practical guide to performance management.* http://police.homeoffice.gov.uk/news-and-publications/publication/performance-and-measurement/Practical_Guide_to_Police_P1.pdf?view=Binary

Home Office (2009). *Performance and measurement.* http://police.homeoffice.gov.uk/performance-and-measurement/performance-assessment/faqs1/#

Horsnell, M. (1989). PC who exposed his colleagues faces discipline hearing – PC Ronald Walker. The Times, Wednesday, 20 Sept.

Horvath, M.A.H. & Brown, J.M. (eds). (2009). *Rape: Challenging contemporary thinking.* Cullompton,: Willan Publishing.

Hough, M. (2004). Crime against statistics: Michael Howard can't really believe what he is saying about violence in Brixton. *Guardian*, Thursday, 14 Oct. http://www.guardian.co.uk/politics/2004/oct/14/prisonsandprobation.conservatives

Hough, M., Maxfield, M., Morris, B. & Simmons, J. (2007). The British Crime Survey after 25 years: Process, problems and prospects. In M. Hough & M. Maxfield (eds.), *Surveying crime in the 21st century* (pp. 7–32). Cullompton: Willan Publishing.

House of Commons (2008). *Transport Committee: Seventh Report.* http://www.parliament.the-stationery-office.co.uk/pa/cm200708/cmselect/cmtran/313/31302.htm (accessed 1 May 2008).

Howard League (1985). *Unlawful sex: Offences, victims and offenders in the criminal justice system of England and Wales.* London: Waterlow.

Howard, M. (1970). *Studies in war and peace.* London: Temple Smith.

Howitt, D. (2001). *Forensic and criminal psychology.* Harlow: Prentice Hall.

Huff, C.R. (2003). Wrongful conviction: Causes and public policy issues. *Criminal Justice Magazine, 18*(1). http://www.abanet.org/crimjust/spring2003/conviction.html (accessed 27 Aug. 2008).

Hufton, D. & Buswell, H. (2000). *Training needs analysis for initial and supervisory investigators.* Harrogate: National Police Training.

Hulse, L. & Memon, A. (2006). Fatal impact? The effects of emotional arousal and weapon presence on police officers' memories for a simulated crime. *Legal & Criminological Psychology, 11,* 313–325.

Hutchinson, J. & Gigerenzer, G. (2005). Simple heuristics and rules of thumb: Where psychologists and behavioural biologists might meet. *Behavioural Processes, 69,* 97–124.

Ihlebaek, C., Løve, T., Eilertson, D.E. & Magnussen, S. (2003). Memory for a staged criminal event witnessed live and on video. *Memory, 11,* 319–327.

Inbau, F.E., Reid, J.E., Buckley, J.P. & Jayne, B.C. (2001). *Criminal interrogation and confessions* (4th edn.). Gaithersberg, MD: Aspen.

Innes, M. (2003). *Investigating murder: Detective work and the police response to criminal homicide.* Oxford: Oxford University Press.

Innocence Project (n.d). Innocence Project website: www.theinnocenceproject. org (accessed 12 Aug. 2008).

IPCC (2007). *Stockwell One. Investigation into the shooting of Jean Charles de Menezes at Stockwell underground station on 22 July 2005* http://www .ipcc.gov.uk/stockwell_one.pdf (accessed 9 Nov. 2007).

Irving, B. (1980). *Police interrogation: A case study of current practice.* Research Study No. 2. Royal Commission on Criminal Procedure. London: HMSO.

Irving, B.L. & McKenzie, I.K. (1989). *Regulating custodial interviews: The effects of the Police and Criminal Evidence Act 1984* (Vol. 2). London: Police Foundation.

Jackson, A. & Jackson, J. (2004). *Forensic science.* Harlow: Pearson Education.

Jackson, J.L. & Bekerian, D.A. (eds.) (1997). *Offender profiling: Theory, research and practice.* Chichester: John Wiley.

Jackson, J.L., Van Koppen, P.J. & Herbrink, J.C.M. (1993). *Does the service meet the needs? An evaluation of consumer satisfaction with specific profile analysis and investigative advice as offered by the Scientific Research Advisory Unit of the National Criminal Intelligence Division (CRI), The Netherlands.* Leiden: NSCR.

Jalbert, N.L. & Getting, J. (1992). Racial and gender issues in facial recognition. In F. Lösel., D. Bender & T. Bleisener (eds.), *Psychology and law: International perspectives* (pp. 309–316). New York: Walter de Gruyter.

Janes, D. (2007). *Edwardian murder: Ightham and the Morpeth train robbery.* Stroud: Sutton Publishing.

Jansson, K. (2007). *British Crime Survey: Measuring crime for 25 years.* http://www.homeoffice.gov.uk/rds/pdfs07/bcs25.pdf

Johnston, L. (2000). Private policing: Problems and prospects. In K. Leishman., B. Loveday. & S. Savage (eds.), *Core issues in policing* (pp. 67–82). London: Longman.

Johnston, L. & Shearing, C. (2003). *Governing security: Explorations in policing and justice.* London: Routledge.

Jones, R.V. (1978). *Most secret war: British scientific intelligence 1939–1945.* London: Hamish Hamilton.

Jordan, J. (2004). Beyond belief? Police, rape and women's credibility. *Criminal Justice, 4,* 29–59.

Kanin, E.J. (1994). False rape allegations. *Archives of Sexual Behaviour, 23*(1), 81–87.

Kapardis, A. (1997). *Psychology and law: A critical introduction.* Cambridge: Cambridge University Press.

Kassin, S.L. & Wrightsman, L.S. (1985). Confession evidence. In S. Kassin & L. Wrightsman (eds.), *The psychology of evidence and trial procedure* (pp. 67–94). Beverley Hills: Sage Publications.

Kassin, S.M., Tubb, V.A., Hosch, H.M. & Memon, A. (2001). On the "general acceptance" of eyewitness research: A study of experts. *American Psychologist*, 56, 405–416.

Kebbell, M.R. & Hatton, C. (1999). People with mental retardation as witnesses in court. *Mental Retardation*, 3, 179–187.

Kebbell, M.R., Hatton, C. & Johnson, S.D. (2004). Witnesses with intellectual disabilities in court: What questions are asked and what influence do they have? *Legal and Criminological Psychology*, 9, 1–13.

Kebbell, M.R. & Milne, R. (1998). Police officers' perception of eyewitness factors in forensic investigations: A survey. *The Journal of Social Psychology*, 138, 323–330.

Kebbell, M.R. & Wagstaff, G.F. (1999). *Face value? Evaluating the accuracy of eyewitness information*. Police Research Series Paper No. 102. London: Home Office, Policing and Reducing Crime Unit.

Kebbell, M.R., Wagstaff, G.F. & Covey, J.A. (1996). The influence of item difficulty on the relationship between eyewitness confidence and accuracy. *British Journal of Psychology*, 87, 653–662.

Kelly, L. (2002). *A research review on the reporting, investigation and prosecution of rape cases*. London: HMCPSI.

Kelly, L. (2008). Contradictions and paradoxes: International patterns of, and responses to, reported rape cases. In G. Letherby, K. Williams, P. Birch & M. Cain (eds.), *Sex as crime?* Cullompton: Willan Publishing.

Kelly, L., Lovett, J. & Regan, L. (2005). *A gap or a chasm? Attrition in reported rape cases*. Home Office Research Study 293. London: Home Office.

Keppel, R.D. (2000). Investigation of the serial offender: Linking cases through modus operandi and signature. In L.B. Schlesinger (ed.) *Serial offenders: Current thought, recent findings* (pp. 121–133). Boca Raton, FL: CRC Press.

Kershaw, C., Nicholas, S. & Walker, A. (2008). *Crime in England and Wales*. http://www.homeoffice.gov.uk/rds/pdfs08/hosb0708.pdf

Kind, S. (1987). *The scientific investigation of crime*. Harrogate: Forensic Science Services.

King, M.A. & Yuille, J.C. (1987). Suggestibility and the child witness. In S.J. Ceci, M.P. Toglia & D.F. Ross (eds.), *Children's eyewitness memory*. New York: Springer.

Kingsley, D. (2002). *Threading together forensic evidence* http://www.abc. net.au/science/news/stories/s558189.htm (accessed 9 Nov. 2007).

Kleinig, J. (1996). *The ethics of policing*. Cambridge: Cambridge University Press.

Klippenstine, M.A., Schuller, R.A. & Wall, A.-M. (2007). Perceptions of sexual assault: The expression of gender differences and the impact of target alcohol consumption. *Journal of Applied Social Psychology*, 37(11), 2620–2641.

Kocsis, R.N. (2003). An empirical assessment of the content in criminal psychological profiles. *International Journal of Offender Therapy and Comparative Criminology*, 47(1), 37–46.

Kocsis, R.N. & Irwin, H.J. (1997). An analysis of spatial patterns in serial rape, arson and burglary: The utility of the circle theory of environmental range for psychological profiling. *Psychiatry, Psychology and Law*, 4(2), 195–206.

Köhnken, G. (1992). *The cognitive interview: A meta-analysis.* Paper presented at the third European Conference on Psychology and Law, Oxford.

Köhnken, G., Milne, R., Memon, A. & Bull, R. (1999). The cognitive interview: A meta-analysis. *Psychology, Crime and Law, 5*(1–2), 3–27.

Kramer, G.P., Kerr, N.L. & Carroll, J.S. (1990). Pretrial publicity: Judicial remedies and jury bias. *Law and Human Behavior, 14*, 409–438.

Krulewitz, J.E. (1982). Reactions to rape victims: Effects of rape circumstances, victim's emotional response, and sex of helper. *Journal of Counseling Psychology, 29*, 645–654.

LaFree, G.D. (1981). Official reactions to social problems: Police decisions in sexual assault cases. *Social Problems, 28*, 581–594.

Laming, D. (2003). *The Victoria Climbié inquiry: Report of an inquiry.* London: HMSO.

Laming, D. (2004). *Human judgement: The eye of the beholder.* London: Thomson Learning.

Layder, D. (1998). *Sociological practice: Linking theory and social research.* London: Sage.

Lee, M. & Punch, M. (2006). *Policing by degrees,* Groningen: de Hondsrug Press.

Lees, S. (2002). *Carnal knowledge: Rape on trial* (2nd edn.). London: Women's Press.

Lees, S. & Gregory, J. (1993). *Rape and sexual assault: A study of attrition.* London: Islington Council Police and Crime Prevention Unit.

Lefford, A. (1946). The influence of emotional subject matter on logical reading. *Journal of General Psychology, 34*, 127–151.

Leippe, M.R. (1980). Effects of integrative and memorial cognitive processes on the correspondence of eyewitness accuracy and confidence. *Law and Human Behavior, 4*, 261–274.

Leippe, M.R. (1994). The appraisal of eyewitness testimony. In D.F. Ross, J.D. Read, M.P. Toglia (eds.), *Adult eyewitness testimony: Current trends and developments.* New York: Cambridge University Press.

Leippe, M.R., Manion, A.P. & Romanczyk, A. (1992). Eyewitness persuasion: How and how well do factfinders judge the accuracy of adults' and children's memory reports? *Journal of Personality and Social Psychology, 63*, 181–197.

Leippe, M.R., Wells, G. & Ostrom, T. (1978). Crime seriousness as a determinant of accuracy in eyewitness identification. *Journal of Applied Psychology, 63*, 345–351.

Light, L.L., Kayra-Stuart, F. & Hollander, S. (1979). Recognition memory for typical and unusual faces. *Journal of Experimental Psychology: Human Learning & Memory, 5*, 212–228.

Lindsay, R.C.L. (1986). Confidence and accuracy of eyewitness identification from line-ups. *Law and Human Behavior, 10*, 229–239.

Lindsay, R.C.L. (1994). Expectations of eyewitness performance: Jurors' verdicts do not follow from their beliefs. In D.F. Ross, J.D. Read & M.P. Toglia (eds.), *Adult eyewitness testimony: Current trends and developments* (pp. 362–384). New York: Cambridge University Press.

Lindsay, R.C.L., Lea, J.A. Nosworth, G.J., Fulford, J.A., Hector, J., LeVan, V. & Seabrook, C. (1991). Biased lineups: Sequential presentation reduces the problem. *Journal of Applied Psychology, 76*, 796–802.

Lindsay, R.C.L., Pozzulo, J.D., Craig, W., Lee, K. & Corber, S. (1997). Simultaneous lineups, sequential lineups and showups: Eyewitness identification decisions of adults and children. *Law and Human Behavior, 21*, 391–404.

Lindsay, R.C.L., Wallbridge, H. & Drennan, D. (1987). Do the clothes make the man? An exploration of the effect of line-up attire on eyewitness identification accuracy. *Canadian Journal of Behavioral Science, 19*, 463–478.

Lindsay, R.C.L. & Wells, G.L. (1983). Improving eyewitness identifications from lineups: Simultaneous versus sequential lineup presentations. *Journal of Applied Psychology, 70*, 556–564.

Lipton, J.P. (1977). On the psychology of eyewitness testimony. *Journal of Applied Psychology, 66*, 79–89.

Littlewood, J. (1953). *A mathematician's miscellany*. London: Methuen.

Loader, I. (1999). Governing policing in the 21st century. *Criminal Justice Matters, 38*(Winter), 9–10.

Loftus, E.F. (1979). *Eyewitness testimony*. Cambridge, MA: Harvard University Press.

Loftus, E.F. & Davies, G. (1984). Distortions in the memory of children. *Journal of Social Issues, 40*, 51–67.

Loftus, E.F., Greene, E.L. & Doyle, J.M. (1989). The psychology of eyewitness testimony. In D.C. Raskin (ed.) *Psychological methods in criminal investigation and evidence* (pp. 3–46). New York: Springer.

Loftus, E.F. & Hoffman, H.G. (1989). Misinformation and memory: The creation of memory. *Journal of Experimental Psychology: General, 118*, 100–104.

Loftus, E.F. & Ketcham, K.E. (1983). The malleability of eyewitness accounts. In S.M.A. Lloyd-Bostock & B.R. Clifford (eds.), *Evaluating witness evidence: Recent psychological research and new perspectives* (pp. 159–171). Chichester: Wiley.

Loftus, E.F., Loftus, G.R. & Messo, J. (1987). Some facts about "weapon focus". *Law and Human Behavior, 11*, 55–62.

Loftus, E.F., Miller, D.G. & Burns, H.J. (1978). Semantic integration of verbal information into a visual memory. *Journal of Experimental Psychology: Human Learning and Memory, 4*, 19–31.

Loftus, E.F. & Palmer, J.C. (1974). Reconstructions of automobile destruction: An example of the interaction between language and memory. *Journal of Verbal Learning and Verbal Behavior, 13*, 585–589.

Long, M. (2003). Leadership and performance management. In T. Newburn (ed.), *Handbook of policing* (pp. 628–655). Cullompton: Willan Publishing.

Loveday, B. (2000a) Policing performance. *Criminal Justice Matters, 40* (Summer), 23–24.

Loveday, B. (2000b) *Managing crime: Police use of crime data as an indicator of effectiveness*. Institute of Criminal Justice Studies, University of Portsmouth.

Lovett, J., Regan, L. & Kelly, L. (2004). *Sexual assault referral centres: Developing good practice and maximising potentials*. Home Office Research Study 285. London: Home Office.

Lundrigan, S. & Canter, D. (2001). A multivariate analysis of serial murderers' disposal site location choice. *Journal of Environmental Psychology, 21*, 423–432.

Luus, C.A.E. & Wells, G.L. (1991). Eyewitness identification and the selection of distractors for line-ups. *Law and Human Behavior, 15*, 43–57.

Luus, C.A.E. & Wells, G.L. (1994). The malleability of eyewitness confidence: Co-witness and perseverance effects. *Journal of Applied Psychology, 66*, 482–489.

Maass, A. & Köhnken, G. (1989). Eyewitness identification: Simulating the "weapon effect". *Law and Human Behavior, 13*, 396–408.

MacDonald, I. (1999). Best Value – Worst Practice? *Police Research and Management, Winter*, 41–50.

MacEachin, D. (1999). Foreword. In R. Heuer, *Psychology of intelligence analysis*. Washington, DC: Center for the Study of Intelligence, Central Intelligence Agency.

Macpherson, W. (1999). *The Stephen Lawrence inquiry*. London: TSO.

Magnussen, S., Wise, R.A., Raja, A.Q., Safer, M.A., Pawlenko, N. & Stridbeck, U. (2008). What judges know about eyewitness testimony: A comparison of Norwegian and US judges. *Psychology, Crime and Law, 14*(3), 177–188.

Maguire, M. (2002). Crime statistics: The "data explosion" and its implications. In M. Maguire, R. Morgan & R. Reiner (eds.), *The Oxford handbook of criminology* (3rd edn., pp. 322–375). Oxford: Oxford University Press.

Maguire, M. (2007). Crime data and statistics. In M. Maguire, R. Morgan & R. Reiner (eds.), *Oxford Handbook of Criminology* (4th edn., pp. 241–301). Oxford: Oxford University Press.

Maguire, M., Noaks, L., Hobbs, R. & Brearley, N. (1992). *Assessing investigative performance*, Cardiff: University of Wales.

Maguire, M. & Norris, C. (1992). *The conduct of supervision of criminal investigations*. The Royal Commission on Criminal Justice, Research Study 5. London: HMSO.

Malpass, R.S. & Devine, P.G. (1981a). Realism and eyewitness identification research. *Law and Human Behavior, 4*, 347–358.

Malpass, R.S. & Devine, P.G. (1981b). Eyewitness identification: Lineup instructions and the absence of the offender. *Journal of Applied Psychology, 66*, 482–489.

Mark, R. (1978). *In the office of constable*. London: Williams Collins Sons.

Mawby, R.C. (2002). *Policing images: Policing, communication and legitimacy*. Cullompton: Willan Publishing.

May, T. (2001). *Social research: Issues, methods and process*. Maidenhead: McGraw-Hill.

McCarthy, M. (1986). Yard in secret swoop on Kent police stations – raids follow allegation of crime statistics fraud. *The Times* (London), Tuesday, 12 Aug.

McCartney, C. (2006). *Forensic identification and criminal justice: Forensic science, justice and risk*. Cullompton: Willan Publishing.

McCloskey, M. & Egeth, H. (1983). Eyewitness identification: What can psychologists tell a jury? *American Psychologist, 38*, 550–563.

McCloskey, M. & Zaragoza, M. (1985). Misleading postevent information and memory for events: Arguments and evidence against memory impairment hypotheses. *Journal of Experimental Psychology, 114*, 3–18.

McConville, M. & Baldwin, J. (1982). The role of interrogation in crime discovery and conviction. *British Journal of Criminology, 22*, 165–175.

McConville, M., Sanders, A. & Leng, R. (1991). *The case for the prosecution*. London: Routledge.

McGrath, M. (2000). Criminal profiling: Is there a role for the forensic psychiatrist? *Journal of the American Academy of Psychiatry and Law, 28*, 315–324.

McGurk, B.J., Carr, M.J. & McGurk, D. (1993). *Investigative interviewing courses for police officers: An evaluation*. Police Research Series: Paper No. 4. London: Home Office Police Department.

McGurk, B., Platton, T. & Gibson, R.L. (1994). Detectives: A job and training needs analysis. In *Rights and Risks: The Application of Forensic Psychology* (pp. 24–31). Leicester: British Psychological Society, No. 21.

Melton, G.B. & Thompson, R.A. (1987). Getting out of a rut: Detours to less traveled paths in child witness research. In S.J. Ceci, M.P. Toglia & D.F. Ross (eds.), *Children's eyewitness memory*. New York: Springer.

Memon, A. & Bartlett, J.C. (2002). The effects of verbalisation on face recognition. *Applied Cognitive Psychology*, *16*, 635–650.

Memon, A. & Bull, R. (1991). The cognitive interview: Its origins, empirical support and practical implications. *Journal of Community and Applied Psychology*, *1*, 292–307.

Memon, A. & Gabbert, F. (2003). Unravelling the effects of a sequential lineup. *Applied Cognitive Psychology*, *6*, 703–714.

Memon, A., Gabbert, F. & Hope, L. (2004). The ageing eyewitness. In J.R. Adler (ed.), *Forensic psychology: Concepts, debates and practice* (pp. 96–114). Cullompton: Willan Publishing.

Memon, A., Hope, L., Bartlett, J. & Bull, R. (2002). Eyewitness recognition errors: The effects of mugshot viewing and choosing in young and old adults. *Memory and Cognition*, *30*, 1219–1227.

Memon, A., Vrij, A. & Bull, R. (2003). *Psychology & Law: Truthfulness, accuracy and credibility of victims, witnesses and suspects* (2nd edn.). Chichester: Wiley.

Milne, R. & Bull, R. (1999). *Investigative interviewing: Psychology and practice*. Chichester: John Wiley.

Milne, R. & Bull, R. (2003). Does the cognitive interview help children to resist the effects of suggestive questioning? *Legal and Criminological Psychology*, *8*(1), 21–38.

Milne, R., Bull, R., Köhnken, G. & Memon, A. (1995). The cognitive interview and suggestibility. *Issues in Criminological and Legal Psychology*, *22*, 21–27.

Mokros, A. & Alison, L. (2002). Is profiling possible? Testing the predicted homology of crime scene actions and background characteristics in a sample of rapists. *Legal & Criminological Psychology*, *7*, 25–43.

Morgan, J.B. (1990). *The police function and the investigation of crime*. Aldershot: Avebury.

Morris, B. (2007). History of criminal investigation. In T. Newburn, T. Williamson & A. Wright (eds.), *Handbook of criminal investigation* (pp. 15–40). Cullompton: Willan Publishing.

Morris, R.M (2006). "Crime does not pay": Thinking again about detectives in the first century of the Metropolitan Police. In C. Emsley & H. Shpayer-Makov (eds.), *Police detectives in history 1750–1950* (pp. 79–134). Aldershot: Ashgate.

Moston, S. & Stephenson, G.M. (1993). The changing face of police interrogation. *Journal of Community and Applied Social Psychology*, *3*, 101–115.

Moston, S., Stephenson, G.M. & Williamson, T.M. (1992). The effects of case characteristics on suspect behaviour during police questioning. *British Journal of Criminology*, *32*, 23–40.

MPA (2008). *Appendix 1: Crime data recording scrutiny report*. http://www.mpa.gov.uk/downloads/committees/mpa/080228-07-appendix1.pdf

Muncie, J. (1996). The construction and deconstruction of crime. In J. Muncie & E. McLaughlin (eds.), *The problem of crime* (pp. 5–64). London: Sage Publications.

Narby, D.J., Cutler, B.L. & Penrod, S.D. (1996). The effects of witness, target and situational factors on eyewitness identifications. In S.L. Sporer, R.S. Malpass & G. Köhnken (eds.), *Psychological issues in eyewitness identification*. Mahwah, NJ: Erlbaum.

NCF (1997). *National police training: Criminal investigation training foundation course (curriculum document)*. Bramshill, Hampshire: National Crime Faculty, a Division of National Police Training.

New Jersey v. Fortin, 162 N.J. 517 (2000).

Newburn T. (2002). Community safety and policing. Some implications of the Crime and Disorder Act 1998. In G. Hughes, E. McLaughlin & J. Muncie (eds.), *Crime prevention and community safety. New directions* (pp. 102–122). London: Sage.

Newburn, T. (2003). Policing since 1945. In T. Newburn (ed.), *Handbook of policing* (pp. 84–106). Cullompton: Willan Publishing.

Newburn, T. (2007). *Criminology*. Cullompton: Willan Publishing.

Newburn, T. & Neyroud, P. (eds.) (2008). *Dictionary of policing*. Cullompton: Willan Publishing.

Newburn, T., Williamson, T. & Wright, A. (2007a). The future of investigation. In T. Newburn, T. Williamson & A. Wright (eds.), *Handbook of criminal investigation* (pp. 652–656). Cullompton: Willan Publishing.

Newburn, T., Williamson, T. & Wright, A. (eds.) (2007b). *Handbook of criminal investigation*. Cullompton: Willan Publishing.

Neyroud, P. & Beckley, A. (2001). *Policing, ethics and human rights*. Cullompton: Willan Publishing.

Nicholas, S., Kershaw, C. & Walker, A. (2007). *Crime in England and Wales 2006/07*. Home Office Statistical Bulletin. http://www.homeoffice.gov.uk/rds/crimeew0607.html (accessed 14 Nov. 2007).

Nicol, C., Innes, M., Gee, D. & Feist, A. (2004). *Reviewing murder investigations: An analysis of progress reviews from six police forces*. Home Office Online Report 25/04. http://www.homeoffice.gov.uk/rds/pdfs04/rdsolr2504.pdf (accessed 10 Nov. 2007).

Niederhoffer, A. (1967). *Behind the shield: The police in urban society*. New York: Doubleday.

Norris, N. (1992). Problems in police training. *Policing*, 8(3), 210–221.

Northamptonshire Police (2007). *Managing performance group*. 13 Sept. 2007. http://www.northants.police.uk/foi/default.aspx?category=13&id=676

NPIA (2007). *Professionalising Investigation Programme (PIP)*. http://www.npia.police.uk/en/10093.htm

NPIA (2008a). *PIP Investigation policy guidance*. http://www.npia.police.uk/en/10094.htm

NPIA (2008b). *Murder investigation manual practice advice*. http://www.npia.police.uk/en/6671.htm

NPIA (2008c). *Guide to the national investigators' examination*, version 14: *2009 exams*. http://www.npia.police.uk/en/docs/Guide_to_the_National_Investigators_Examination_2009_.pdf

NPIA (2008d). *SIO Register*. http://www.npia.police.uk/en/10175.htm

NPIA (2008e). *Initial police learning*. http://www.npia.police.uk/en/5984.htm?IPLDP-curriculum

NPIA & ACPO (2005). *Guidance on investigating serious sexual offences*. Bedfordshire: ACPO/Centrex.

NPT (1999). Memorandum by National Police Training. In Home Affairs Committee, *Police training and recruitment* (Vol. 2, pp. 311–348). London: HMSO.

O'Connor, D. (2005). *Closing the gap: A review of the "fitness for purpose" of the current structure of policing in England & Wales*. London: HMIC.

O'Donnell, C. & Bruce, V. (1982). The Batman effect: Selective enhancement of facial features during familiarisation. *Perception*, 29, 76.

O'Hara, C. & O'Hara, G. (1973). *Fundamentals of criminal investigation* (5th edn.). Illinois: Charles C. Thomas.

Oliver, I. (1987). *Police, government and accountability*. London: Macmillan.

Ormerod, D. (1999). Criminal profiling: Trial by judge and jury, not criminal psychologist. In D. Canter & L. Alison (eds.), *Profiling in policy and practice* (pp. 207–261). Aldershot: Ashgate.

O'Rourke, T.E., Penrod, S.E., Cutler, B.L. & Stuve, T.E. (1989). The external validity of eyewitness identification research: Generalising across subject populations. *Law and Human Behavior, 13*, 385–395.

Ossorio, P. (1985). Pathology. In K. Davis & T. Mitchell (eds.), *Advances in descriptive psychology* (Vol. 4). Greenwich, CT: JAI Press.

Osterburg, J.W. & Ward, R.H. (2000). *Criminal investigation: A method of reconstructing the past* (3rd edn.). Cincinnati: Anderson Publishing.

Packer, H.L. (1968). *The limits of criminal sanction*. Stanford: Stanford University Press.

Palmiotto, M.J. (ed.) (2003). *Policing and training issues*. Upper Saddle River, NJ: Prentice Hall.

Palmiotto, N. (2004). *Criminal investigation* (3rd edn.). University Press of America.

Parker, E.S., Birnbaum, I.M., Weingartner, H., Hartley, J.T., Stillman, R.C. & Wyatt, R.J. (1980). Retrograde enhancement of human memory with alcohol. *Psychopharmacology, 69*, 219–222.

Parker, J.F., Haverfield, E. & Baker-Thomas, S. (1986). Eyewitness testimony of children. *Journal of Applied Social Psychology, 16*, 287–302.

Parker, J.F. & Ryan, V. (1993). An attempt to reduce guessing behaviour in children's and adults' eyewitness identification. *Law and Human Behavior, 17*, 11–26.

Parkinson, S. & Marsh, I. (2000). Management, measurement and performance: The impact of accountability in the Merseyside Police Service. In *Criminal Justice Matters, 40*(Summer), 25–26.

Parliamentary Office of Science and Technology (2006). *The National DNA Database*. Postnote February 2006 no. 258.

Pawson, R. & Tilley, N. (1997). *Realistic evaluation*. London: Sage Publications.

Pearse, J. & Gudjonsson, G.H. (1996). Police interviewing techniques at two south London police stations. *Psychology, Crime and Law, 3*, 63–74.

Penrod, S. (2005). Eyewitnesses. In L.E. Sullivan & M.S. Rosen (eds.). *Encyclopedia of law enforcement* (Vol. 1). Thousand Oaks: Sage.

Perfect, T.J., Watson, E.L. & Wagstaff, G.F. (1993). Accuracy of confidence ratings associated with general knowledge and eyewitness memory. *Journal of Applied Psychology, 78*, 144–147.

Peterson, C., Dowden, C. & Tobin, J. (1999). Interviewing preschoolers: Comparisons of yes/no and wh- questions. *Law & Human Behavior, 23*, 539–556.

Pezdek, K. & Blandon-Gitlin, I. (2005). When is an intervening lineup most likely to affect eyewitness identification accuracy? *Legal and Criminological Psychology, 10*, 247–263.

Phillips, C. & Brown, D. (1998). *Entry into the criminal justice system: A survey of police arrests and their outcomes*. Home Office Research Study 185. London: Home Office, Research and Statistics Directorate.

Pickel, K. (1999). The influence of "context" on the weapon focus effect. *Law and Human Behavior, 23*, 299–313.

Pickel, K.L., Narter, D.B., Jameson, M.M. & Lenhardt, T.T. (2008). The weapon focus effect in child eyewitnesses. *Psychology, Crime & Law, 14*(1), 61–72.

Pinizzotto, A.J. (1984). Forensic psychology: Criminal personality profiling. *Law and Human Behaviour, 14*(3), 215–233.

Pinizzotto, A.J. & Finkel, N.J. (1990). Criminal personality profiling: An outcome and process study. *Law and Human Behavior, 14*(3), 215–233.

Police and Criminal Evidence Act (1984). (Codes of Practice) Order 1988. London: HMSO.

Pollard, B. (1983). Police effectiveness and public acceptability. In T. Bennett (ed.), *The Future of policing* (Cropwood Conference Series No 15, pp. 117–126). Cambridge: Institute of Criminology,.

Poythress, N., Otto, R.K., Darkes, J. & Starr, L. (1993). APA's expert panel in the congressional review of the U.S.S. Iowa incident. *American Psychologist, 48*, 8–15.

Pozzulo, J.D. & Lindsay, R.C.L. (1997). Increasing correct identifications by children. *Expert Evidence, 5*, 126–132.

Pozzulo, J.D. & Lindsay, R.C.L. (1998). Identification accuracy of children versus adults: A meta-analysis. *Law and Human Behavior, 22*, 549–570.

Pringle, P. (1958). *The thief takers*. London: Museum Press.

Pynoos, R. & Eth, S. (1984). The child as witness to homicide. *Journal of Social Issues, 40*, 87–108.

Rachlin, H. (1996). *The making of a detective*. New York: W.W. Norton.

Rainbow, L. (2008). Taming the beast: The UK approach to the management of behavioural investigative advice. *Journal of Police and Criminal Psychology, 23*, 90–97.

Rand Corporation (1975). *The criminal investigation process* (Vols. 1–3). Santa Monica, CA: Rand Corporation.

Rathmell, A. (2002). Towards postmodern intelligence. *Intelligence and National Security, 17*(3), 87–104.

Rawlings, P. (2002). *Policing: A short history*. Cullompton: Willan Publishing.

Read, J.D. (1995). The availability heuristic in person identification: The sometimes misleading consequences of enhanced contextual information. *Applied Cognitive Psychology, 9*, 91–121.

Read, J.D. & Desmarais, S.L. (2007). Lay beliefs about eyewitness memory. In B.L. Cutler (ed.), *Encyclopaedia of psychology and law*. London: Sage.

Read, J.D., Lindsay, D.S. & Nichols, T. (1998). The relationship between confidence and accuracy in eyewitness identification studies: Is the conclusion changing? In C.P. Thompson, D. Bruce, J.D. Read, D. Hermann, D. Payne & M.P. Toglia (eds.), *Eyewitness memory: Theoretical and applied perspectives* (pp. 107–130). Mahwah, NJ: Erlbaum.

Read, J.D., Vokey, J.R., Hammersley, R. (1990). Changing photos of faces: Effects of exposure duration and photo similarity on recognition and the accuracy–confidence relationship. *Journal of Experimental Psychology: Learning, Memory, and Cognition, 16*, 870–882.

Read, J.D., Yuille, J.C. & Tollestrup, P. (1992). Recollections of a robbery: Effects of arousal and alcohol upon recall and person identification. *Law and Human Behavior, 16*(4), 425–446.

Reiner, R. (1988). Keeping the Home Office happy. *Policing, 4*(1), 28–36.

Reiner, R. (1992). Police research in the United Kingdom: A critical review. In M. Tonry & N. Morris (eds.), *Modern policing* (pp. 435–508). Chicago: University of Chicago Press.

Reiner, R. (1998). Process or product? Problems of assessing individual police performance. In J. Brodeur (ed.), *How to recognize good policing: Problems and issues* (pp. 55–72). London: Sage.

Reiner, R. (2000). *Politics of the police* (3rd edn.). Oxford: Oxford University Press.

Reiner, R. (2007). *Law and order: An honest citizen's guide to crime and control.* Cambridge: Polity Press.

Reppetto, T.A (1978). The detective task: The state of the art, science craft? *Police Studies: The International Review of Police Development, 1*(3), 5–10.

Ressler, R.K. & Burgess, A.W. & Douglas, J.E. (1988). *Sexual homicides: Patterns and motives.* New York: Lexington Books.

Ressler, R.K., Burgess, A.W., Hartman, C.R., Douglas, J.E. & McCormack, A. (1986). Murderers who rape and mutilate. *Journal of Interpersonal Violence, 1,* 273–287.

Ressler, R.K. & Shachtman, T. (1992). *Whoever fights monsters.* London: Pocket Books.

Ricci, C.M., Beal, C.R. & Dekle, D.J. (1996). The effect of parent versus unfamiliar interviewers on children's eyewitness memory and identification accuracy. *Law and Human Behavior, 20*(5), 483–500.

Rips, L. (1994). *The psychology of proof deductive reasoning in human thinking.* Cambridge, MA: MIT Press.

Roach, J. (2007). Those who do big bad things also usually do little bad things: Identifying active serious offenders using offender self-selection. *International Journal of Police Science and Management, 9*(1), 66–79.

Rose, D. (1996). *In the name of the law: The collapse of criminal justice.* London: Vintage.

Rose, M.P., Nadler, J. & Clarke, J. (2006). Appropriately upset? Emotion norms and perceptions of crime victims. *Law and Human Behaviour, 30,* 203–219.

Rose, R.A., Bull, R. & Vrij, A. (2003). Enhancing older witnesses' identification performance: Context reinstatement is not the answer. *Canadian Journal of Police and Security Services, 1,* 173–184.

Ross, D.F., Read, J.D. & Toglia, M.P. (eds.) (1994). *Adult eyewitness testimony: Current trends and developments,* New York: Cambridge University Press.

Rossmo, D.K. (1993). Geographic profiling: Locating serial killers. In D. Zahm & P.F. Cromwell (eds.), *Proceedings of the international seminar on environmental criminology and crime analysis.* Coral Gables, FL: Florida Criminal Justice Executive Institute.

Rossmo, D.K. (2000). *Geographic profiling.* Boca Raton, FL: CRC Press.

Rossmo, K. (1997). Geographic profiling. In J.L. Jackson & D.A. Bekerian (eds.), *Offender profiling: Theory, research and practice.* New York: John Wiley & Sons.

Rossmo, K. (2006). Criminal investigation failures: Avoiding the pitfalls. *FBI Law Enforcement Bulletin, 75*(9), 1–8.

Royal College of Pathologists (2009). *FAQs: Careers.* http://www.rcpath.org/index.asp?PageID=1381 (accessed 15 Feb. 2009).

Roycroft, M. (2007). What solves hard to solve murders? *Journal of Homicide and Major Incident Investigation, 3*(1).

Saferstein, R. (2004). *Criminalistics: An introduction to forensic science* (8th edn.). Upper Saddle River, NJ: Pearson/Prentice Hall.

Salfati, C.G. & Taylor, P. (2006). Differentiating sexual violence: A comparison of sexual homicide and rape. *Psychology, Crime and Law, 12*(2), 107–126.

Sampson, F., Connor, P., Hutton, G., McKinnon, G. & Johnston, D. (eds.) (2008). *Blackstone's police investigators' manual 2008*. Oxford: Oxford University Press.

Sanders, A. (1977). *Detective work: A study of criminal investigations*. New York: The Free Press.

Sanders, A. & Young, R. (2007). From suspect to trial. In M. Maguire, R. Morgan & R. Reiner (eds.), *The Oxford handbook of criminology* (4th edn., pp. 953–989). Oxford: Oxford University Press.

Sanders, G.S. (1986). On increasing the usefulness of eyewitness research. *Law and Human Behavior, 10*, 333–335.

Sandow-Quirk, Mary (2002). A failure of intelligence. *Prometheus, 20*(2), 131–142.

Savage, S. (2007). *Police reform: Forces for change*. Oxford: Oxford University Press.

Savage, S.P., Charman, S. & Cope, S. (2000). The policy-making context: Who shapes policy? In F. Leishman., B. Loveday. & S. Savage (eds.), *Core issues in policing* (pp. 30–51). London: Longman.

Scheck, B., Neufeld, P. & Dwyer, J. (2000). *Actual innocence: Five days to execution and other dispatches from the wrongly convicted*. New York: Doubleday.

Schmechel, R.S., O'Toole, T.P., Easterly, C. & Loftus, E.F. (2006). Beyond the Ken? Testing jurors' understanding of eyewitness reliability evidence. *Jurimetrics, 46*, 177–214.

Schuster, B. (2007). Police lineups: Making eyewitness identification more reliable. *NIJ Journal, 258*. http://www.ojp.usdoj.gov/nij/journals/258/police-lineups.html#note6 (accessed 30 Aug. 2008).

Searcy, J.H., Bartlett, J.C. & Memon, A. (1999). Age differences in accuracy and choosing in eyewitness identification and face recognition. *Memory and Cognition, 27*, 538–552.

Searcy, J.H., Bartlett, J.C. & Memon, A. (2000). Relationship of availability line-up conditions and individual differences to false identification by young and older eyewitnesses. *Legal and Criminological Psychology, 5*, 219–236.

Searcy, J.H., Bartlett, J.C., Memon, A. & Swanson, K. (2001). Ageing and line-up performance at long retention intervals: Effect of meta-memory and context reinstatement. *Journal of Applied Psychology, 86*, 207–214.

Searcy, J.H., Bartlett, J.C. & Siepel, A. (2000). Crime characteristics and lineup identification decisions. Unpublished manuscript.

Senior, P., Crowther-Dowey, C. & Long, M. (2007). *Understanding modernisation in criminal justice*. Maidenhead: Open University Press.

Sexual Offences Act (2003). http://www.legislation.hmso.gov.uk/acts/acts2003/30042–b.htm (accessed 6 June 2008).

Shapiro, P.N. & Penrod, S. (1986). Meta-analysis of facial identification studies. *Psychological Bulletin, 100*, 139–156.

Shaw, J.S. & McClure, K.A. (1996). Repeated postevent questioning can lead to elevated levels of eyewitness confidence. *Law and Human Behavior, 20*, 629–654.

Shepherd, E. (1993). Resistance in police interviews: The contributions of police perceptions and behaviour. In E. Shepherd (ed.), *Aspects of police interviewing*. Issues in Legal and Criminological Psychology, No. 18. Leicester: British Psychological Society.

Shulsky A.N. & Schmitt G.J. (2002). *Silent warfare: Understanding the world of intelligence* (3rd edn.). Washington, DC: Brassey's.

Simon, D. (1991). *Homicide: A year on the killing streets*. New York: Ivy Books.

Skolnick, J.M. (1994). *Justice without trial: Law enforcement in democratic society* (3rd edn.). New York: Macmillan.

Smith, A. (2006). *Crime statistics: An independent review*. London: *Home Office*. http://www.homeoffice.gov.uk/rds/pdfs06/crime-statistics-independent-review-06.pdf

Smith, A.D. & Winograd, E. (1978). Adult age differences in remembering faces. *Developmental Psychology, 14*, 443–444.

Smith, N. & Flanagan, C. (2000). *The effective detective: Identifying the skills of an effective SIO*. London: Research, Development and Statistics Directorate.

Smith, S.M., Stinson, V. & Prosser, M.A. (2004). Do they all look alike? An exploration of decision-making strategies in cross-race facial identifications. *Canadian Journal of Behavioural Science, 36*, 144–153.

Smith, V.L., Kassin, S.M. & Ellsworth, P.C. (1989). Eyewitness accuracy and confidence: Within-versus between-subject correlations. *Journal of Applied Psychology, 74*(2), 356–359.

Snook, B., Wright, M., House, J. & Alison, L. (2006). Searching for a needle in a needle stack: Combining criminal careers and journey-to-crime research for criminal suspect prioritization. *Police Practice and Research, 7*, 217–230.

Snow, J. (1855). *On the mode of communication of cholera*. http://www.deltaomega.org/snowfin.pdf. (accessed 14 Nov. 2007).

Softley, P. (1980). *Police interrogation*. Home Office Research Study No. 61. London: HMSO.

Soukara, S., Bull, R., Vrij, A., Turner, M. & Cherryman, J. (2007). What really happens in police interviews of suspects? Tactics and confessions. Unpublished manuscript.

Southgate, P. (1988). Conclusions. In P. Southgate (ed.), *New directions on police training* (pp. 230–240). London: HMSO.

Spinney, L. (2008). Line-ups on trial. *Nature, 453*(7194), 442–444.

Sporer, S.L. (1993). Eyewitness identification accuracy, confidence and decision times in simultaneous and sequential line-ups. *Journal of Applied Psychology, 78*, 22–33.

Sporer, S.L., Köhnken, G. & Malpass, R.S. (1996). Introduction: 2000 years of mistaken identification. In S.L. Sporer, R.S. Malpass & G. Köhnken (eds.), *Psychological issues in eyewitness identification*. Mahwah, NJ: Erlbaum.

Sporer, S.L., Penrod, S.D., Read, D. & Cutler, B.L. (1995). Choosing, confidence and accuracy: A meta-analysis of the confidence–accuracy relation in eyewitness identification studies. *Psychological Bulletin, 118*, 315–327.

Spottiswoode, C. (2000). *Improving police performance: A new approach to measuring police efficiency: Technical annexes*. London: Public Services Productivity Panel.

SRA (2008). *Guidelines on the assessment of character and suitability*. http://www.sra.org.uk/documents/students/student-enrolment/character-guide.pdf

Statistics Commission (2006). *Report no. 30. Crime statistics: Users' perspective*. http://www.statscom.org.uk/uploads/files/reports/Crime_Statistics_Review-final.pdf

Steblay, N.M (1992). A meta-analytic review of the weapon focus effect. *Law and Human Behavior, 16*, 413–424.

Steblay, N., Dysart, J., Fulero, S. & Lindsay, R.C.L. (2001). Eyewitness accuracy rates in sequential and simultaneous lineup presentations: A meta-analytic review. *Law and Human Behavior, 25*, 459–473.

Steele, C.M. & Josephs, R.A. (1990). Alcohol myopia: Its prized and dangerous effects. *American Psychologist*, 45, 921–933.

Stelfox, P. (2007). Professionalising criminal investigation. In T. Newburn, T. Williamson & A. Wright (eds.), *Handbook of criminal investigation* (pp. 628–651). Cullompton: Willan Publishing.

Stelfox, P. & Pease, K. (2005). Cognition and detection: Reluctant bedfellows? In M. Smith & N. Tilley (eds.), *Crime science: New approaches to preventing and detecting crime* (pp. 191–207). Cullompton: Willan Publishing.

Stephens, M. (1988). *Policing: Critical issues*. London: Harvester Wheatsheaf.

Stevens, J. (2002). *The search for the truth in the criminal justice system*. http://www.le.ac.uk/press/press/scalesofjustice2.htm.

Stewart, E. (1998). Operational decision making. *Police Research and Management*, 2(3), 73–86.

Stockdale, J.E. (1993). *Management and supervision of police interviews*. Police Research Series, Paper 5. London: Home Office.

Stradling, S. & Harper, K. (1988). The tutor constable attachment, the management of encounters and the development of discretionary judgement. In P. Southgate (ed.), *New directions on police training* (pp. 199–218). London: HMSO.

Technical Working group for Eyewitness Evidence (1999). *Eyewitness evidence: A guide for law enforcement*. Washington, DC: US Department of Justice, Office of Justice Programs.

Temkin, J. (1997). Plus ça change: Reporting rape in the 1990s. *British Journal of Criminology*, 37, 507–528.

Temkin, J. (2002). *Rape and the legal process* (2nd edn.). Oxford: Oxford University Press.

Temkin, J. & Krahé, B. (2008). *Sexual assault and the justice gap: A question of attitude*. Oxford: Hart Publishing.

Thomas R. (2000). *Detective fiction and the rise of forensic science*. Cambridge Studies in Nineteenth-Century Literature and Culture. Cambridge: Cambridge University Press.

Thompson, D.J. Hermann, D.J., Read, D., Bruce, D., Payne, D. & Toglia, M. (eds.), *Eyewitness memory: Theoretical and applied perspectives*. Hillside, NJ: Erlbaum.

Tilley, N. & Ford, A. (1996). *Forensic science and crime investigation*. Crime Detection and Prevention Series, Paper 73. London: Home Office.

Timm, H. & Christian, K.E. (1991). *Introduction to private security*. Pacific Grove, CA: Brooks/Cole.

Tong, S. (2005). *Training the effective detective: A case-study examining the role of training in learning to be a detective*. Unpublished PhD dissertation, University of Cambridge.

Tong, S. & Bowling, B. (2006). Art, craft and science of detective work. *Police Journal*, 79, 323–329.

Tooley, V., Brigham, J.C., Maas, A. & Bothwell, R.K. (1987). Facial recognition: Weapon effect and attentional focus. *Journal of Applied Social Psychology*, 17, 845–849.

Trent, S., Patterson, E. & Woods, D. (2007). Challenges for cognition in intelligence analysis. *Journal of Cognitive Engineering and Decision Making*, 1(1), 75–97.

Tulving, E. (1974). Cue-dependent forgetting. *American Scientist*, 62, 74–82.

Turtle, J.W. & Yuille, J.C. (1994). Lost but not forgotten: Repeated eyewitness recall leads to reminiscence but not hypermnesia. *Journal of Applied Psychology*, *79*, 260–271.

Turvey, B. (1998). *Deductive criminal profiling: Comparing applied methodologies between inductive and deductive criminal profiling techniques*. http://www.corpus-delicti.com/Profiling_law.html (accessed 9 Nov. 2007).

Turvey, B.E. (1999). *Criminal profiling: An introduction to behavioural evidence analysis*. London: Academic Press.

Tweney, R. & Chitwood, S. (1995). Scientific reasoning. In S. Newstead & J. Evans (eds.), *Perspectives on thinking and reasoning* (pp. 241–260). Hove: Lawrence Erlbaum.

UEA (1987). *Police probationer training: The final report of the stage II review*. London: HMSO.

Underwood, B.J. (1969). Attributes of memory. *Psychological Review*, *76*, 559–573.

Valentine, T. & Heaton, P. (1999). An evaluation of the fairness of police line-ups and video identifications. *Applied Cognitive Psychology*, *13*, 59–72.

Valentine, T. & Mesout, J. (2008). Eyewitness identification under stress in the London Dungeon. *Applied Cognitive Psychology*, *23*(2), 151–161.

Valentine, T., Pickering, A. & Darling, S. (2003). Characteristics of eyewitness identification that predict the outcome of real lineups. *Applied Cognitive Psychology*, *17*, 969–983.

Waddington, P.A.J. (1999). *Policing citizens*. London: London College Press.

Wakefield, H. & Underwager, R. (1998). Coerced or nonvoluntary confessions. *Behavioral Sciences and the Law*, *16*, 423–440.

Walby, S. & Allen, J. (2004). *Domestic violence, sexual assault and stalking: Findings from the British Crime Survey*. Home Office Research Study 276. London: Home Office.

Walker, A., Kershaw, C. & Nicholas, S. (2006). *Crime in England and Wales 2005/06*, Home Office Statistical Bulletin. http://www.homeoffice.gov.uk/rds/pdfs06/hosb1206.pdf

Walker, C. & Stockdale, R. (1995). Forensic evidence and terrorist trials in the UK. *Cambridge Law Journal*, *54*(1), 69–99.

Walker, M.A. (1992). Do we need a clear-up rate? *Policing and Society*, *2*, 293–306.

Ward, C. (1995). *Attitudes towards rape*. London: Sage.

Wason, P. & Johnson-Laird, P. (eds.) (1968). *Thinking and reasoning: Selected readings*, Harmondsworth: Penguin Books.

Waters, I. (2000). Quality and performance monitoring. In F. Leishman., B. Loveday & S. Savage (eds.), *Core Issues in policing* (2nd edn., pp. 264–287). London: Longman.

Weatheritt, M. (1986). *Innovations in policing*. London: Croom Helm in association with the Police Foundation.

Weber, N. & Brewer, N. (2003). The effect of judgment type and confidence scale on confidence–accuracy calibration in face recognition. *Journal of Applied Psychology*, *88*, 490–499.

Weingardt, K.R., Toland, H.K. & Loftus, E.F. (1994). Reports of suggested memories: Do people truly believe them? In D.F. Ross, J.D. Read, M.P. Toglia (eds.), *Adult eyewitness testimony: Current trends and developments*. New York: Cambridge University Press.

Wells, G.L. (1078). Applied eyewitness testimony research: System variables and estimator variables. *Journal of Personality and Social Psychology, 36*, 1546–1557.

Wells, G.L. (1984). The psychology of line-up identifications. *Journal of Applied Social Psychology, 14*, 89–103.

Wells, G.L. (1993). What do we know about eyewitness identification? *American Psychologist, 48*, 553–571.

Wells, G.L. & Bradfield, A.L. (1998). "Good you identified the suspect": Feedback to eyewitnesses distorts their reports of the witnessing experience. *Journal of Applied Psychology, 83*, 360–376.

Wells, G.L., Ferguson, T.J. & Lindsay, R.C.L. (1981). The tractability of eyewitness confidence and its implications for triers of fact. *Journal of Applied Psychology, 6*, 688–696.

Wells, G.L. & Lindsay, R.C.L. (1985). Methodological notes on the accuracy–confidence relationship in eyewitness identifications. *Journal of Applied Psychology, 70*, 413–419.

Wells, G.L. & Loftus, E.F. (eds.) (1984). *Eyewitness testimony: Psychological perspectives*. New York: Cambridge University Press.

Wells, G.L. & Loftus, E.F. (2003). Eyewitness memory for people and events. In A.M. Goldstein (ed.), *Handbook of psychology* (Vol. 11): *Forensic psychology* (pp. 149–160). New York: John Wiley & Sons.

Wells, G.L. & Luus, C.A.E. (1990). Police line-ups as experiments: Social methodology as a framework for properly conducted line-ups. *Personality and Social Psychology Bulletin, 3*, 285–293.

Wells, G.L., Malpass, R.S., Lindsay, R.C.L., Fisher, R.P., Turtle, J.W. & Fulero, S.M. (2000). From the lab to the police station: A successful application of eyewitness research. *American Psychologist, 55*, 581–598.

Wells, G.L. & Olson, E.A. (2001). The other-race effect in eyewitness identification: What do we do about it? *Psychology, Public Policy, and Law, 7*, 230–246.

Wells, G.L. & Olson, E. (2003). Eyewitness identification. *Annual Review of Psychology, 54*, 277–295.

Wells, G.L., Rydell, S.M. & Seelau, E.P. (1993). On the selection of distractors for eyewitness lineups. *Journal of Applied Psychology, 78*, 835–844.

Wells, G.L., Seelau, E., Rydell, S. & Luus, C.A.E. (1994). Recommendations for conducting lineups. In D.F. Ross, J.D. Read & M.P. Toglia (eds.), *Adult eyewitness testimony: Current trends and developments*. New York: Cambridge University Press.

Wells, G.L., Small, L., Penrod, S., Malpass, R.S., Fulero, S.M. & Brimacombe, C.A.E. (1998). Eyewitness identification procedures: Recommendations for lineups and photospreads. *Law and Human Behavior, 22*, 60–647.

Wells, R. (1987). The will and the way to move forward in policing. In J. Benyon & J. Solomos (eds.), *The roots of urban unrest* (pp. 75–90). Oxford: Pergamon Press.

West, A. (2001). A proposal for an investigative science course: Any takers? *Police Research & Management, 5*(2), 13–22.

Whitaker, B. (1964). *The police*. Harmondsworth: Penguin Books.

Wike, R. (2006). *Where terrorism finds support in the Muslim world*. Pew Research Center publications: http://pewresearch.org/pubs/26/where-terrorism-finds-support-in-the-muslim-world (accessed 14 Nov. 2007).

Wilcock, R.A., Bull, R. & Vrij, A. (2007). Are old witnesses always poorer witnesses? Identification accuracy, context reinstatement, own-age bias. *Psychology, Crime & Law, 13*(3), 305–316.

Williamson, T.M. (1993). From interrogation to investigative interviewing. Strategic trends in police questioning. *Journal of Community and Applied Social Psychology*, *3*, 89–99.

Willis, J. (1995). New wine in old bottles: The sentencing discount for pleading guilty. *Sentencing Law in Context*, 1(special issue, ed. A. Kapardis), 39–78.

Wilson, O.W. (1962). *Police planning*. Springfield: Charles C. Thomas.

Wilson, P.R., Lincoln, R. & Kocsis, R. (1997). Validity, utility and ethics of criminal profiling for serial violent and sexual offenders. *Psychiatry, Psychology and the Law*, *4*(1), 1–12.

Wise, R.A. & Safer, M.A. (2004). What US judges know and believe about eyewitness testimony. *Applied Cognitive Psychology*, *18*, 427–443.

Wood, D. & Tong, S. (in press). The future of initial police training: A university perspective, *International Journal of Police Science and Management*.

Wright, A. (2000). Managing the future: An academic's view. In F. Leishman., B. Loveday & S. Savage (eds.), *Core issues in policing* (2nd edn., pp. 288–299). London: Longman.

Wright, A. (2002). *Policing: An introduction to concepts and practice*. Cullompton: Willan Publishing.

Wright, D.B. & Skagerberg, E.M. (2007). Postidentification feedback affects real eyewitnesses. *Psychological Science*, *18*(2), 172–178.

Yarmey, A.D. (1979). *The psychology of eyewitness testimony*. New York: Free Press.

Yarmey, A.D. (2001). Expert testimony: Does eyewitness memory research have probative value for the courts? *Canadian Psychology*, *42*, 92–100.

Yarmey, A.D., Jones, H.T. & Rashid, S. (1984). Eyewitness memory of elderly and young adults. In D.J. Muller, D.E. Blackman & A.J. Chapman (eds.), *Psychology and law*. Chichester: John Wiley & Sons.

Yarmey, A.D. & Kent, J. (1980). Eyewitness identification by elderly and young adults. *Law and Human Behavior*, *4*, 359–371.

Yarmey, A.D., Yarmey, M.J., Yarmey, A.L. (1996). Accuracy of eyewitness identifications in showups and lineups. *Law and Human Behavior*, *20*(4), 459–477.

Young, J. (1988). *Risk of crime and fear of crime*. http://www.malcolmread.co.uk/JockYoung/RISK.htm

Young, M. (1991). *An inside job: Policing and police culture in Britain*. Oxford: Clarendon Press.

Yuille, J.C. (1986). Meaningful research in the police context. In J.C. Yuille (ed.), *Police selection and training: The role of psychology*. Dordrecht: Martinus Nijhoff.

Yuille, J.C. & Cutshall, J.L. (1986). A case study of eyewitness memory for a crime. *Journal of Applied Psychology*, *71*, 291–301.

Yuille, J.C., Davies, G.M., Gibling, F., Marxsen, D. & Porter, S. (1994). Eyewitness memory of police trainees for realistic role plays. *Journal of Applied Psychology*, *79*, 931–936.

Yuille, J.C. & Tollestrup, P.A. (1990). Some effects of alcohol on eyewitness memory. *Journal of Applied Psychology*, *75*, 268–273.

Zander, M. (1994). Ethics and crime investigation by the police. *Policing*, *10*(1), 39–47.

Zaragoza, M.S. & Koshmider, J.W. III (1989). Misled subjects may know more than their performance implies. *Journal of Experimental Psychology: Learning, Memory and Cognition*, *15*, 246–255.

Index

Indexed by Terry Halliday

Printed and bound by CPI Group (UK) Ltd, Croydon, CR0 4YY

1